RULE #1

RULE #1

The Simple Strategy for Successful Investing in Only 15 Minutes a Week!

Phil Town

 CROWN PUBLISHERS NEW YORK

Copyright © 2006 by Philip B. Town

Rule #1 trademark used by permission of Philip B. Town
All rights reserved.
Published in the United States by Crown Publishers, an imprint of the Crown Publishing
Group, a division of Random House, Inc., New York.
www.crownpublishing.com

Crown is a trademark and the Crown colophon is a registered trademark of
Random House, Inc.

Library of Congress Cataloging-in-Publication Data is available upon request.

ISBN-13: 978-0-307-33613-2
ISBN-10: 0-307-33613-1

Printed in the United States of America

Design by Robert Bull and Lauren Dong

10 9 8 7 6 5 4 3 2 1

First Edition

To Alaina and Danielle

Without you none of this would have happened.

Contents

RULE #1

Make Money No Matter What

Change your thoughts, and you change your world.
—Norman Vincent Peale (1898–1993)

T his book is a simple guide to returns of 15 percent or more in the stock market, with almost no risk. In fact, Rule #1 investing is practically immune to the ups and downs of the stock market — and by the end of this book I'll have proved it to you.

Rule #1 investing is important today for many reasons, the least of which being that baby boomers currently have an average of about $50,000 in the bank to retire on, twenty years from now. They *think* they need a million but aren't going to get there. Younger generations have a hard time paying off debt, saving money, and even thinking about investing on their own in the market. If people do nothing but invest in low-risk government bonds that pay about 4 percent, they're guaranteeing themselves a stressful retirement. On the other hand, striving for a 15-percent return by *guessing* what to invest in ("speculating" in investor-speak) is a guaranteed way to lose money. Rule #1 solves the problem of how to get high returns with low risk, and it can get you to retirement a lot sooner with a lot less money than you imagine.

I didn't invent The Rule. It was first set by Columbia University's Benjamin Graham and then, more famously, adhered to by Graham's student and the world's most successful professional investor—Warren Buffett. According to Buffett, "There are only two rules of investing: Rule #1: Don't lose money . . . and Rule #2: Don't forget Rule #1."

The reason I'm writing about The Rule is that I'm *not* a Buffett or a

Graham. If you have to be a genius to use The Rule, there's not much point in writing about it, is there? I'm an ordinary person just like you. I like things simple and straightforward. I didn't go to business school or work on Wall Street. I learned how important The Rule is in the school of hard knocks. If you could invest without the danger of losing your money, wouldn't you be more willing to take control and do it yourself?

Because the answer to that question is obviously yes, I get invited to show at least 500,000 people a year how easy it is to apply Rule #1. I've been speaking about Rule #1 on Peter Lowe's monster arena tour, "Get Motivated," where I'm introduced as "the man who's taught more people how to invest than anyone in the country." On that tour, I've shared arena stages with Rudy Giuliani, Bill Clinton, George H. W. Bush, Gerald Ford, Jimmy Carter, Margaret Thatcher, Colin Powell, Mikhail Gorbachev, and General Tommy Franks—and spoken to more than two million people about The Rule. Now it's time for me to finally reach you.

Before I learned Rule #1 and started touring, I mostly got dirty for a living and didn't dare dream of buying expensive real estate or traveling the world in luxury. I dug ditches, washed rental equipment, pumped gas, drove trucks, bussed tables, and machined leg braces. I was an average high school student and it took me four tries to get through college. During my nearly four years in the Army, I spent two years with Special Forces (aka the Green Berets) and four months in Vietnam.

On March 1, 1972, I finished my military service in Vietnam and returned to the United States. On my last day in the army, I was walking through SeaTac Airport in Seattle, proudly wearing my uniform and green beret, when a man ran up, spat on me, and ran off. I'd been away from the United States so long that I had no idea how much Americans despised me for what I'd been sent overseas to do. After years of serving my country, it took me only a few days as a civilian to discover that many people thought I was a fool (or worse) for putting my life on the line.

I felt unemployable, but I finally found a job as a river guide. And after a couple of years of guiding in California, Utah, and Idaho, I ended up in the Grand Canyon. By then my hair was as long as everyone else's, I wore black leather, grew a goatee, lived in a teepee in the woods near Flagstaff, Arizona, and drove around on a really loud black Harley-Davidson, scaring people. I was as far from Wall Street and the world of investing as possible. I was still getting dirty for a living. Except now I had an attitude.

Life changed in 1980, when I took the trustees from Outward Bound down the canyon for two weeks. Outward Bound is an educational program that challenges people of all ages in various settings, usually in adventurous wilderness expeditions, so that they learn about teamwork, leadership, building a better world, self-discovery, and so on. Because Outward Bound makes the participants do all their own work, we decided to do the same to the trustees; instead of rowing them down the river, we put them on small rafts and forced them to do most of the paddling. After seven days we got to Crystal, the nastiest rapid in the Grand Canyon. Eighty thousand cubic feet of water per second crashes into a granite wall, turns 90 degrees, and drops 35 feet. At the wall, the drop and the volume of water creates a huge recirculating hole (famously known as "the Hole"). In all my trips down the canyon, I'd never been near that hole, and the only person I knew who had . . . well, he'd barely gotten out alive. He'd emerged with deep lacerations and almost a broken back. We always maneuvered the boats way to the right of the Hole and snuck by it. But this time we were paddling, and I needed my crew's help to drive the boat to the right side of the river. We started off okay, drifting down the right side, but when I told my charges to paddle for the right shore, we went nowhere. In fact, we kept drifting closer and closer to the Hole. "Paddle faster! Harder! Your lives depend on it!"

But we just kept going backwards toward the Hole. Then I told my guys to paddle as if *my* life depended on it, and all that did was get them banging paddles against one another. They were all sucking wind, and meanwhile we were still going backwards. There was nothing to do but turn the boat around and hit the Hole straight on. That way, maybe only *some* of us would die. Just then I noticed a little seam of water between the wall and the Hole, and I screamed over the noise of the rapids for my crew to paddle toward the upper edge of the Hole as hard as they could. I thought maybe we could surf the wave off the base of the cliff. It was a total long shot, and I had a flash of us getting crushed against the cliff before drowning in the Hole. Maybe the guys saw it, too, or maybe they finally realized the Hole was the end. Either way, they suddenly made that paddle boat fly, and we skidded along the lip of the Hole. We all stared for a moment down into its open vortex like mice looking into a washing machine. To this day I don't understand how we managed to slide past that rapid. We hit that little seam of water perfectly, missed the wall, missed the Hole, and came out the other side. And we didn't even get wet. Very exciting. When we came ashore, one of the guys vomited while I had to explain to the owner of the company, who happened to be along on the trip, why it wasn't really my fault that I'd just taken six of his VIPs on a joyride to the edge of disaster.

Later that evening, one of the rafters gave me a bear hug, eyes full of emotion, and said, "How can I thank you for saving my life?" I didn't have the heart to tell him I'd nearly killed him. This man, a guy I'll call "the Wolf" because his surname roughly translates as "wolf," was a self-made millionaire. Naturally, as he was talking and thanking me, I was thinking he was going to give me some money for "saving" his life. Instead, he started into the old feed-a-man-a-fish story. You know: Feed a man a fish, you've fed him for a day. Teach a man to fish, you've fed him for a lifetime. . . . I wasn't really listening. He could keep the fish. I just wanted the money. But he'd made up his mind to teach me how to invest, and he wasn't accepting complete apathy and a bad attitude for an answer.

Around the fire that night he asked me how much money I made. I told him $4,000 during the rafting season and that I drew unemployment for the other six months. That shut him up for a couple of days. But he persevered, piqued my curiosity, and eventually got me started. I borrowed $1,000, and five years later I was a millionaire. By then I'd mastered the basics of what I now call Rule #1 investing. At the time I didn't know that The Rule is used by the best investors in the world and has been for the last 80 years. All I knew was that it made me money. That's what I'm going to teach you in this book.

Yes, there are lots of ways to get rich. Maybe you can learn to hit home runs and sign a major-league contract; invent the next hot gizmo;

buy a winning lottery ticket; or work on your acting and become the highest paid celebrity in Hollywood. But for people like you and me, how achievable are these goals, really? It's so much easier to learn how to invest with Rule #1 and be done with it. I did. You don't even have to be that smart, either. It's so simple.

Most Americans are trapped in mutual funds that, at best, ride the waves of the market. They diversify to spread the risk. They're in it for the long haul. They're doing everything the experts tell them to do. Except they still lose lots of money in market downturns. Consider the following: In 1906 the Dow Jones Industrial Average—a key index of the stock market's rise and fall—hit 100. In 1942 it was also at 100. In other words, if you bought a diversified portfolio of stocks anytime from 1906 to 1942, your rate of return was zero or worse (most likely worse). Thirty-six years. That's a very, very long run. From 1942 to 1965 the market went up and gave investors a wonderful 11 percent compounded rate of return for 22 years (not counting dividends). But then the Dow got to 1,000 and it never went over that for the next 18 years, until 1983. And then the market took off again—from 1,000 to 11,000 in 17 years. And now it's drifting along sideways again. Obviously (at least to us amateurs) the market explodes upwards, gets massively overpriced, and flattens out for two or three decades. The key word here, if you didn't already notice, is the word *decades.*

Of course, there are other possibilities for the market than just going sideways. As I write this, America's president is trying to reformulate Social Security by moving $2 trillion back into the hands of workers so they can privately invest it. If he's successful, that money will flow into mutual funds and drive the market straight up. For a while. Then the baby boomers will start retiring and possibly pull out their trillions, which could crash the market to 2002 levels. Some argue that China and India will offer such robust markets that American companies will continue to grow earnings, which will in turn prop up stock prices. But are *you* willing to count on that? Where does all this confusion leave the ordinary small investor like you and me? It leaves us with only one way to invest—by employing Rule #1 within the context of today's market.

Just as Buffett has modified his investment principles in response to changes in the marketplace, I've had to take Rule #1 principles further as a result of three major influences on the market in the last 20 years: (1) the impact of institutional money, such as mutual funds, pension funds, banking funds, and insurance funds; (2) the impact of Efficient Market Theory (which I'll explain); and (3) the impact of the Internet and personal computers on the ordinary individual's capacity to access information cheaply and use it to his advantage.

Rule #1 is the result of the one tried-and-true investing strategy meeting institutional control of the market at a time when the tools of investing are available to anyone with a computer. For the first time in history, the little guy who doesn't have eight hours a day to conduct exhaustive market research can implement Rule #1, and the tools already on your computer make it possible for you to become a successful Rule #1 investor in just 15 minutes a week. You possess an enormous number of built-in advantages—from what you know and what information you can access, to how fast you can move in and out of the market. The totality of these advantages makes it possible to outperform the so-called experts. If you're a good shopper who knows how to find wonderful things at attractive prices, you'll have no trouble learning Rule #1, which is based on the same concept.

If Rule #1 is so great, why hasn't it been available to people before now? Because now, for the first time, the tools on your computer make Rule #1 possible for everyone in just minutes a week.

As this book will make evident, the confluence of technology, money, and strategy is creating a revolution in investing at a time when small investors like us need it the most.

My hope is that this book will restore your faith in investing. If you're willing to believe in Rule #1, I'll teach you how to move financial mountains. All it takes is a little faith, a little practice, and a little effort. I'll retrain you if you've lost hope in the market, and I'll train you if you're a new investor—even if you have no financial experience whatsoever and just want to get started with something that's risk-free and guaranteed to provide financial security.

Whether you're a seasoned investor or a novice, you're going to let go of old and wrongheaded ivory-tower theories. Leave your mutual

Authors Levitt and Dubner state clearly in their book *Freakonomics* what the Internet has truly given us all: access to previously secret information and the power to use that information to our advantage. They write: "Information is the currency of the Internet. As a medium, the Internet is brilliantly efficient at shifting information from the hands of those who have it into the hands of those who do not. . . . The Internet has proven particularly fruitful for situations in which a face-to-face encounter with an expert might actually *exacerbate* the problem of asymmetrical information—situations in which an expert uses his informational advantage to make us feel stupid or rushed or cheap or ignoble." In the investing world, guess who, by their hoarding of information, tries to make us feel stupid and dependent on them for information? Yes, the so-called experts, meaning many—but not all—money managers, brokers, and financial planners.

funds and those managers behind. In doing so, you'll escape mediocrity and learn to depend on yourself to open the door to true wealth.

You want to know what gets me really pumped up? Imagine a world where high school kids learn Rule #1 and at 15 years old start compounding money at 20 percent a year. Young people who can find $1,000 a year to buy great companies will have more than $45 million to retire on at age 65. That means they'll be able to do whatever they want in their working lives with no worries about retirement. They could be entrepreneurs, teachers, soldiers, astronauts, scientists, firemen, artists, or missionaries. Doesn't matter, because they know they'll have a fortune as early as their fifties. And I get even more pumped up when I think about *my* generation, the baby boomers, being able to retire comfortably because they learned to invest with high rates of return in businesses they're proud to own, without the fear of losing what they worked so hard to gain. Rule #1 is for *everyone*, regardless of age, wealth, IQ, or social status. Used properly, it'll ensure you never have to worry about money again. I know you're ready, so let's begin.

To become a true Rule #1 investor, you'll have to learn how to perform some basic calculations. At first this might seem scary, but it shouldn't be any scarier than learning something new in school and having to wait until you get used to what you're seeing and doing. Believe me, I'm a math phobe, too, and I hate anything that's complicated. What I want you to do is pretend you're back in fourth grade and you have to learn your multiplication tables. Once you get used to working with the numbers and making routine calculations, it'll be as easy as

One of the less touted benefits of Rule #1 investing is the ability to retire comfortably with a lot less money. For example, let's say you save $300,000 by the time you retire (excluding your house, etc.) and then take the advice of most professionals—putting that $300,000 mostly in bonds, which, on average, will provide an annual income of about $15,000 a year. That's about $1,300 a month (and a bit more if they amortize the principle). Not nearly enough to maintain a middle-class lifestyle. That is why financial planners suggest you accumulate ten times your current income—which for many people means they need about $1 million socked away. One million is a very scary number for most; invested safely in bonds, it'll provide about $50,000 a year in income.

A Rule #1 investor, however, can create a yearly income stream of $50,000 with only a *$300,000* nest egg! That benefit alone argues for a Rule #1 approach. And the reason the numbers work out that way is that Rule #1 investors reap 15 percent returns a year. Few baby boomers are currently in a financial situation where they can envision having a million dollars in the next 15 years. And those who *can* see a million in their future . . . well, with a million bucks, a Rule #1 investor is knocking out about *$12,000* a month income instead of $4,000. With $12,000 a month income, a millionaire can retire like, well . . . a millionaire.

knowing what two times two is. By the end of the book, you'll have acquired some pattern recognition skills that make Rule #1 investing second nature.

To facilitate the learning process and simplify the calculations as much as possible, I've designed a website that works in tandem with this book. You'll find many references to the site www.ruleoneinvestor. com—throughout, and you may want to acquaint yourself with it before beginning. There you'll find various calculators and trusted links to financial sites. But the vast majority of what you need in order to learn the Rule #1 ropes awaits you here; I use the website more like a chalkboard that allows me to interact with you—if you want. It also affords you the opportunity to go to the chalkboard and test your Rule #1 methods using my tools.

When I'm assuring someone that he or she can do this, I often tell the story of a woman I met a few years back in a workshop, whom I'll call Julie. Julie had been a stay-at-home mom for 20 years, and prior to that, she'd taught high school art classes. She hated math, had no history of working with numbers, and wasn't even in charge of the bills at home. But upon seeing an advertisement for a seminar where I was among the speakers, she got curious. She then signed up for a workshop, and within a few months she was well on her way to becoming a master Rule #1 investor, having speedily learned how to manipulate the numbers. Her husband, who'd previously managed all of their investments and household finances, was forced to surrender. Once Julie took charge of their portfolio, they watched it grow from $45,000 to more than $72,000—a 60-percent return—in a few months. Meanwhile, Julie's husband's 401k retirement account, which

I'll be using a lot of examples in the book that include numbers, such as stock prices, growth percentages, earnings per share, etc. The numbers are used for explaining the concepts and teaching you Rule #1 investing. Because these figures derive from mid-2005—or earlier—they probably won't reflect the actual, current numbers as you read this. Don't let that affect your learning experience. Accept them as examples only.

had $50,000 in it, increased by $462 during the same period. If Julie could do the math, so can you.

For those independent types who'd rather not use the time-saving cal-culators offered on www.ruleoneinvestor.com, make a beeline for the website anyway and pick up tools I provide that will allow you to do essentially the same thing with Excel. Trust, though, that the more comfortable you become with Rule #1 thinking, the more this will become an "in your head" process. Eventually, your primary use of the web will be in gathering financial data, accessing online market tools, and getting the most up-to-date information. You may also opt to visit my site for the sole purpose of accessing new information I post, as well as to link yourself to other online resources.

I'll try to define as much as I can along the way, but if you ever come across a term you don't understand and that you want clarified, flip to the glossary at the end of the book.

If you ever need a sounding board, e-mail me from my website. I'll post answers to all the popular questions.

Chapter 1

The Myths of Investing

An expert is a person who avoids small error as he sweeps on to the grand fallacy.

—BENJAMIN STOLBERG (1891–1951)

THE GOLD standard of low-risk investing is a ten-year United States Treasury bond, which, at the time of this writing, has a return of about 4 percent. Invest in nothing but these bonds and you're guaranteed a 4-percent haul. The only problem with such a strategy, especially for the millions of soon-to-be-retired baby boomers, is that, at 4 percent, it takes 18 years to double your money. In addition, after 18 years, even with a low inflation rate of 2 to 3 percent, most of the gain is absorbed by higher prices, leaving you with only slightly more buying power than you had 18 years earlier. Despite this reality, investors buy billions of dollars of these 4-percent bonds.

Why in the world would anyone want to own a bond that barely keeps pace with inflation and realizes almost no real gain in wealth? Because almost everyone is convinced that a higher rate of return necessarily means a lot more risk. And they're more afraid of losing money in an attempt to get a higher return than of their inability to retire comfortably.

The fact is, a higher rate of return is not necessarily contingent on incurring significantly more risk. Let me explain.

HIGH RETURNS DON'T NECESSARILY MEAN MORE RISK

During a talk at the America West Arena in Phoenix, Arizona, I asked the audience, "How many of you drove your cars here today?" Most people raised their hands. "Okay, almost everybody. And how many of you took a huge risk driving here?" A few hands went back up. "You guys took a *huge* risk driving here?" I asked incredulously. "Either you drivers didn't really take a risk and are just clowning around, or at last we've found the problem with Phoenix traffic — you people with your hands up don't know how to drive. Is that it?" Everybody laughed. "Okay, so it wasn't so terrifying to drive down here. But now imagine that you're coming here but instead of *you* doing the driving, it's your eleven-year-old nephew behind the wheel. Are you taking a lot of risk now?" People laughed and nodded yes. "The trip was the same — going from A to B. But when you put someone in the driver's seat who doesn't know how to drive, a relatively safe trip becomes an incredibly risky trip."

Exactly the same thing holds true for your journey to financial freedom. If you don't know what you're doing, your journey is going to be either very slow or very dangerous. That's why most people think that going fast (going after a high rate of return) is dangerous — because they don't know how to drive the financial car, and not because going fast is *necessarily* dangerous. It's only dangerous if you don't know what you're doing. And the essence of Rule #1 is knowing what you're doing — investing with certainty so you *don't lose money!*

Now, you're probably wondering, "What about mutual funds? What about all those techniques we learn to minimize risk and maximize returns?" Well, folks, I hate to be the bearer of bad news, but here's the truth: Being a mutual fund investor is a whole lot riskier than being a Rule #1 investor. Investing in a mutual fund is, in many ways, like handing your car keys to that 11-year-old nephew.

THE MUTUAL FUND SCAM

If you own mutual funds that are attempting to beat the market, and you're hoping your fund manager can give you a nice retirement, you're highly likely to be the victim of a huge scam. You're not alone — 100 million investors are right there with you. *Fortune* magazine reports that since 1985 only 4 percent of all the fund managers beat the S&P 500 index, and the few who did it did so by only a small margin. In other words, almost no fund managers have done what they're paid by you to do — beat the market. That significant fact went unnoticed through the roaring 1980s and 1990s as the stock market surged with double-digit growth, bringing your fund manager along for the joyride. But now the ride is over, and investors are starting to notice that their fund managers are pretty much useless. This is not a new observation.

Several years ago, Warren Buffett said this about your fund manager: "Professionals in other fields, like dentists, bring a lot to the layman, but people get nothing for their money from professional money managers." The key word here is *nothing*. And yet, what do you do? You give your hard-earned money to one of these guys and hope he can deliver those 15-percent-or-better returns, like the ones you got in the 1990s. Why? Because you don't want to invest your own money, and because you've been convinced by the entire financial services industry that you can't do it yourself.

Come on, get real. From 2000 to 2003, mutual funds lost half their value. You could have lost 50 percent of your money without the help of a professional. In fact, in 1996 a monkey was hired to compete with the best fund managers in New York. He beat them two years in a row. When I told this story one day to an audience in Los Angeles, someone from the upper deck in the Arrowhead Pond Arena yelled out, "What's the name of the chimp?" This is proof that some people will do anything to avoid investing their own money.

Peter Lynch, one of the few fund managers who made above-market returns and then got out before the market leveled him, wrote in his book *One Up on Wall Street* that the amateur investor has "numerous built-in advantages, which, if exploited, should result in outperforming the market and the experts." In other words, you should be doing this yourself. But you don't. The reason you don't is that the entire financial services industry perpetuates three myths of investing to keep people investing with them in spite of the industry's dismal performance over any long period.

THE THREE MYTHS OF INVESTING

Myth 1. You Have to Be an Expert to Manage Money.

The first myth I want to bust is that it takes a lot of time and expertise to manage your money. It would if investing were hard to learn or if getting the information to make a decision took a lot of time. I'll prove to you that it doesn't, even though the financial services industry wants us to believe it does. The industry stands to make billions from commissions and fees if it can keep you thinking you can't do it on your own.

The Internet has changed everything. Now the tools that used to cost $50,000 a year are available for less than two bucks a day and take only minutes a day to use instead of 50 hours a week. And the Internet tools are more accurate, more timely, and easier to apply than anything your fund manager had just a couple of years ago. All you need is a little instruction and a brief learning period. But don't bother to ask your broker, financial planner/adviser, certified public accountant (CPA), or fund manager if you should do this on your own. You know what *they're* going to say. Something like, "But that's what I do for you, so you don't have to worry about it." Well, you should worry about it. A lot. It's your money and you're the only one who really cares about what happens to it.

Even the pros like Jim Cramer, a guy who's in your corner and who wants to see you invest on your own, doesn't really know what it's like to be one of us. Like the rest of the top of the financial industry, Jim's Ivy League, incredibly smart, loves playing with stocks all day and night, lives it and breathes it and has no sense of what it's like to be you and me out there digging ditches someplace and hoping we can retire.

For these guys it's a game. A serious game, but still a game. Jim's a trader and loves to speculate. Following his approach, you've got to put in five to ten hours a week minimum and you're playing a very dangerous game with money you can't afford to lose against really rich, really smart, and really motivated guys — guys just like Jim.

If you think you can win at that game, be my guest. And if you do win, my hat goes off to you. You're a lot smarter than the rest of us. For everybody else, me included, there has to be another way. Most of us don't have five hours a week for investing. Let's face it. We've got kids to raise, lives to live, and jobs that already take more time than we have. We also don't want to be chained to watching the stock market or to become frantic day traders. What fun would that be? We're just looking for something to invest in that gets really great returns without the risk of losing money and without spending a lot of time at it.

Rule #1 is investing for the rest of us.

Myth 2. You Can't Beat the Market.

Okay, it's true that 96 percent of all mutual fund managers have not been able to beat the market in the last 20 years. But you're not a fund manager and you're not judged by whether you beat the market. Your financial skill is judged by whether you're living comfortably when you're 75. You shouldn't care whether you beat the market. If the market goes down 50 percent but your fund manager loses only 40 percent of your money, he may have beaten the market, but does that seem good to you? Rule #1 investors expect a minimum annual compounded rate of return of 15 percent a year or more. If we can get that, we don't care what the market did. We're going to retire rich anyway. Judged by that standard, Rule #1 investors . . . well, rule.

The myth that you can't beat the market was started in the 1970s by, among others, Professor Burton Malkiel of Princeton University, who did lots of research purporting to prove that nobody beats the market. (We'll be going into greater detail regarding Malkiel's theories later on in this book, but we must mention him here to debunk this myth.) His book, *A Random Walk Down Wall Street,* still sells. He influenced a generation of professors in business schools who, as a body, subscribed to what has become known as Efficient Market Theory (EMT). EMT says markets in general (and the stock market in particular) are efficient — that is, they price things according to their value. In the stock market, the ups and downs of the market are caused by rational investors responding minute by minute to the events that may affect their investments. According to EMT, the market is *so* efficient that everything that can be known about a company is already, minute by minute, figured into the price of its stock. In other words, the price of the stock at all times equals the value of the company.

If that's true, say the professors who believe in EMT, then it's simply not possible to find a stock that's undervalued, and it's equally impossible to pay too much for a stock. Why? Because price is always equal to value. So there are no deals in the market, and there are no rip-offs. This situation, EMT theorists say, accounts for the fact that almost no fund managers ever beat the market. These fund managers are smart guys, and if none of them beats the market for long periods, then the market must be perfectly pricing everything.

But some people do beat the market for long periods, and the point of this book is to show you how. You'll soon realize how false EMT really is.

In 1984, Warren Buffett gave a lecture at Columbia Business School in which he showed that at least 20 investors, who he'd predicted would have high rates of return, all beat the target of 15 percent handsomely for periods longer than 20 years. All of these investors hailed from the same school of investing, which he called "Graham-and-Doddsville" because all had either learned from professors Graham and Dodd, from Buffett, or from someone who was copying Buffett—the same way I learned from my teacher and the way you're learning from me. (Benjamin Graham was Buffett's teacher at Columbia; David Dodd was another professor at the school.) The compounded annual rate of return for these investors over eight decades ranged from 18 percent to 33 percent per year. The point Buffett was making to the Columbia students was that the people he knows who make over 15 percent a year for long periods *all do it similarly.* They all start with Rule #1.

After the 2000 to 2003 stock market debacle, when some very good businesses saw their stock values drop by 90 percent, Professor Malkiel was interviewed, and as we'll see in Chapter 8, he came as close to a retraction of his theory as an academician ever could when he admitted that "the market is generally efficient . . . but do[es] go crazy from time to time." Oh. It's efficient but sometimes it's not. Funny, but I thought that was what Buffett and Graham had been saying for 80 years. Buffett quips that he hopes the business schools will continue to turn out fund managers who believe in EMT so that he'll continue to have lots of misinformed fund managers to buy businesses from when they price them too cheap, and to sell businesses to when they're willing to pay too much.

The chart on page 18 shows how Rule #1 investors have fared over the last several decades, as compared with the performance of the S&P 500 and the Dow Jones Industrial Average.

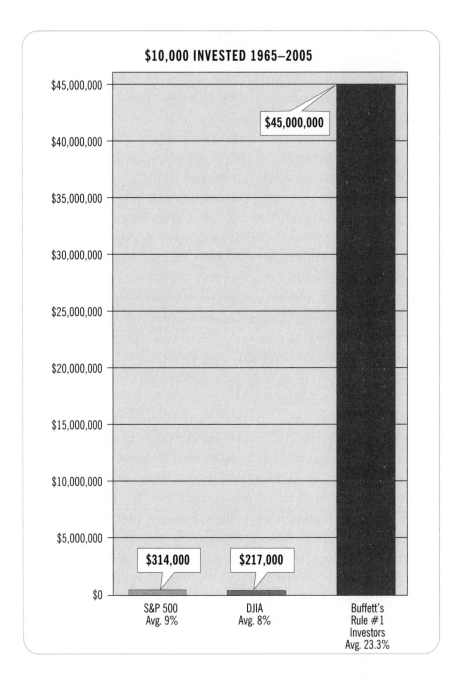

$10,000 INVESTED 1965–2005

S&P 500
Avg. 9%
$314,000

DJIA
Avg. 8%
$217,000

Buffett's
Rule #1
Investors
Avg. 23.3%
$45,000,000

How Rule #1 investors have fared in comparison with the market's most popular indexes. This chart may appear erroneous or exaggerated, but it's not. Rule #1 investors outperform the S&P 500 and the Dow Jones Industrial Average by a long shot—routinely. The magic of compound growth is what

Myth 3. The Best Way to Minimize Risk Is to Diversify and Hold (for the Long Term).

Diversify and hold. Everybody knows that's the safest way to invest in the stock market, right? But then again, at one time everybody knew the earth was flat. The fact is, a long-term diversified portfolio would have had a zero rate of return for 37 years from 1905 to 1942, for 18 years from 1965 to 1983, and from 2000 to 2005. Sixty years out of 100. If you know how to invest—meaning you understand Rule #1 and know how to find a wonderful company at an attractive price—then you *do not* diversify your money into 50 stocks or an index mutual fund. You focus on a few businesses that you understand. You buy when the big guys—the fund managers who control the market—are fearful, and you sell when they're greedy. Shocking, no? (And if you don't know what I mean by this, you will by the end of this book. Promise.)

Today more than 80 percent of the money in the market is invested by fund managers (pension funds, banking funds, insurance funds, and mutual funds). As I indicated in the Introduction, this is what is known as "institutional money." Out of $17 trillion, the big guys manage more than $14 trillion of it. In other words, the fund managers *are* the market; when they move billions of dollars into a stock, the price of that stock goes up. When they take their money out, the price of that stock goes down. Their effect on the market is so huge that if they decide to sell suddenly, they can generate a massive crash. Understanding this fact is central to Rule #1: The fund managers control the price of almost all the stocks in the market, but they can't easily get out when

---

explains the massive difference between compounding at 8 or 9 percent per year versus compounding a little over 23 percent per year.

Such a huge difference isn't so obvious at first glance. Because 23 percent is just three times bigger than 8 percent, one would automatically think the dollars should just be three times bigger. But compounding growth is not linear, it's what is called geometric. Compounding grows a rate of return not only on the original dollar invested, but also on the accumulating dollar returns ("interest on interest"). Because 23 percent produces a higher dollar return every year, which, in turn, has a 23 percent return on it, the accelerating dollar amount explodes after several years and rockets far from the lower 8-percent compounded return.

Cool, huh?

they want to. You and I, however, can be in or out of the market within seconds. In Chapter 11 we'll explore in detail what this means for us.

So what happens in the long run if the baby-boom money that drove the market up starts to come out as the baby boomers retire? Or what if some other event draws money out of the market? As mutual funds drop in value, investors react by withdrawing money faster from the funds, which ultimately puts the market into free fall. The irony is that while, in theory, investing for the long run in a diversified mutual fund lowers risk, such an investment strategy in this market actually *raises* risk. In this market there's no such thing as a "balanced portfolio" that reduces your exposure to market risk, no matter how loudly the financial services industry salesmen shout it. If this market crashes, fund managers who play these games may find themselves rearranging deck chairs on the *Titanic*.

If you don't think a total stock market meltdown can happen in a modern economy, think again. It just happened over the last ten years in Japan, whose stock market lost 85 percent of its value from 1992 to 2002. It hasn't recovered yet. And Japan's boomers are about ten years older than America's (political and economic factors prompted a baby boom in Japan prior to the start of World War II). If America's market tanks 85 percent, the Dow will be at 1500. It happened during the 1930s. It can happen again.

Diversification spreads you out too thin and guarantees a market rate of return — meaning whatever happens to the whole market happens to you. Obviously there are hundreds of great businesses available to buy, but if you have a job and a family and don't want to be married to your computer, you don't have time to keep up with more than a few. If you buy businesses you don't keep up with, you'll inevitably violate Rule #1 with respect to some, causing your overall return to drop.

As Rule #1 business buyers, we pick a few choice businesses in different sectors of the market. So even though we aren't "diversifying" like mutual fund managers by buying dozens — if not hundreds — of different companies at once, we'll be setting up a portfolio that reflects different categories of businesses. But exactly how many companies you can buy into will depend on how much money you have to invest, and I'll tell you what the right proportional relationship is.

Diversification is for people who have 30 years to go, have no desire whatsoever to learn how to invest, and are going to be happy with an 8-percent yearly return and a minimum standard of living in retirement. Our goal is to find wonderful companies, buy them at really attractive prices, and then let the market do its thing—which means eventually the market will price these businesses correctly at their value; in a few weeks, months, or years we're a lot richer than we are right now. That's what we *want* to do. But to do that, we have to stop being ignorant investors being taken advantage of by the entire financial services industry and start being knowledgeable Rule #1 investors who, instead of being the prey, outfox the predators.

> In the mid-1960s my dad suggested I put money in a diversified mutual fund. I invested $600 and forgot about it. Eighteen years later my investment was worth $400. Imagine if I were 45 years old in the mid-1960s and I invested $60,000 instead of $600. How depressing would it have felt 18 years later at age 63 to discover my $60,000 had become $40,000 instead of the $240,000 I was planning on for my retirement? A goal of this book is to spare you from ever having to look into that financial abyss.

DOLLAR COST AVERAGING WILL NOT PROTECT YOU

Although dollar cost averaging (DCA) is technically not a myth, I get a lot of questions about it and constantly have to prove to people that DCA is not the investor's lifesaver it's purported to be. A favorite sales tool for fund managers and brokers, DCA is the strategy of buying stocks or mutual funds every month with the same amount of money, regardless of the price of the stock or fund. For example, you buy $100 worth of shares in Microsoft every month, no matter what the price per share is. So if the price is down, your money buys more shares. If it's up, your money buys fewer shares. The objective of dollar cost averaging is to minimize your investment risk by making the average cost per share of stock smaller.

This method of protecting yourself has two huge flaws: (1) In a long sideways or down market, DCA is pretty much the same as buy-and-hold; and (2) for DCA to work, you have to put in *the same amount every month, no matter what.* So between 1929 and 1930, when $100,000 of stocks became worth $10,000, you'd still have needed to be willing to buy in. Between 2000 and 2002, when the tech stock index lost 85 percent of its value, you'd have needed to be willing to keep buying all the way down to the bottom. First, that assumes you have a job and the spare cash to spend on stocks during a recession or depression, and, second, it assumes you'd still be willing to throw in good money after taking that kind of a loss. Instead of trusting DCA, Rule #1 investors know the value of a wonderful business and buy it when it's undervalued. In other words, as I'll shortly show, we buy one dollar of value for fifty cents and repeat. We do not buy one dollar for ten dollars and hope our profligacy will be counterbalanced by an opportunity to sometimes — maybe — buy the same stock for an inexpensive price.

> With DCA from 1905 to 1942, your rate of return in a Dow index fund would have been 1 percent as opposed to zero percent with buy-and-hold. From 1965 to 1983, your rate of return would have been 2 percent instead of zero percent. From 2000 to 2005, your rate of return would have been 3 percent instead of 0 percent. In other words, over the majority of the last 100 years of stock investing, it would've been better to just buy a government bond and forget about it than to DCA in a Dow index fund.

Because Rule #1 investors require a 15-percent return, we have to throw out strategies that fail to achieve that minimum in all kinds of markets. And because DCA failed to achieve even treasury bond rates of return in several sideways markets in the last 100 years, it cannot be a useful Rule #1 strategy.

The truth is, the financial services industry cares about your money only because it takes commissions and fees whether it makes you any money or not. It perpetuates the Three Myths of Investing and extols the virtues of dollar cost averaging so you and I will give managers our money. The last thing they want is for you to invest successfully on your own. They want you to believe you'll lose your money if you do this yourself. They're hoping your fear of loss will compel you to keep giving them your money in spite of the likelihood they'll be *less* effective than you are in reaping a high return.

THE THREE MYTHS VS. RULE #1	
Myth	**Rule #1**
It's hard and it takes too long.	It's simple, taking at most only 15 minutes a week.
You can't beat the market.	You can take advantage of regular mispricing to reap a 15-percent return or more.
Diversify, buy, and hold	Buy a dollar for 50 cents, and sell it later for a dollar. Repeat until very rich.

RULE #1 VS. REAL ESTATE

Okay, so let's say you don't buy into the myths of investing, but you do buy into the myth about real estate being a better investment than businesses. You know I'm going to shoot you down on this argument. If you think that because real estate lets you leverage your investment, the rate of return is much higher than a business/stock investment and is, therefore, a better place for beginning investors to put their money, think again.

This is a commonly held idea that's completely mistaken. I've owned a lot of real estate, everything from subdivisions to huge farms, apartments, commercial property, and single-family homes. I've bought into hot real estate markets like Del Mar, California, and Jackson Hole, Wyoming, and slow ones like Fairfield, Iowa. If we're going to do a real estate versus business/stock ownership returns comparison, we could pit the hottest real estate markets against the hottest Rule #1 investors. But it seems better to use the average real estate market and the average Rule #1 investor.

A reasonably good growth rate in a real estate market over a 30-year period is about 4 percent. A reasonably good rate of return for a Rule #1 investor is about 15 percent. True, Jackson Hole and Del Mar real estate appreciated at 10 percent per year for 30 years (in big bursts). And it's equally true that experienced Rule #1 investors nail 25 percent per year return on investments (ROIs) for 30 years. But these are exceptional cases.

A return on investment (ROI) is simply the return you get from an investment—the dollars you put in and the dollars you get out within a certain time period—which can reflect either a profit or loss. It's usually expressed as an annual percentage return. For example, if you invest $100 into a business and it returns to you $150 after the first year, your ROI is 50 percent. Technically, ROI is calculated by dividing your total amount invested into your profit. (Extra tidbit: This is slightly different from ROIC—return on investment *capital*—which is a more complicated calculation that's very specific about what constitutes dollars in and dollars out. You'll come to understand ROIC very soon, as it's an excellent indicator of the health of a business.)

So let's look at the difference between investing $50,000 right now in real estate versus $50,000 right now in a business with Rule #1. This is an especially interesting contrast considering real estate and the stock market might not go up at all for the next 15 years! (If that happens, the real estate example below will seem wildly optimistic!)

Here are the numbers: We buy a $250,000 house for $50,000

down with a 6-percent, 30-year fixed mortgage. Our payments are $1,200 a month, but we rent it for $1,200 and cover our mortgage payments. We are, however, in the hole for insurance, maintenance, advertising, and taxes.

On the other hand, let's assume we never miss a month's rent and can increase the rent by 4 percent a year. By our ninth year, we've been able to increase rents enough to cover everything. From there on to the thirtieth year, it's all cash flow. Then we sell the place. At that point the house is worth $811,000 and is totally paid for. Also, we've pocketed rental income we've reinvested wisely and made the same return on that as on our house overall—about 10 percent per year for an additional $230,000. Total return equals $1,041,000. Our compounded ROI for 30 years is 10.6 percent. Quite respectable, although I didn't deduct for management and maintenance, which I expect we'll do ourselves. This isn't an insignificant headache, and gathering up the investment dollars from such an endeavor isn't easy. We had to do a lot of work (and hoping) to get that 11-percent return. Nonetheless, let's compare that to our 15-percent minimum Rule #1 return.

First, as Rule #1 investors, we incur almost *no management responsibility*—a significant advantage. We have to spend about 15 minutes a week, and that's it. We're required to know how to do Rule #1 investing, of course, but it's easier to learn than real estate investing once you see the advantages. We buy a wonderful business (actually *a part of* a business via shares of stock) at an attractive price with our $50,000. We then sell it when it gets unattractive and buy another. We do that for 30 years, averaging 15 percent. (And as with the real estate example above, we're not being taxed on our gains—in this case, we're buying and selling in a tax-protected IRA, which you'll learn about later.) After 30 years, my investment is worth $3.3 million. My 30-year compounded ROI is 15 percent, only 4 percentage points higher than the real estate transaction, but I have $2 million more in my bank account.

It gets better. Now let's compare the two investments when you're 60 and retired. If you invested in real estate, what you do at this point is take the $1.2 million and put it into a nice 5-percent bond that pays you $5,000 per month. After taxes, you keep $4,000 a month. That's a whopping $1,650 in today's money. Better hope Social Security is still working. Or you keep working your real estate, dealing with renters and fixing toilets, and the rent money is your income: about $3,800 a month. Your only other choice is to re-leverage your investment and buy more real estate — which is a whole lot different from being retired, isn't it?

At least now you know the truth: Real estate is nice and I have a lot of money in it, but it really doesn't begin to compete with a consistent 15-percent Rule #1 return. My advice: Go find a wonderful business at an attractive price and live like a king when you retire.

But if you're a Rule #1 investor, it's no big deal to spend 15 minutes a week on your investments, so you'll continue to invest the $3.3 million at 15 percent and then live on the 15-percent increase each year. Translation: You're receiving about $40,000 a month. That's not a typo. Of course, you do have to pay taxes on that, so you'll end up with about $30,000 a month, which is only $12,000 in today's dollars. Do you think you can squeak by on $12,000 a month when you're retired versus $1,650 in today's dollars?

So there's how I look at it. You can stay ignorant of The Rule, opt exclusively for real estate, and try to live on the result the rest of your life — or you can become a Rule #1 investor.

WHY BOTHER LEARNING RULE #1?

I can't reiterate this enough: The first reason you should bother to learn The Rule is that you can make 15 percent a year or more with very little risk, and that'll change the way you and your family live forever. You can't do that in real estate, in a mutual fund, or by randomly picking stocks out of a hat. The second reason is that when you invest by The Rule, it almost doesn't matter what amount of money you start with; in 20 years you can retire comfortably. Take a look at this chart:

Amount to start	Monthly savings (additions to account)	Amount in 20 years	Annual income in 20 years
$1,000	$300	$470,000	$70,000
$10,000	$300	$650,000	$97,000
$50,000	$300	$1,450,000	$215,000

Similar to what we just went through in comparing Rule #1 returns to real estate returns, if you could retire with a permanent income of $70,000 a year 20 years from now, starting today with just $1,000, would you want to learn to do that? It's possible, as we've seen, if you accumulate money for 20 years and from then on consume only the gains, leaving the principle untouched. So if you start with $1,000 your principle is almost $500,000 in 20 years, and if you continue to make 15 percent a year, you have $70,000 a year to live on — without ever touching that half a million. If you start today with $50,000, your principle in 20 years will be $1.45 million, allowing you to live off a $215,000 (15 percent) gain each year. Think you can handle that kind of retirement? The key is to bank 15 percent or more returns a year from all that you've amassed over those initial 20 years (and beyond), which will beget ever higher returns. And if you don't think you have 20 working years left before your targeted retirement date, you can still generate a decent amount of money following The Rule, and make that money continue to work for you in retirement.

MEET DOUG AND SUSAN CONNELLY

Let's look at an overall picture of Rule #1 investing in the real world.

It's 2003. Doug and Susan Connelly are a couple in their late forties with two kids in high school. They live on a combined income of about $60,000 a year. Doug works as a salesman for a small business and Susan is a teacher in a private school. They listened to me speak at a motivational seminar and decided to learn The Rule.

What's driving them to invest on their own is the simple fact that they *must* if they want to have a decent retirement. At this point they have only $20,000 in an IRA, although their $200,000 home will be paid for by the time they're ready to retire. They think they can add about $5,000 a year pre-tax to their IRA. Here's the problem: They know that if they put the $20,000 plus $5,000 a year into a bond at 4 percent, they'll have only $190,000 to live on if they retire in 20 years. The $190,000 in their IRA at 4 percent will provide them with about $650 a month pre-tax. Add in Social Security and a paid-for house and they think they can squeeze by, but it isn't the life they want. They want to travel, eat in restaurants when they desire, and drive a car that won't break down. Doug likes to play golf, and it isn't getting any cheaper. Susan would love to go to New York and see a Broadway show once in a while, but at $100 a seat, dinner at $100 per person, and a hotel at $250 a night, she knows that kind of outing is too pricey on their probable income.

And even more important to Doug and Susan is being able to cover their medical bills. They know health care is getting more and more expensive and insurance doesn't cover it all. They read an article in *Newsweek* that featured interviews with retirees who were paying $600 a month out of pocket for medicine not covered by either their health insurance or Medicare. The Connellys don't want to burden their kids, and they don't want to lose everything they have or be forced to finish their lives in some government nursing home because of an unexpected health problem. They know they need more money.

They got excited about Rule #1 investing because of the math: If The Rule can get them a 15-percent-a-year return in their IRA where they don't pay tax, they'll have more than $840,000 in their IRA for retirement in 20 years instead of $190,000. Second, they can continue investing while retired, compounding the $840,000 at 15 percent. That'll give them more than $10,500 a month to live on pre-tax, plus Social Security, without touching the $840,000. That's significantly better than the $650 they can expect from a bond. They've decided it's well worth learning The Rule to secure that better life.

Retirement Strategy	Year 2005 retirement capital	Year 2025 retirement capital	Year 2025 income to supplement Social Security
Playing it "safe"	$20,000 plus $5,000 / year	$190,000	$7,700 annually
Rule #1	$20,000 plus $5,000 / yr	$840,000	$126,000 annually

THE POWER OF MONEY MAKING MONEY

Doug and Susan can retire much sooner and/or far better than they thought they could because of the power of compound growth, which dictates that not only money earns a return on investment (ROI), but the ROI earns an ROI. (Recall the difference in compounding at 8 or 9 percent a year versus 23 percent.) This is how money can make even more money over time. Example: You invest $1,000 and it gets an ROI of 10 percent each year. After the first year your investment is worth $1,100. In the second year you get an ROI of 10 percent on that $100 profit as well as your original $1,000. This brings your total to $1,210, and so on. If you leave your investment to compound at 10 percent per year, 50 years later that $1,000 becomes $117,391 . . . and you are dead. So we need to speed this up a bit. To do that, we have to get a better ROI.

The reason we make Rule #1 the foundation of our investment philosophy is that we understand that the power of compounding money at 15 percent a year or more depends on not losing it — *ever.* A 50-percent drop in price requires a 100-percent rise in price just to break even. If the price of a stock drops 80 percent, it has to go up 400 percent to break even. Oracle was at $40 a share in 2000 and dropped to $10. That's an 80-percent drop. It has to double once from $10 to $20 and then double again from $20 to $40 just to break even. Four hundred percent! Think about that. For the market to go up 400 percent,

the Dow, for example, would have to go from 10,000 to 40,000. And
that could take at least three decades! Meanwhile, your portfolio is a
permanent disaster and a 15-percent minimum yearly return is out of
reach.

Let's return for a moment to Doug and Susan Connelly, but this
time assume only Susan came to learn about Rule #1 and each has a sep-
arate portfolio (a stubborn couple, they both practice their own methods of investing and don't want to mix accounts). Let's also assume each
has $20,000 to invest now, plus an additional $5,000 a year, as in the
example above. After 10 years of investing and reaping 15 percent a
year, Doug loses half his money in a market crash. Susan, a Rule #1 investor, does not. She then teaches Doug about Rule #1, and from the
end of the tenth year onward, they both manage to make 15 percent a
year. Twenty years from now, Doug has $420,000; Susan has
$840,000. This means Doug has $63,000 a year to live on while Susan
is living comfortably on $126,000 a year. The permanent $63,000-per-
year difference in annual income 20 years later is Doug's one-time violation of Rule #1.

And this isn't even close to what's actually happened to thousands
of students of mine who've related their investing horror stories. For
example, I met Robert at a presentation I did in Texas. He had all his
retirement invested in Enron stock at the urging of his trusted bosses.
He was so angry about it that when I showed the class proof that Enron
insiders were getting out even while they told their employees to stay
in, he had to go out into the hall and cool off before breaking something. Such anger is very real, the outward manifestation of serious
emotional problems that ferment when we work hard to build wealth
and then see it taken away because of ignorance. There wasn't a person
in that room who didn't see a piece of themselves in Robert's anger
and pain.

Another guy whom I'll call Chris told me he started with about
$50,000 in 1990 and built it up to more than $1 million by 2000. Then
he lost it all simply because he couldn't believe it wouldn't go back up
and his broker kept telling him to "double down" — put more and more
into the stocks that were going down so he'd make his fortune when
they went back up. But they didn't ever go up, and it wiped him out. He

was starting over with $1,000 and the realization that even if the market does go up in the long run, the long run is longer than he has.

These are people to admire. They got knocked down hard and still got up. But although we salute their guts and perseverance, the truth is we don't want to have their experience if we can avoid it. My feeling is, learn Rule #1 and avoid making the mistake in the first place.

Get knocked down seven times. Get up eight times.

—JAPANESE PROVERB

If you've never bought a stock before, don't know how to open a brokerage account, or don't know what an IRA is, don't worry. I'll be guiding you through the process in Chapter 15. First I want you to become very familiar with the Rule #1 methodology, and then we'll tackle those smaller issues and get you started on the right foot.

The impact of compounding rates of return can work for you or against you. Which way it works depends on whether you're able to invest with certainty in companies that won't lose your money. Only then will your compounded rate of return be certain to be positive and high enough to make a difference in your life. Almost any sort of positive compounded rate of return will eventually make you rich. The question is *when*. Obviously, the larger the positive compounded rate of return, the faster you get rich—as long as you don't violate Rule #1.

Think of it like a board game in which if you land on the wrong square you get sent back to the beginning and have to start over. That's exactly what kills most institutional (mutual fund) portfolios. At some point the big guys—your mutual fund managers—all land on that square. Your job as a little investor is to learn how to avoid landing on that square. If you don't get sent back to the beginning, you're going to be *very* comfortable financially.

Ask yourself this question: If you thought you could retire in 10 to 20 years by working on it just 15 minutes a week with less risk than you're taking right now in your mutual funds, would you want to learn how? I'm guessing the answer is an enthusiastic "yes," so listen up as we turn now to a discussion of Rule #1's specific working method.

Chapter 2

Rule #1 and the Four Ms

It is possible to fail in many ways . . . while to succeed is possible only in one way.

—Aristotle (384–322 B.C.), *Nichomachean Ethics*
(an early Rule #1 investor)

SOME THINGS don't change. Rule #1 is one of those things. It's been the basis of excellent investing for the last hundred years and it will be the basis of excellent investing a hundred years from now. A Rule #1 investor looks at stocks as businesses that have a determinable value, and then waits patiently for market fluctuations to bring her that business at a great price. Here are The Rule's main tenets:

RULE #1 IN A NUTSHELL

First, understand that Rule #1 literally is "Don't Lose Money," but what it means in practical terms is to invest with certainty. Certainty comes from this: *buying a wonderful business at an attractive price*. Memorize the following:

Knowing you will make money comes from buying a wonderful business at an attractive price.

The word *wonderful* actually encompasses three simple elements that we'll explore in depth in upcoming chapters. First, *wonderful* implies that the business has *Meaning* to you — that you understand it enough to want to own the whole thing if you could, that you'd be proud to own it, and that the business reflects your values. On a second level, *wonderful* means that the business meets certain criteria in terms of financial strength and predictability; in particular, it must have a so-called *Moat*. And, third, it must have *good Management*. If you don't know what I mean by "Moat" and "good Management," don't worry. I'll be taking you through exactly what a Moat is, how to identify one, and how to spot good Management. I'll spell out all the criteria you need to confidently label a company "wonderful."

It's not enough, however, for the business to be just wonderful. We need to buy this business at an attractive price. By "attractive" I mean we can buy the business with a very big *Margin of Safety* (MOS). To me a nice MOS is buying a dollar of value for fifty cents. So, once I know what a business is worth, I want to buy it for half that price. Obviously, doing that will make me very rich at some point.

Figuring out the value of a business is either easy or impossible. If a business is "wonderful," then by definition it's a business that's predictable. If it's predictable, we can determine a value. If it's not a predictable business, it's impossible to know what it's worth. And I'll tell you exactly how to spot businesses that are predictable and thus can be valued, as well as teach you how to calculate their value quickly. Rule #1 investing comes down to four straightforward steps:

1. Find a wonderful business.
2. Know what it's worth as a business.
3. Buy it at 50 percent off.
4. Repeat until very rich.

Seems simple enough. Why doesn't everybody do it? Here's Buffett's answer to that very question: "It is extraordinary to me that the idea of buying dollar bills for 50 cents takes immediately with people or it doesn't take at all. It's like an inoculation. If it doesn't grab a person right away, I find that you can talk to him for years and show him records and it doesn't make any difference. They just don't seem able to grasp the concept, simple as it is."

When I was taught Rule #1 investing, the first truth I learned was the following:

The price of a thing is not always equal to its value.

For example, if I want to buy a new car, I have a pretty good idea what it's worth before I walk into a dealership — I know its sticker price and I know it's sold for a range of prices, usually less than the sticker price. I don't plan on paying whatever the dealer asks. But suppose I don't know what the car is worth? The dealer can get away with selling it to me for a lot more than its value — above its sticker price. If I pay $200,000 for a Mercedes-Benz that has a retail value or sticker price of $100,000, when I sell it I'm going to lose a lot of money. But if I could buy it for $50,000, when I sell it I'm going to *make* money. Buying stocks as businesses is just like that, except there is no sticker price on the window. We have to figure out what the sticker price is, and then pay less.

In essence, Rule #1 is just about being a good shopper.

If you're the type who waits to buy until there's a red-tag sale, where items get priced well below their actual values (you know that flat-screen TV is worth $5,000, but you can get it for $2,500), you're already set to be a good Rule #1 investor. All it takes is learning how to determine the values of wonderful companies and waiting for the market to sell you those companies at discounted prices.

If we wouldn't expect a car always to be priced right, why would we expect a business always to be priced right?

Businesses are different from cars and other salable goods in one important respect: The Sticker Price of a business is determined by the kind of surplus cash it can produce for its owners in the future. Rule #1 investors can look at a business and quickly figure out what kind of surplus it can produce in the future, deriving from that the Sticker Price of the business. And that's exactly what I'm going to show you how to do.

Once you know how to calculate a company's Sticker Price, which is its value regardless of the price it's selling for on the market, you're on your way to investing with certainty and abiding by Rule #1.

THE FOUR Ms

In thinking about the process you'll be undertaking in finding wonderful companies at attractive prices, it helps to think of what I've just outlined and what I call "the Four Ms": *Meaning, Moat, Management,* and *Margin of Safety.* Right now these four words may not make a whole lot of sense to you, but we'll be going into great detail on each of them. They'll be your signposts as you travel the path to the perfect investment. They are an easy way of recalling the steps to take from beginning (when you're just thinking about investing in a certain business) to end (when you're ready to buy that business with your hard-earned money).

The trick to understanding the essence of the Four Ms is to turn them into questions you must answer in evaluating a business and deciding whether it can be a good investment. (How you go about answering these questions in a methodical, step-by-step process is the focus of the next several chapters.)

1. Does the business have *Meaning* to you?
2. Does the business have a wide *Moat*?
3. Does the business have great *Management*?
4. Does the business have a big *Margin of Safety*?

If you can answer a big unconditional YES to all four of these questions, you'll know if this business is one you want to buy. A few requirements follow these questions:

The first question, "Does the business have *Meaning* to you?," demands you buy it only if you'd be willing to make this business the sole financial support of your family for the next 100 years. In other words, you'd better know what you're buying, because if it goes down, your family is going to starve. It also demands you act as if you're the sole owner. In other words, you better know what this business does, and be confident it operates from a set of values you feel comfortable with.

The second question, "Does the business have a wide *Moat?*," demands the business be able to defend itself against attacks by competitors, as if they were attacking armies trying to sack the castle. In other words, you'd better be able to accurately predict this business's long-term future.

The third question, "Does the business have great *Management?*," demands you be confident that the people running the business are doing so as if it were their family's only means of support for the next 100 years. In other words, you'd better be convinced they're not going to rip you off for their short-term benefit.

The fourth question, "Does the business have a big *Margin of Safety?*," demands you know the value of the business and can get it on sale. In other words, you'd better be able to buy this business cheap enough that you can sell it later without losing money — even if you were wrong to buy it in the first place.

For a beginning investor, these four questions can be intimidating and scary. There's a knee-jerk tendency to think, "I can't figure that out," and be done with investing on your own. But I've got good news. First, it used to take a lot of time to figure this stuff out, but now it's fast with access to the right tools. Second, you only have to find a few businesses you can say yes to, and you're pretty much set for a while. From that point on, you just monitor your businesses and let the money roll in. Once I show you how to access and use the Tools, you'll be able to keep close watch on your businesses and avoid losing any money — even if you make a few mistakes along the way or the market begins to do weird, unpredictable things.

> *There are opportunities to buy wonderful companies at attractive prices — they really do exist — if you're willing to do your homework and say good-bye to mutual funds.*

If you're finding yourself already a bit overwhelmed, take a deep breath. Central to this book is training you to answer these four questions in regard to any company so that you can become a confident individual investor. Be patient. It seems impossible to imagine now, but eventually you'll be practicing Four M thinking without conscious effort. You'll be viewing the investment universe through a Rule #1 lens.

That which we persist in doing becomes easier, not that the task itself has become easier, but that our ability to perform it has improved.
—Ralph Waldo Emerson

Now, on to those Four Ms in detail.

Chapter 3

Buy a Business, Not a Stock

An invasion of armies can be resisted, but not an idea whose time has come.

—VICTOR HUGO (1802–1885), *HISTOIRE D'UN CRIME*, 1852

THE FIRST M question—*Does the business have Meaning to you?*—implies two other questions: (1) Do you want to own the whole business? and (2) Do you understand it well enough to own all of it?

When I'm shopping for a great business to buy, I say to myself, "Phil, if you buy this, you will own the whole thing and all that that implies." I repeat this to myself even if I'm going to buy only a small piece via purchasing a few shares of stock. There is a very good reason for reciting such a mantra. It gets me thinking like a business owner and not a stock investor, which is critical to becoming a successful Rule #1 investor.

BE PROUD OF WHAT YOU OWN

If we buy the business as a business and not as a stock speculation, then it becomes personal. I want it to be personal. I want to be proud of what I own. This is an important starting place for deciding what to put our money into. What we decide to invest in gets our vote for continuing to do business, whatever that may be. If we buy Coca-Cola, for example, we're tacitly endorsing the company. In effect, we're saying we want Coke's products and want Coke's way of doing business to proliferate. If we buy a business that exploits child labor in a third-world factory, we're supporting the exploitation of children. Maybe that's okay with you, but the key point here is to own what you're proud to say is yours. Our vote may not count for much at the ballot box, but as owners of a business, it counts a lot. If our decision to own a particular business is a voice in the way the world works, I think we should consider what we're saying.

Approaching Rule #1 investing with an awareness of what it is you think is good or bad in the world will help you make good investment decisions *for you*. This doesn't mean it'll safeguard you from buying businesses that won't fail, or that aligning your values with your companies assures you maximal success from a financial standpoint. It just means the world has enough hypocrites in it, so why join them? If you think something is bad for the world, then don't own the business behind it. Stand for whatever you want with your money and realize that it's a personal choice.

> Investing is one of the most morally charged and important things we can do. If we're privileged enough to be among the few who have more money than is necessary to survive, we must be careful how we allocate that excess capital. Ultimately, it could determine how the world works for our children.

I'm not writing this book to tell you what to invest in. I hope that's clear. I'm writing this book so you'll know how to find great investments, and I'm leaving it up to you to select the five or ten companies you like the best. Think of investing your money like planting seeds in the ground. Imagine that you'll reap what you sow. Act as if that's true.

And buy every business with the 10-10 Rule in mind.

THE 10-10 RULE

The 10-10 Rule: I won't own this business for ten minutes unless I'm willing to own it for ten years.

The 10-10 Rule is just a way of thinking about investing. In fact, as you'll see, we might buy the business today and sell it in a month and then buy it back three months later and then sell it again a few weeks after that. The fact that we buy it *as if* we're going to keep it for ten years does not preclude us from buying and selling this business over and over.

The reason it's important to buy using the 10-10 Rule is that it makes us much more disciplined investors.

Most investors assume they're going to lose money on some of their investments as the market for their stock moves up and down. Because of that expectation, they diversify to reduce the risk of overall losses. But no business owner would be so casual about losing money in several of his businesses, as if that were just the way things went. Can you even imagine a business owner deciding to buy five more businesses to "lower his risk"? How crazy would that be? If his one business is too risky, why would diversifying into five more businesses make the first one *less* risky? If the first business is too risky, then he should sell it and get into a business he understands better. The 10-10 Rule helps us remember just how long we're "willing" to own this business so we're always thinking as a long-term investor.

As Rule #1 investors, we're going to own only a few businesses. Since that's the case, we must prepare ourselves to be certain we own the right few businesses — businesses that won't lose our money.

We have the luxury of waiting patiently until we can find wonderful companies at attractive prices, and we make it a habit never to put up our money until we're certain we're not going to lose money. If the company is in fact wonderful, and if the price we pay is in fact attractive, we know we're going to make money.

But what kind of business should you own? Should you and I own the same kinds of businesses? Are you and I the same kind of people?

Do we love and understand the same kinds of things? Obviously, every one of us is unique, with a talent all his or her own. Every person I took down the river was in some way unique. We are different with a purpose. Acting in harmony with who you are means *investing* in harmony with who you are. So what kinds of businesses should you own? The ones you understand. Those businesses tend to be about who you are.

UNDERSTAND YOUR BUSINESS

As I keep drumming in, the objective of Rule #1 is to invest with certainty so we don't lose our money. If we don't *understand* what we're buying, the only thing we can know for certain is that we don't have a clue what's going to happen to this business in the future. And if we don't have a clue what's going to happen in the future, how are we going to figure out what this thing is worth today? Obviously, we need to understand the business so we can predict the future with some degree of certainty and then arrive at a value today. Just as obviously, it's a lot easier to understand businesses we already know a lot about than businesses we've never heard of. So we're going to start our search for a wonderful business by discovering the kinds of businesses we already understand.

You're probably wondering to what *degree* you must truly understand a business. For example, if you really love cereal, your favorite brand is Cheerios, that particular brand is manufactured by General Mills, and the company has never done you wrong, can it truly be said that you *understand* General Mills? Or should you have a detailed knowledge of the behind-the-scenes manufacturing and retailing process of Cheerios? Must you know the supply chain, the box-manufacturing procedure, the labor costs, the marketing and advertising, the ways in which shelf space is fought for? These are all good questions, but way beyond the scope of what I mean by "understand your business." *Meaning* is just the first step. So if you like Cheerios and feel good about the company that produces the brand, General Mills, that's enough to get you past the first M. By the time you finish the other three Ms, you'll easily know enough about this business to make a good Rule #1 decision.

How much do you need to know to check off the first M? Not much, really. Just enough to get comfortable. You don't have to make a big deal of this. You don't have to know intricate details of marketing, the future product delivery pipeline, or much else except that you like what they do and it isn't hard to see that they can keep doing it better than anybody else. By the time you get done with the 4M process, you're going to know enough to put your money in with confidence. And, as you'll see, we have Tools that help us escape without harm if we goof. *Meaning,* in the Rule #1 sense, is just about understanding what a company does and how it does it—enough to be happy to put your name on the business and expect to keep it there for the next hundred years or so. According to Mr. Buffett, quoting Matthew 6:21: "For where your treasure is, there will your heart be also."

The only certainty I had when I started investing was that I wouldn't know a wonderful business from a terrible business. And the first thing I learned was that I knew a lot more about businesses than I thought.

Let's do a quick exercise: Draw three circles that intersect in the middle. Label the first circle "Passion." Label the second circle "Talent," and label the third circle "Money." (I must credit author and business

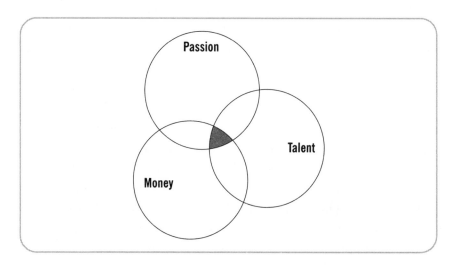

researcher Jim Collins for this idea of the three circles, which he uses to evaluate companies, especially those that go from "good" to "great.")

Write everything you're seriously passionate about in the first circle — the things you love to do or would do if you had the time or the money. Write everything you're talented at in the second circle — everything you're really good at, whether in a professional or recreational sense. And in the third circle write down everything that either makes you money or that you spend money on.

 Ask yourself these three questions:

1. What do you love to do, professionally and as recreation?
2. What things are you really good at?
3. What do you do to make money or what do you spend money on?

Your answers—especially the ones that recur with respect to all three questions—will help you begin to pick your own wonderful companies.

For example, if I did this when I first started investing, I would have written that I was into river guiding, I was talented at river guiding, and I made money river guiding. Simple. And once I saw that "river guiding" was in all three circles, all of a sudden it would have been crystal clear that I might have a fairly easy time understanding a river touring business. It also wouldn't take me long to see that a river touring business was similar to other businesses — like an African safari business or even a cruise line. What's more, there's probably a connection to a business like Disneyland or Magic Mountain, another popular theme park.

What you're looking for in the Three Circles is something that shows up in more than one circle — a word that points to a product, an industry, or a certain business. Anything that's in two or all three circles is something you probably understand much better than most of the rest of us. It's probably something that has Meaning to you, which automatically makes it an industry worth researching.

Go online to Yahoo! and click on "Finance," then "Industries," and then "Industry Index." As you'll see, just about every business in the world falls into one of these 12 categories or "sectors." (This is to get you thinking about what you'd like to buy — before even learning about the technical analyses we'll be doing shortly. Once you've learned all the Rule #1 ropes, you'll initially spend lots of time hunting around these sites and searching for businesses to put to the entire Rule #1 test.)

The list of sectors reproduced here from Yahoo! isn't *the* list. There is no master list of sectors. Different data companies list different numbers of sectors by splitting or combining some. Each data company will have its way of categorizing and naming companies within sectors, but all will be relatively similar. I'll guide you through more of this sector hunting in Chapter 13.

Each sector is made up of industries similar to one another. The adventure travel industry is in one of these sectors, but which one? Don't be afraid to click around and see for yourself. Since adventure travel might have something to do with Services, try that. You just click on "Services" and the website brings up a bunch of industries that are all service related in some way (see list on page 46).

Sectors > Services
Click on column heading to sort
Description ▲
Sector: Services
Advertising
Broadcasting & Cable TV
Business Services
Casinos & Gaming
Communications Services
Hotels & Motels
Motion Pictures
Personal Services
Printing & Publishing
Printing Services
Real Estate Operations
Recreational Activities
Rental & Leasing
Restaurants
Retail (Apparel)
Retail (Catalog & Mail Order)
Retail (Department & Discount)
Retail (Drugs)
Retail (Grocery)
Retail (Home Improvement)
Retail (Specialty)
Retail (Technology)
Schools
Security Systems & Services
Waste Management Services

From here on, it's just common sense. Look down the list at the left and see if any industry could include the adventure travel industry. How about Recreational Activities? Click on that, and the list on page 47 is what comes up:

Hmmm. Does any of these companies look like an adventure travel company? Yeah! American Classic Voyages, Carnival Corporation, Royal Caribbean, and Vail Resorts seem like they might be in the ballpark. But there are also other interesting companies on the list: Blockbuster is where I get videos; Netflix is where I get DVDs; and I've been to Six Flags a bunch of times. Just like that, I'm in the ballpark of businesses that I, a former river guide, might know something about! Down in the canyon after all our passengers were asleep, we guides would sometimes sit around in the dark and talk about how great it would be to go on a cruise and let somebody else row the boat, unload the gear, cook the food, and bag the poop. River tours and ocean cruises have a whole lot in common.

What else can I shop for? Almost anything I like to do or buy is represented by a business in some sector and industry.

If I think I know something about the outdoor equipment companies, I can find them in the Recreational Products industry. About a hundred companies make products like snow machines, motorcycles, golf clubs, power boats, and skis. In the Apparel group are other companies that pop out at me. I buy Columbia Sportswear and Quicksilver for outdoor gear— they make good river shorts and snowboard bindings. Just like that, based

Sectors > Services	Football Equities, Inc. (FBLQ.PK)
Click on column heading to sort.	Fortune Diversified Indus (FDVI.OB)
	GameTech International (GMTC)
Description ▲	GWIN, Inc. (GWNI.OB)
	Int'l Thoroughbred Breede (ITGB.PK)
Sector: Services	International Speedway (ISCA)
Industry: Recreational Activities (More Info)	Intra-Asia Entertainment (IRAE.OB)
	Life Time Fitness, Inc. (LTM)
All-American SportPark, I (AASP.OB)	Littlefield Corporation (LTFD.OB)
American Classic Voyages (AMCVQ.PK)	Magnum Sports & Entertain (MAGZ.PK)
American Skiing Company (AESK.OB)	Malibu Enter. Worldwide (MBEW.PK)
AMF Bowling, Inc. (AMBWQ.PK)	Millennium Sports Mgmt. (MSPT.PK)
Bally Total Fitness Holdi (BFT)	Movie Gallery, Inc. (MOVI)
Blockbuster Inc. (BBI)	Netflix, Inc. (NFLX)
Bowl America Incorporated (BWLA)	Pacific Systems Control T (PFSY.PK)
Bull Run Corporation (BULL.PK)	Physical Spa & Fitness (PFIT.OB)
Call Now, Inc. (CLNWE.OB)	Renaissance Entertainment (FAIR.PK)
Canterbury Park Holding C (ECP)	Royal Caribbean Cruises L (RCL)
Carnival Corporation (CCL)	Royal Olympic Cruise Line (ROCLF.PK)
Carnival plc (ADR) (CUK)	Six Flags, Inc. (PKS)
Cedar Fair, L.P. (FUN)	Skyline Multimedia Entert (SKYL.PK)
Championship Auto Racing (CPNT.PK)	Speedway Motorsports, Inc (TRK)
Commodore Holdings Ltd. (CCLNQ.PK)	Sports Club Company (SCY)
Dale Jarrett Racing Adven (DJRT.OB)	Tix Corp. (TIXC.OB)
Diamondhead Casino (DHCC.OB)	Vail Resorts, Inc. (MTN)
Diversicon Holdings Corp. (DVSH.PK)	VCG Holding Corp. (PTT)
Dover Motorsports, Inc. (DVD)	Video City, Inc. (VDCY.PK)
eCom eCom.com, Inc. (ECEC.PK)	Warner Music Group Corp. (WMG)
Entertainment Technologie (ETPI.PK)	West Coast Entertainment (WCEC.PK)
Equus Gaming Company L.P. (EQUUS.PK)	World Wrestling Entertain (WWE)
Family Golf Centers, Inc. (FGCIQ.PK)	
First National Entertain. (FNAT.PK)	

only on my experience in the army and as a guide, snowboarder, motorcycle rider, and general consumer, I find 17 businesses I might be interested in owning. I'll put their symbols on a spreadsheet (see page 48).

When I was looking at industries the hard way back in the 1980s, it was slower because I was doing it in a public library by flipping through thick data books. But I got to the same place eventually — a list of businesses that I could probably come to understand pretty easily with a little homework. You can do this easily. Just by answering the three questions about what you're talented at, what you love, and how you make or spend your money, you'll quickly have a list of dozens of compa-

From my river days:

ZQK	Quicksilver
COLM	Columbia
HDI	Harley-Davidson
HED	Head
BUD	Anheuser-Busch
IDR	Intrawest
MTN	Vail Resorts
BKS	Barnes & Noble
BGFVE	Big Five Sporting Goods
CAB	Cabelas

From where I shop all the time:

WFMI	Whole Foods Market, Inc.
WMT	Wal-Mart
WAG	Walgreens
SBUX	Starbucks
OSI	Outback Steakhouse

From my Special Ops days:

SWB	Smith & Wesson
RGR	Ruger

nies you already have a pretty good understanding of. Armed with that list, you can start shopping.

If you've lived awhile, been a consumer of products and services, worked a job or two, you know about a whole lot of businesses. It really isn't rocket science to find something that has meaning to you. Look at the kinds of companies Warren Buffett has owned: soft drinks, fast food, candy, razors, amusement parks, TV, newspapers, banks, mobile homes, furniture stores, diamond stores. . . . There are tons of companies out there you'll be able to understand just fine. In fact, there'll be so many, you're going to have to narrow down your list through careful analyses and Rule #1 evaluations.

Rule #1 investors don't do anything they aren't certain about. No gray areas. It's either clear and certain they understand the business, or it isn't. Many times throughout this book, you're going to hear me warn you to be certain you understand the business. Since, as a Rule #1 investor, you own the whole thing, nothing will mess you up as an owner quite as fast as not being certain what the business is you're about to buy.

SAMPLE CIRCLES FROM STUDENT KATHY

I encourage all of my students to draw up their own Three Circles and see what emerges on paper. When one of my workshop students went through the exercise, she was surprised by how many businesses could flow from all three circles. Here are her results:

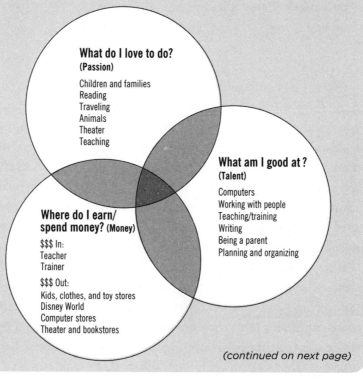

What do I love to do?
(Passion)

Children and families
Reading
Traveling
Animals
Theater
Teaching

What am I good at ?
(Talent)

Computers
Working with people
Teaching/training
Writing
Being a parent
Planning and organizing

Where do I earn/
spend money? (Money)

$$$ In:
Teacher
Trainer

$$$ Out:
Kids, clothes, and toy stores
Disney World
Computer stores
Theater and bookstores

(continued on next page)

Kathy noticed right away that teaching and children were in all three circles while training, computers, and theater were in two circles. These five areas of interest led her to eight industries:

Interest	Industry
Teaching and training	Education and training
	Publishing
Children	Apparel stores
	Catalogs
	Toy stores
Computers	Personal computers
	Application software
Theater	Movie production—theaters

These eight industries encompass more than 300 businesses that Kathy can look at with some degree of comfort because her experience as a parent and a teacher has given her a lot of familiarity with businesses in these industries.

Once you begin to actually practice Rule #1, you'll begin to see what areas of the market you understand and what areas you should avoid. (You'll also discover areas you'll want to explore and attempt to understand, and take the necessary steps to do that.) But some of that understanding might come from sheer trial and error. You'll likely have at least one experience where you think you know a certain business and industry well, only to see it fail once you've invested in it. Result: a feeling of being slapped in the face. Have I ever misunderstood an industry and gotten burned? Of course, and it was part of my learning curve.

It happened when I invested in a computer company that had a lot of brains, money, and a historic leader (Steve Jobs) behind it. The year was 1985 and Steve Jobs had left Apple to build a much better operating system than both Windows and Apple, which he called NeXT. He was encouraging investors like me to invest in either NeXT itself or in companies that were developing software that would run on the NeXT computer. Because I'd been contemplating investing in a software company, I'd been in contact with programmers and computer geeks. I thought I knew the computer world, and every programmer said the NeXT computer was the best platform for developers, the best operating system, the prettiest box, the hottest new thing. It had everything, except that it wasn't compatible with Microsoft Windows. And Microsoft's products reigned supreme. Microsoft was, for all intents and purposes, untouchable.

If you went to desktop publishing shows between 1988 and 1991, you probably spotted the distinctive NeXT grayscale monitors; they'd almost disappeared by 1993. I lost $5 million, which paled in comparison with how much other investors lost, including Ross Perot, Carnegie-Mellon and Stanford universities, and Compaq Computer. I'll admit, from the start this wasn't a very Rule #1–esque investment since neither NeXT nor the software company had the established history they needed to pass the Four M test in its entirety. But at the time I was eager to jump aboard, and when you have someone like Steve Jobs asking for help, well . . .

My experience taught me two valuable lessons: (1) businesses that lack the history to make a prediction of the future possible are inherently risky; and (2) don't touch businesses you don't understand. If Warren Buffett admits he won't invest in Microsoft because he doesn't understand computer technology, what was I doing investing in software for a totally new computer? I was young and foolish and thought I could break The Rule and get away with it. Now I'm older and wiser . . . well, older anyway, and I want to help you avoid my mistakes.

You're going to start this process by searching for businesses you think you understand, and from there put them to a numbers test. Do your best to avoid listening to any arrogant or emotional voices within you that can steer you in the wrong direction. Rule #1 is so simple and straightforward that it's easy to think it can be improved upon. If you attempt to do so, you'll lose money.

You don't necessarily have to use the Internet to conduct an initial search. An effective starting point for finding businesses you understand is simply to consider where you repeatedly shop and what you repeatedly buy. You might not understand the intricacies of, say, the shoe

Once you actually have a list of wonderful companies that appear to meet all the Rule #1 criteria, the full extent of which
you'll learn step-by-step in this book, that list will become your
Watch List. It will contain the companies that require only 15
minutes a week to monitor.

industry, but if you wear only Nike shoes and routinely buy Nike apparel (and happen to like everything you see and hear about Nike),
that's a good start. Look at your credit card statements and checkbook
to see where your money goes. And then ask yourself, "What would I
be proud to own?" My guess is you'll have 15 or more on your list just
from being alive and working.

And then the real homework begins. You have to know if any of
these companies has a *Moat*.

Chapter 4

Identify a Moat

Learning is not compulsory . . . neither is survival.
                                        —W. Edwards Deming (1900–1993)

Question two: *Does the business have a wide Moat?*
The first thing you want to know when you're about to buy a business (with the "I'm buying the whole enchilada" mentality, because you understand it and are proud to own it) is whether or not its future is predictable. Obviously, you want a company that will be a winner—a business that will continue to grow for decades into the future. But if you can't predict with a high degree of certainty that it'll be a winner, then its future isn't predictable, and as a Rule #1 investor, you don't buy a company with an uncertain future.

This chapter begins a learning process that will enable you to *know* if a business will succeed and continue to perform well for at least the next 20 years. For a company to have that degree of predictability, it must possess some sort of lasting competitive edge, or, as Mr. Buffett puts it, a "durable competitive advantage that protects it from attack, like a moat protects a castle." In other words, we're looking for a business that has a great big, wide, hard-to-get-across-and-attack-the-castle Moat. We want massive protection from the attacking competitors who want a piece of the action.

Finding a business with a wide Moat is key to finding a successful business to own, because a business with a wide Moat is much more predictable for the next 20 years than a business with no Moat.

Some of you may already be familiar with the Moat concept. Even so, I'd encourage you to read what follows as a reminder of how critical this concept can be. After providing a primer on Moat characteristics, I'll then show exactly which financial numbers you need to "see" a huge Moat.

WHAT IS A MOAT?

The idea of the Moat is really simple. If an industry looks as if it might be very easy to get into, there probably isn't a Moat. On the other hand, if it looks as though it might be really hard to get into and be successful, you'll probably find some wide-Moat businesses.

For example, when I was a kid, my family had a little farm in Oregon with one cherry tree. All I had to do to get into the cherry business was climb up into the cherry tree and pick cherries, get my grandfather to take me to the cherry collection station, where they'd weigh my haul, measure a random sample, and pay me. That was it. No barriers whatsoever to my being in the cherry business. The reason there was no barrier was that nobody at a grocery store particularly cared which farm the cherries came from. A cherry is a commodity, which means a cherry from one farm is pretty much indistinguishable from a cherry from another farm. Commodity businesses don't have Moats. If you own a commodity business, you have exactly zero protection from competitors. If they want to take your castle, there isn't much to stop them. If they can both grow and sell cherries cheaper than you, you might be out of business. We don't want to own businesses without Moats because it's really hard to make money. Ask anybody who owns a farm, pharmacy, deli, gas station, or T-shirt shop. These are all hard businesses to make money in, because they're essentially commodity businesses.

What if, instead of wanting to compete in the cherry business, I wanted to go toe-to-toe with Coke and Pepsi? Looks like they make a lot of money. But do you think that might be hard? Let's say I even have a tree that magically grows cans full of a cola drink that tastes exactly like the Real Thing. Can I pick the colas, go to the store, sell them cheap, and compete with Coke? No. The store owner has only so much space in his cooler. Coke and Pepsi already have taken every inch of that space because customers come into the store specifically to buy Coke or Pepsi. The reason customers show up to buy those brands is that Coke and Pepsi are on TV all day advertising. Those ads don't cost the store owner a dime (plus some merchants receive strong incentives to stock their stores with Coke or Pepsi either solely or prominently). Why in the world would the store owner give up an inch of his Coke or Pepsi space to my unknown cola? Answer: He won't. Not an inch.

So how am I going to sell my cola? If I can't answer that question easily, it's pretty good evidence that Coke and Pepsi have a wide protective Moat that's preventing competitors like me from taking their castles. Even if I could grow colas for free, I still probably couldn't get shelf space in a store.

What that wide Moat means to a business owner is that the business is very hard to compete against. A Coke is much more expensive than a generic cola, but nobody who wants a Coke cares. You can't compete with Coke by lowering your price, and that's also a sign of a wide Moat. It is hard to compete against eBay because it has the biggest online auction market in the world. Gillette is very hard to compete against because it has such a large number of dedicated Gillette fans. Same with Disney, Wrigley, and Apple.

What's even more spectacular about businesses with wide Moats is they can keep up with inflation. In other words, they can raise prices as their costs go up. People will still buy Coke, a Gillette razor, or a grande latte at Starbucks, even if these items cost more today than they did yesterday.

Moats aren't just about loving the product. Lots of people hate Microsoft but use Windows anyway because it has such a huge library

> 👉 A Rule #1 company will always be one that can ride any inflation wave. That's the purpose of the Moat around the castle: protection from inflation and competition. Moat businesses aren't affected by inflation because they're able to raise their prices as the cost of doing business goes up. Wide-Moat companies—Rule #1 companies—can do that because they have some kind of monopolistic position in the market. The essence of a monopoly is the ability to raise prices at will.

of software running on it that they're somewhat forced to use it. (Remember my NeXT story? My fellow investors and I couldn't swim across Microsoft's Moat and attack the castle.) A competitor like Linux can give away its operating system (for free) and still not make much of a dent in Microsoft's market. Switching from one operating system to another can be so painful as to be prohibitive. And while people in small towns might hate what the local Wal-Mart did to their neighbor's hardware store business, they still buy the hammer at Wal-Mart because it's so cheap they can't help themselves. Wal-Mart has a Moat based on price.

Moats can be created by trade secrets that keep other businesses from copying them. In addition to possessing a brand Moat, Coke's trade-secret taste is so well liked that Coke couldn't even compete with itself. It tried a new formula — New Coke — and blew a hole in its revenue. People have enjoyed Coke just the way it is for nearly 100 years. If other companies could copy it, they would. But they can't quite get it right. When you want a Coke, you've got to buy a Coke. Even if you could copy Coke perfectly, you'd have to compete with its brand and its world-wide distribution. Nice Moat.

The pharmaceutical giant Pfizer gets its Moat from patents on drugs. That's a Moat supported by law. Intel gets its Moat from its long experience in building chips. You'd have to hire Intel's people to get what they know.

A utility like PG&E protects itself by government law. It's the only utility that can provide power in its region, and therefore it has a monopoly. To get power in California, you have to buy it from PG&E or build your own power source. Utilities are like toll bridges. To get over the body of water, you have to pay the toll or build your own boat. Toll-bridge companies are often government-created monopolies, but they don't necessarily have to be. Most advertising and media companies are also examples of toll-bridge businesses. If you want to advertise in a Washington, D.C., newspaper, you're probably going to do it in the *Washington Post*. You have to pay the toll to the *Post*. Time Warner is a toll-bridge company. So is Google.

In effect, a business that has a Moat has some kind of durable leg-up that protects it from competition. It doesn't have to be a "monopoly" in a classic sense (meaning it has exclusive control over a particular area of the market), but it should be a company that is well known for being number one or number two in its industry.

THE FIVE MOATS		
TYPE	**DEFINITION**	**EXAMPLE**
Brand	a product you're willing to pay more for because you trust it	Coke, Gillette, Disney, McDonald's, Pepsi, Nike, Budweiser, Harley-Davidson
Secret	a business that has a patent or trade secret that makes direct competition illegal or very difficult	Pfizer, 3M, Intel
Toll	a business with exclusive control of a market—giving it the ability to collect a "toll" from anyone needing that service or product	media companies, utilities, ad agencies
Switching	a business that's so much a part of your life that switching isn't worth the trouble	ADP, Paychex, H&R Block, Microsoft
Price	a business that can price products so low no one can compete	Wal-Mart, Costco, Bed Bath & Beyond, Home Depot, Target

The reason Rule #1 investors like Moats so much is that Moat companies permit more accurate predictions about their future. Companies with one or more of the Five Moats can survive and grow much more easily than companies that have to fight off competition from some low-priced product. Since, as Rule #1 investors, we're going to buy a business as if it's the only source of income for our families for the next 100 years, we want to be certain about the Moat.

SUSTAINABLE MOATS

If you're a company committed to protecting itself from potential invaders, your Moat must also be *sustainable*. Remember, you and I are counting on this business being around for 20 years, so the durability of the product and the industry is critical. The company has to do more than just offer a good product. Coke's advantage had been around for 100 years. The company sustains its advantage by protecting the secret of its syrup recipe as though the recipe were the lifeblood of the company—which it is. But Coca-Cola also protects its distribution system and fights against Pepsi for every retail outlet. The combination protects the company's Moat, but if the firm lets its guard down and fails to defend its Moat, the Pepsi hordes will eventually cross it and attack the castle.

Microsoft continues to protect its Moat by improving technology and evolving with consumer and business demands. It doesn't assume it can remain untouchable by relying on outdated or useless technology. As I write this, Google is causing Bill Gates extreme concern as it tunnels under his Moat with its search engine. He may be right to be worried because Google has figured out how to make a lot of money without charging anyone for their website and without making anyone change their computer or their computer's operating system. Google is built on top of Linux, so it doesn't have to use any Microsoft products. Google's Moat, which Gates is trying to figure out how to cross so he can destroy his competitor, is its huge lead in intelligent searches. It's a *Secret* Moat. And it's already become a *Brand* Moat. Can Google leverage its consumer connections so effectively that no one cares about running on

Windows anymore? In certain tech circles, this is *the* question. So you see, the battle rages. Is Microsoft's Moat durable? Is Google's?

You don't have to identify multiple Moats around one company to consider it a potentially good investment—although you're likely to find that the wider the Moat, the more likely it is a combination of several Moat categories. Coca-Cola and Microsoft, for example, both have acquired a reputable brand identity while exhibiting other Moat characteristics. Don't fuss over counting the Moats around a business; rather focus on identifying the one Moat among others that seems hardest to cross, and have confidence that the company can sustain that Moat for a very long time.

If you want a motorcycle that's hard-core, tough, and respected by the serious bikers, there's only one — a Harley. Anything else could get you a beating at the big biker rallies in Sturgis and Daytona every year. The look, sound, feel, and personality of the motorcycle are what Harley owners buy. There's no second choice. Harleys have been around for decades and will be around for decades more. But back in the 1970s the company had to fight to compete against the Japanese. Honda spent millions trying to compete with Harley. Honda makes a better motorcycle from a technical point of view, and it's much less expensive. But it doesn't sound like a Harley, it doesn't ride rough like a Harley, and it doesn't get respect like a Harley. Not surprisingly, Honda has been unsuccessful in convincing motorcycle riders that its bike is a Harley even when it looks almost exactly like one. Today the Japanese import Harleys to Japan because the bikes are so different from motorcycles produced in their own country. You want a Harley, you've got to buy a Harley. That Moat came from Harley's determining what made a Harley unique, and then defending that turf with patents, lawyers, and marketing. Harley has found its sustainable Brand Moat — the Harley look, sound, and feel. Can we predict that they'll be in business in 20 years?

A company with a wide sustainable Moat is much less likely to go
out of business than a company without one. Its earnings are also much
more predictable over the long term. Therefore, companies with sustainable Moats make for more predictable investments.

A lot of investors make the mistake of thinking the price of the
stock and whether it goes up or down has something to do
with how well it's competing with other companies—or, in my
terms, how wide its Moat is. For example, over the last seven
years, Pepsi stock has massively outperformed Coke stock. But
remember, we don't buy stocks, we buy businesses. As business buyers, we must understand that there are many forces
affecting stock prices—forces that often have nothing to do
with the quality of the company or the width of its Moat.

Here's a great example (refer to the charts on page 62): In
1998 Pepsi had a value of $44 per share and Coke had a value of
$42 per share (we'll be going into the details of figuring out val-
ues—Sticker Prices—in Chapter 9). On the market, Pepsi was
selling for $30 per share, about 30 percent under its value.
Coke, on the other hand, was selling for $90 per share, about
200 percent over its value. Since then, Coke's market price has
gone down and Pepsi's price has gone up. What a surprise!

Understand that Moat tells us whether a company is likely
to be around in 20 years, not what price we should be paying
for it right now. Wide-Moat businesses are often massively
overpriced and, as a result, can drop in price like there is no tomorrow. But if, in fact, a company has a huge Moat, the existence of that Moat almost guarantees there'll be a tomorrow
brighter than today. That "tomorrow" is, of course, what we
Rule #1 investors count on: the payoff for buying a stock when
everyone else is undervaluing it.

Sometimes people just learning Rule #1 think that because
companies with obvious Moats are usually priced well above
what they're worth, those companies are *always* priced well

above what they're worth. Not true. Emphatically not true. If it were true, to get a big Margin of Safety, you and I would have to find businesses with wide Moats before anyone else noticed the Moats were there. I don't know about you, but I'm just not smart enough to do that consistently. Me, I'm going to just keep doing what works: identifying obvious wide-Moat businesses and then buying them for a lot less than they're worth whenever I can.

If you bought Coke in 1980, your rate of return as of 2005, 25 years later, would've been 12 percent. If you bought Pepsi in 1980, your rate of return would've also been 12 percent. So we have two companies with almost identical products, Brand Moats, and compounded long-term returns in the market. But look at their price charts and see the apparent difference. There's no real difference in rate of return, but it sure seems as if Pepsi did better. In fact, what happened is that Coke got massively overvalued in the late 1990s and, since then, has been re-priced by the market.

Our job is to find businesses with obviously wide Moats, buy them when the market has mispriced them too low, then sell them when the market has mispriced them too high. Doing it the opposite way, buying Coke at $90 when it's worth $40, is a bad idea. We want to be sellers at $90. These overpriced wide-Moat companies do have a way of crashing, which gives us our chance to buy them back at great prices and ride them up for another 10 or 20 years until they become overvalued again. But to do that, you have to be confident in the Moat.

Figuring out whether a business has a Moat can be a challenge if you try to do it based on instinct alone. Rule #1 investors, however, take the guesswork out of identifying a Moat by looking at five numbers in particular. These five numbers put the magnifying glass on businesses, allowing us to truly see what's going on inside and whether we can keep these firms on our list of wonderful companies.

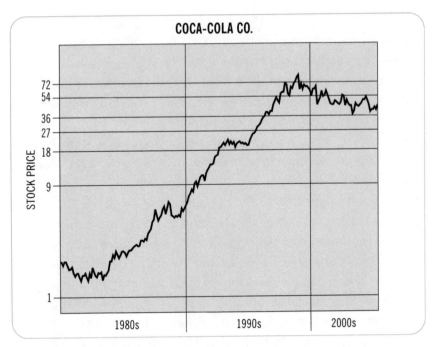

Your 25-year compounded rate of return in Coke is 12 percent.

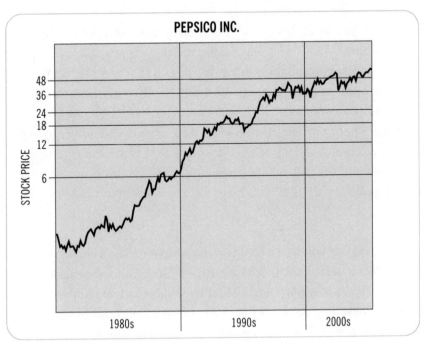

Your 25-year compounded rate of return in Pepsi is 12 percent.

THE BIG FIVE

If a business has at least one of the Five Moats, it'll show up in the Big Five numbers. These numbers are proof of the existence of a Moat. Businesses without Moats do not have good Big Five numbers. If you can't spot good Big Five numbers, I promise you that you're on the thin ice of "hope" in trying to predict the future for that business. The firm may not have the Moat—or the future—you think it does. The Big Five numbers are so important that I *never* buy a business that has a bad Big Five. Here are the Big Five:

1. Return on Investment Capital (ROIC)
2. Sales growth rate
3. Earnings per Share (EPS) growth rate
4. Equity, or Book Value per Share (BVPS), growth rate
5. Free Cash Flow (FCF or Cash) growth rate

All of the Big Five should be *equal to or greater than* 10 percent per year for the last 10 years.

Return on Investment Capital (ROIC or ROC or ROI)	≥ 10% per year for 10 years
Sales (or Revenue) growth rate	≥ 10% per year for 10 years
Earnings per Share (EPS) growth rate	≥ 10% per year for 10 years
Equity (or Book Value or BVPS) growth rate	≥ 10% per year for 10 years
Free Cash Flow (FCF) growth rate	≥ 10% per year for 10 years

Although hundreds of numbers are tracked on financial websites like Yahoo! Finance and MSN Money for lots of businesses, these five numbers are not always tracked for free. Because Rule #1 investors focus on these five, I'm going to show you how—step-by-step—to create each of these critical growth-rate numbers yourself from information that *is* free. That will be the focus of Chapter 6. First, however,

*Go to
www.ruleoneinvestor.com
to obtain useful
information and trusted
links to financial sites that
will assist you in gathering
the raw data you need to
successfully evaluate
businesses.*

we're going to discuss in the next chapter what each of these five numbers tells us, and how they help us identify wide-Moat companies. It'll take some time to get used to these numbers, so be patient. Recall how frustrating learning 2 + 2 = 4 was in the first grade? Okay, maybe it wasn't frustrating for you, but you did have to count on your fingers at the start. This is a lot easier than that because we've got computers and calculators to help us out.

Chapter 5

The Big Five Numbers

Mankind have a great aversion to intellectual labor; but even supposing knowledge to be easily attainable, more people would be content to be ignorant than would take even a little trouble to acquire it.
— SAMUEL JOHNSON (1709–1784), QUOTED IN BOSWELL'S
LIFE OF SAMUEL JOHNSON

EVEN IF we think we can identify the Moat in a business without much effort, it doesn't mean we stop there and go on to consider its Management (the third M). First we must *confirm* the strength of this business by looking at the Big Five numbers. These are the five numbers I use to help me determine whether a business can give me at least a 15-percent return a year. In other words, the Big Five are a huge clue to whether this business is predictable and can be trusted to deliver expected rates of return in the future. We'll also, as an afterthought, glance at debt. I don't consider a company's debt one of the Big Five, but it's a number we're going to have to look at once we've checked off the health of the Big Five. (And usually, if our Big Five are all looking good, debt will, too.)

Remember: All of these Big Five numbers should be *equal to or greater than* 10 percent per year for the last 10 years. We must also look at the five-year and one-year numbers, and compare those to the 10-year numbers to make sure business isn't slowing down. But if you want to focus on as few numbers as possible to get used to this evaluation process, you can get started by simply looking at the 10-year average and, if it's above 10 percent, move on to the next step.

Let's consider what each of these Big Five numbers mean. For now, don't worry about where these numbers come from. Focus on understanding what they mean, and then we'll learn how to arrive at them.

ROIC

Return on investment capital (ROIC) is the rate of return a business makes on the cash it invests in itself every year. For example, let's say your kids finance a lemonade-stand business with $200 to get it up and running. Their "investment capital" is the $200. After a week, the kids come back in the house with $300. After subtracting their expenses of $200 they paid for supplies, salaries, and flyers they made at Kinko's, their profit is $100. Their ROIC is their profit divided by their invested capital. In this case they did great: $100 divided by $200 is 50 percent. Pretty amazing return in just a week. By comparison, if they put the $200 in the bank at 2 percent a year, their investment would have grown by less than ten cents. Let's see: $100 or $0.10 — which is better? There's a lesson for your kids in there somewhere.

In any case, ROIC is the percentage return you get back from the cash you've plowed into your business. It's a measure of how effectively a company uses the money (borrowed or owned) invested in its operations. As such, it's also an indicator of how effective a company's Management team is at using the money invested in its operations. A good, solid ROIC is one of the first indications that the managers of this business are on the side of its owners, something that's going to be very important as we continue our research.

If you were to ask me which of the Big Five is the most important number, I'd tell you to go to ROIC first. If a business doesn't have a healthy ROIC — above 10 percent per year on average for the last ten years — move on to another business. A business that has a great Moat almost always boasts an attractive ROIC, because the Moat protects against constant price pressure from competitors. In fact, such a Moat-protected business forces *others* to compete on price, which is a hard way to make money.

We want to see a long history of great ROIC — at least 10 percent per year for the last ten years' average. And we don't want to see ROIC going down; we want to see it going up or at least staying the same. While it's acceptable to just focus on the ten-year average, it's best to look at three numbers for ROIC: (1) the ten-year average, (2) the past five years' average, and (3) last year's average. Having all three ROIC numbers gives a better sense of how a company is doing.

Let's look at some companies' ROIC as of early 2005 and see what they tell us. (Refer to the chart on page 68.) These are all pairs of companies that compete with each other. For example, Apollo competes with ITT Educational; Oracle competes with Sybase; General Motors competes (sort of) with Harley-Davidson; Whole Foods competes with Albertsons; and Dell competes with Gateway. Read this chart from left to right: look at the ten-year ROIC first, then the five-year, and finally the one-year, which is the most recent year. Obviously, we want to see the numbers topping 10 percent in all categories, and it'd be great if they showed growth — if they rise as we move from the ten-year average to the five-year to the one-year.

Just based on the ROIC numbers you see here, which companies would *you* choose to invest in?

We can see by comparing the ROIC numbers over time that ROIC is going up or holding steady for Apollo, Harley-Davidson, Whole Foods, and Dell. It's bouncy at Oracle and ITT, but still way above our 10-percent minimum requirement. Sybase has recovered a bit recently. GM and Albertsons are holding steady lately, but too low for consideration. Gateway's ROIC is dropping like a brick.

Remember: We want ROIC to be staying steady or going up. Apollo and ITT are in the education industry. Both show great numbers, although Apollo is more consistent. Whole Foods competes with Albertsons. The grocery business has really low profit margins to begin with, so give them some slack for that, but look at the difference in the two companies' ROIC. Whole Foods' ROIC is getting bigger. Albertsons' is getting smaller. Who do you think has the Moat?

General Motors and Harley are in similar businesses. Check out GM's low and disappearing ROIC. This is a sign of a company on the edge of going under. Meanwhile, Harley is looking very healthy.

How about Dell and Gateway? Who has the Moat? Not really a

Company	ROIC—10 yr	ROIC—5 yr	ROIC—1 yr
Apollo Group[1]	32%	30%	36%
ITT Educational[2]	171%	313%	46%
Oracle[3]	110%	182%	54%
Sybase[4]	–21%	–24%	12%
GM[5]	3%	1%	1%
Harley-Davidson[6]	16%	18%	18%
Whole Foods[7]	7%	10%	12%
Albertsons[8]	9%	6%	6%
Dell[9]	43%	43%	42%
Gateway[10]	–10%	–50%	–112%

LEGEND TO CHART:

1. Apollo Group (APOL): A provider of higher education programs for working adults, with campuses and learning centers in the United States, Puerto Rico, and British Columbia.
2. ITT Educational Services (ETI): Another provider of education programs, offering degree and non-degree programs throughout the United States.
3. Oracle (ORCL): A company that develops, manufactures, markets, and distributes computer software for businesses.
4. Sybase (SY): Another software company that supports businesses.
5. General Motors (GM): One of the grand old American car companies.
6. Harley-Davidson (HDI): Maker of the heavyweight motorcycle that bears its name.
7. Whole Foods (WFMI): A natural food and nutritional supplement store chain.
8. Albertsons (ABS): A supermarket chain that operates food-drug stores.
9. Dell (DELL): Manufactures a brand of computers, including systems, desktops, notebooks, and enterprise systems.
10. Gateway (GTW): Another computer manufacturer that makes a broad line of desktop and portable PCs and PC-related products.

problem answering that one, is there? Dell has built a monster Moat that Gateway tried to swim across. Looks like Gateway drowned in Dell's Moat. Do you want to put your money in Gateway and hope they use it better than they have in the past? Or do you want to go with something just a bit more predictable, like Dell? I'd go with Dell — at the right price.

Unfortunately, for a Rule #1 investor there's no "right price" for Gateway. It doesn't meet the Moat requirement, which means it doesn't meet the predictability requirement, and therefore we can't make a decision about this business's future. If we can't make that decision, we can't give it a value. No value, no way to know what it's worth today. If we buy it without knowing what it's worth today, we're just guessing that it's cheap and therefore must go up. We can't *know* that it's cheap, since we can't give it a value; therefore, we're gambling, wishing, or hoping. Whatever you want to call it, it isn't investing. See how just a few bits of data lead to a very emphatic conclusion?

ROIC is not the only number we need to look at to confirm we have a company with a very wide Moat. We also need to know that the business is growing for the benefit of us, the owners. For that information, we have to look at four growth *rates*: (1) sales growth rate; (2) earnings per share growth rate; (3) equity growth rate; and (4) free cash growth rate.

The Big Five numbers are calculated for us on some professional sites, but those sites cost money. Free sites like MSN Money or Yahoo! Finance have *some* of the Big Five calculated, and then we have to do the rest ourselves from raw data. To make it easy, I put Rule #1 calculators for each of the Big Five on my website, www.ruleoneinvestor.com. But just to show that you could easily derive these growth rates even if my site wasn't available, in the next chapter I'll show you a neat trick for figuring these out in your head. All you need are ten years of numbers. You can get these numbers from sites like MSN Money or possibly your online broker's website, if it offers research tools. You may want to become familiar with one site in particular for purposes of learning the ropes of Rule #1 methodology, and then you can experiment with other sites and find the one(s) you think are easiest. In this book we'll be using data taken mostly from MSN Money and Yahoo! Finance. This doesn't mean you can't access the same information elsewhere. Refer to my website for links to financial data sites.

THE FOUR GROWTH RATES

We need to find out the sales, EPS, equity, and cash growth rates. These numbers tell us how much the business is growing each year over the previous years and, if they're consistent, give us a huge clue to what rate of growth we should expect in the future. This is critical to figuring out what this business is worth today.

Sales are the total dollars the business took in from selling whatever widgets and digits it sells. Your kids' lemonade stand sold $300 of lemonade. That's the sales number. Simple enough. Sometimes sales is referred to as the "top line" (number) because it's located on the top line in financial reports about the business (specifically, on the income statement). Each year the business will report its sales (and the other numbers as well), which allows us to see if sales grew compared to last year. We like to see ten years of numbers to get an idea if sales are growing consistently. If they are, we can calculate the amount of growth above last year.

If your kids have $300 of sales this year, and next year they have $1,000 of sales, their sales grew by $700. That's nice to know, but the really important number is what the *rate* of growth is. We just let the computer divide $300 into $1,000 and we get 3.33. That means the sales were the same (that's the first 1) plus another 2.3, or 233 percent. So the sales growth rate for this one year is 233 percent. If we want to calculate the sales growth rate for multiple years, we can do that easily. Let's jump forward in time and pretend the kids have had the stand for five years. In the fifth year, we check out how the business is doing by figuring out its average growth rate for those five years. Business is rocking right along, and sales amount to $3,000 for the last year. Five years ago, sales were only $1,000.

The most accurate way to do this calculation is to use my rate calculator, which tells us the growth rate is 25 percent for those five years. (The calculators on my website make this a cinch. I'll take you through the steps of making this calculation roughly in your head or on paper in the next chapter.) We can do that same calculation for ten years, five years, and one year (the most recent year) and see if the rate of sales growth is growing or shrinking. And we repeat that exercise for all four growth rate numbers — sales, EPS, equity, and cash. Nothing to it, once you've done it a couple of times.

The next number is *EPS* (earnings per share), which tells us how much the business is profiting per share of ownership. For example, since your kids' lemonade stand has really taken off, they need to buy a lot more supplies to keep up with demand. They're going to need some outside money to do that. And to get the money, the kids can sell some of their ownership. Let's say it's year seven and they want to sell half of it to you, their dad or mom. First they make their lemonade-stand business into a corporation so they can create lots of little pieces of ownership in the business. Those pieces are called shares of stock. Once they do that, they'll have stock to sell to you. They decide to issue 2,000 shares. They could have decided on any number of shares, be it 10,000 or a million. That wouldn't change the size of the pie — but just create more pieces.

Next they have to figure out what the business is worth so they'll know what to charge for a piece of it. Well, for five years, the business has been growing its earnings fast — at about 25 percent a year. Last year the earnings were $2,000. You tell your kids that if they were a big public company that had a similar track record, lots of fund managers would be happy to pay about two times the growth rate, or about 50 times last year's earnings, to own a piece of the business. So if the business were big and publicly traded, with lots of investors, it'd be worth maybe $100,000. But, you point out, it isn't big and it isn't public, so it isn't worth that much to a private investor. Too many risks. Risks along the lines such as, "Who are you going to sell your piece to, if you want out?" Or, since the business is only five years old and really small, can it grow at that pace when it gets bigger? And where are they going to get more money if they need it to keep growing at that fast pace? What happens if Management wants to leave and go to high school?

So you and your kids agree the business isn't worth $100,000. It's maybe worth a quarter of that. Say $25,000. If the business is worth $25,000, half of it's worth $12,500. So the kids agree to sell half of it to you for $12,500. In exchange for your $12,500, they give you half the issued stock: 1,000 shares. Since you received 1,000 shares of stock in exchange for your $12,500, you paid $12.50 per share of stock. They also issued themselves stock that represents ownership of the other half of the business, so the kids have 1,000 shares, too. They didn't pay anything for theirs. They are the founders of the business, and it's common that founders get their stock for free for doing all the work to make it successful.

Armed with the $12,500 of investment capital you put in the business, plus the cash surplus they had from earnings of $2,000, over the next few years your kids continue to grow the business to a point where it now generates $6,000 in earnings per year. Because the business owners (you and the kids) have 2,000 shares of stock, the $6,000 of earnings is divided into 2,000 pieces of $3 each. That's how we get earnings per share, or EPS. In this case, the EPS is $3. EPS is often called "the bottom line" (number) because it's usually the last line on the financial statement (specifically, on the income statement).

Just as with sales, what we really care about right now is what the EPS growth rate is. And as with sales growth rate, the EPS growth rate is the amount of growth from one year to another expressed in a percentage. If the EPS ten years ago was ten cents per share ($100 divided by 1,000 shares, since Mom and Dad hadn't bought in yet) and the EPS today is $3 per share, the EPS growth rate calculation tells us the ten-year EPS growth rate is 41 percent per year.

That's a great number. Now we want to know if the owners get to keep that money or whether it's getting spent on a bunch of equipment to create next year's spectacular growth. To find that out, we look at the *equity* growth rate.

Equity is what you and the kids would have left over if the kids sold off everything, paid off any debt, and took the money that was left. If the kids decided they wanted to quit the business, of course they would try to sell it. But if nobody wanted to buy it from them, they could just sell off their supply of sugar and lemons and pay off whatever they owe. Let's say they have an $8,000 supply of lemons, sugar, ice machines, glasses, and tables on hand, plus $10,000 in cash and a couple of trucks worth $10,000 (that's what's left over from profits and the $12,500 investment after buying more supplies and equipment). Since they don't owe anybody, the equity totals $28,000 ($8,000 from selling the supplies, $10,000 from selling the trucks, and $10,000 in cash). You and the kids would split that on a per-share basis. Since there are 2,000 shares and $28,000 to split up, each share would get $14. That $14 is called *book value per share* (BVPS) and the $28,000 is called *equity* or *book value.* (Some people call it the *liquidation value*—what the business is worth if it's no longer a business.)

That raw number itself isn't so important to determine value because businesses with a lot of real estate and machinery, like McDonald's, can have a huge equity relative to their value, while businesses that are all about intellectual property, like Google, might have a small equity relative to their value. In other words, equity numbers are vastly different when you contrast a factory-type business with one based on knowledge or intellect. But the *rate* of equity *growth* could be identical and is very, very important. It tells us the business can accumulate surplus, and that in itself makes it exceptional. Hence, equity alone isn't nearly as revealing as *equity growth rate,* which is why we focus more on the growth rate than on the numbers from which we derive the growth.

What's so important about equity growth? Some students of mine have asked me this question and wondered why, if equity is really just a "surplus," equity growth is a good indicator of a company's strength. Well, if a business's equity (the "surplus") isn't growing, the business doesn't have the funds to spend on increasing its market or developing new products. Maybe earnings are simply being channeled back into maintaining the business—for example, by building new manufacturing plants (which may be worthless in five years). Or maybe the company is pursuing a "growth for growth's sake" strategy. That sort of purposeless growth usually shows up in a much lower ROIC, meaning the owners—we Rule #1 investors—are being taken advantage of.

In the 1934 edition of *Security Analysis,* author Benjamin Graham explains that most businesses are not able to accumulate much of an equity surplus because they spend everything they earn to maintain the status quo by replacing and/or keeping up with what they need to stay in business (equipment, R&D, and so on). Noting this, Warren Buffett began looking for the exception: a business that accumulates more and more surplus every year. Finding these exceptions is the key to Rule #1 investing, so we look for businesses that accumulate surplus. That's why we track equity growth; it's a very good sign that the business is exceptional.

Equity, or book value per share, is also an excellent indicator of the long-term growth of what Mr. Buffett calls *intrinsic value* and what I call the "Sticker Price" — the rational value of a business. In the Berkshire Hathaway chairman's letter of February 2005, Mr. Buffett writes, "Despite their shortcomings, yearly calculations of book value are useful at Berkshire as a slightly understated gauge for measuring the long-term rate of increase of our intrinsic value." Therefore, we look very seriously at the equity growth rate to help determine the long-term growth rate, and thus the Sticker Price, of a business.

We figure the equity growth rate just like sales and EPS growth rates. Back when the kids first sold you stock in their business, after you put in the $12,500, the equity in the business was essentially all cash — $14,500. If the business had been liquidated five years ago, each share in the business would've been worth $7.25. If the kids decided to liquidate today, five years later, the equity would be $28,000 and the book value per share $14. We put those two numbers — $14,500 of equity value from five years ago and $28,000 from today — in our calculator, and it tells us the equity or book value growth *rate* for the last five years is 14 percent per year. (Again, I'll be taking you through these calculations in the next chapter; my point here is simply to convey what these numbers mean. I use the term "calculator" loosely, because you'll soon find out how to perform these calculations either roughly in your brain or with the help and accuracy of a real calculator.)

Finally, cash tells us if the company's cash is aligned with its profits. Cash *growth*, in particular, tells us whether its cash is growing with its profits or if the profits are only on paper. We like *real* cash growth.

The kids' lemonade business is a great cash biz. There's some machinery to squeeze the lemons, crush the ice, and serve the juice, and there are a few trucks, but that's about it. That means the profits of the business don't have to be reinvested in expensive hardware that eventu-

Equity is more or less the take-home money if a business is not sold as an ongoing business but instead the machines, supplies, and real estate are sold off, the proceeds of the sales are added to whatever cash the business has in the bank, the debts are paid off, and the remaining cash is divvied up among its owners. Equity doesn't factor the value of the business as an ongoing moneymaker, which is an important part of the real worth of any business, and which, as owners, is ours as well. But early growth rate does give us a very good sense of the growth rate of the real value of the business. We can use that number to figure out what it's going to be worth in ten years. (For more on equity, refer to the Glossary.)

ally becomes worthless and has to be replaced over and over. If this business makes a profit, almost all of it becomes cash in the bank. That cash can be used for business purposes, or it can be given to the owners as a so-called dividend. A dividend is just a pay-out of extra cash the business can't use effectively to grow. Because I'm more or less lazy and prefer to fish than to study annual reports, I really like businesses that can invest the cash for me instead of giving it to me and making me reinvest it myself. Hence, I like businesses that grow fast (and don't pay dividends, but I'll give you the lowdown on dividends at the end of this chapter). Five years ago, your kids' lemonade business had $1,000 in cash. Today they have $10,000 in cash. We plug those numbers into our calculator and get 58 percent for the cash growth rate.

At the end of each quarter, businesses count their cash. Then, the next quarter, they often spend the previous quarter's cash on replacing capital items such as manufacturing machinery. What's left is called "free cash" and is used for paying dividends, or just having it available for working capital—i.e., money to spend on growing the business.

CONSISTENCY

Consistent numbers are what we are looking for. The kids' lemonade business didn't give us enough numbers to see if it was consistently growing (I suppose we could have gathered all of the numbers, but they haven't been in business for at least ten years). I like lots of numbers, and I want to see them going up every year. Here's an example of ten years of the Big Five numbers for Apollo Group:

	ROIC
Last ten years (1995–2004)	32%
Last five years (1999–2004)	30%
Last year (2003–2004)	36%

Year	1995	1996	1997	1998	1999	2000	2001	2002	2003	2004
SALES	163	214	283	391	498	610	769	1009	1310	1798
EPS	.08	.12	.19	.26	.33	.41	.60	.87	1.30	.77
EQUITY	55	88	124	200	231	261	481	700	1027	957
CASH	12	15	36	26	31	83	120	224	287	400

Note: All values except EPS are given in millions of dollars. (EPS is in dollars.)

ROIC is always given as a percentage, while raw values for sales, equity, and cash are typically given in millions of dollars. (EPS is always given in dollars.) We have to take these numbers, however, and create percentages from them that represent growth rates. Only then can we be certain that they meet our 10-percent-per-year on average minimum standard.

In this example, Apollo's ROIC is staying consistent and sales (gross profit), EPS, equity, and cash numbers are all going up almost every year until 2004. It's obvious this business is consistent. Here's what the four numbers look like when we put them on a graph (I converted the numbers to per-share for comparison):

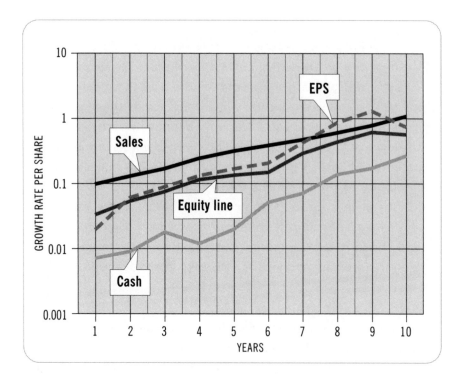

THE FOUR GROWTH RATES

As I've just mentioned, growth rates are different from the raw numbers. The chart above shows the *rates of growth* across all numbers—sales, EPS, equity, and cash—determine to some degree the size of the Moat and the future value of the business, so they're very important. As you can guess, rates are given in percentages, not millions of dollars. In Chapter 6, I'll teach you how to arrive at growth rate percentages in all four categories—sales, EPS, equity, and cash—but for now I want you to become familiar with looking at growth rates and being able to use them to decide on a future growth rate for the business. Ultimately, that's what's important about growth rates: They tell us about the future of the business—and that, in turn, tells us what it's worth today.

A business that can grow its earnings at 15 percent a year indefinitely has a higher value placed on every dollar of current earnings than a business that's going to grow at only 5 percent a year. Moreover, a

Free websites such as MSN Money calculate some of the growth rates, but not all of them. Other websites do calculate and display all the growth rates for various numbers of years, but they charge to access their services. (These subscription-based sites vary in price, too, so it's smart to know what you're getting and how you plan to use the information.) While you might one day join such a subscription-based site to retrieve this information (as most professionals do), it's always good to know how to calculate the rates on your own as a backup. It's like this: I know how to grow corn in case I need to do it someday, but I'd rather pay someone else to do the growing and just buy my corn down at the store.

business that can grow its current dollar of earnings at 15 percent a year probably has a wide Moat, which makes the earnings more *likely* than for the business that grows at 5 percent, with no Moat. It would be nice to be able to buy the wide-Moat company that is rapidly growing its earnings for the same price as the no-Moat company that is dawdling along, but usually nobody is stupid enough to price them the same. That's what makes growth rates so key. What we pay for today is an expected rate of growth. The higher rate is evidence of a Moat, and the Moat makes the expectation more certain. That will become significant in a later chapter.

Remember, we want sales, earnings per share, equity, and cash to be growing faster than 10 percent per year average over the last ten years. And to make sure the rates of growth are not slowing down, we'll look at the five-year and one-year numbers. These are the four growth-rate numbers for Apollo Group, calculated in 2005 for the previous ten years, then five years, and then one year:

Sales			EPS			Equity			Cash		
10	5	1	10	5	1	10	5	1	10	5	1
27%	29%	34%	29%	24%	-41%	53%	46%	2%	51%	68%	39%

Note: All figures are yearly averages.

Read from left to right. Look first at the ten-year growth rate, then the five-year, and finally the one-year—the most recent year. We first want to ensure that all numbers are at least 10 percent, and then we want to see if they are going up or going down as we go from looking at the ten-year average to last year's growth rate.

From these numbers we can see that while the sales rate of growth is getting higher, the EPS rate of growth dropped, and so did equity and cash. If we just looked at a chart of the numbers, Apollo looks pretty good. But if we see those numbers calculated to refer to rates of growth, Apollo suddenly appears to have a problem.

If you want to buy Apollo, you're going to have to decide whether this problem that slammed the brakes on its growth rate, whatever it is, is a one-time situation that Apollo is fixing, or the beginning of a permanent mess that you don't want to own. This is where understanding the business is so critical. If you're not sure you understand, then this isn't an industry for you to be investing in, because these numbers could be showing you a Moat that has been permanently and terminally breached.

Pretty cool, seeing the difference between the numbers and the growth rates derived from them. Calculating growth rates from the numbers is easy, and I'll take you through it in the next chapter. By calculating growth rates of two competing companies, you can really see what's going on and who's got the upper hand (the wider Moat) in the industry.

Here's Apollo Group compared against ITT Educational. (Remember: These numbers reflect rates configured during the writing of this book, in 2005.)

Company	ROIC			Sales			EPS			Equity			Cash		
	10	5	1	10	5	1	10	5	1	10	5	1	10	5	1
Apollo Group	32%	30%	36%	27%	29%	34%	29%	24%	-41%	53%	46%	2%	51%	68%	39%
ITT Educational	171%	313%	46%	12%	14%	18%	25%	27%	26%	19%	29%	23%	29%	11%	-1%

Note: All figures are yearly averages.

Look at the percentages in each category of Big Five percentage growth numbers. Both businesses have great ROIC and sales numbers (all above 10 percent), but whatever hammered Apollo's EPS number lately had no effect on ITT. Apollo's EPS growth rate in the past year was down 41 percent while ITT continued its growth rate at 26 percent. Same with equity; Apollo's equity number plummeted to 2 percent while ITT held at 23 percent. But ITT's cash growth got hammered, reaching −1 percent. I would need to know what's going on before I'd feel good buying either of these right now.

Here's Oracle compared with Sybase:

Company	ROIC			Sales			EPS			Equity			Cash		
	10	5	1	10	5	1	10	5	1	10	5	1	10	5	1
Oracle	110%	182%	54%	12%	3%	15%	26%	18%	16%	31%	19%	29%	35%	16%	11%
Sybase	-21%	-24%	12%	-2%	-2%	1%	-11%	-49%	-21%	4%	12%	-1%	32%	-3%	-3%

Note: All figures are yearly averages.

Oracle and Sybase, two companies that compete in the database market, are both lukewarm on all Big Five numbers. Look at Sybase. See the negative numbers? Its growth rates are going in the wrong direction. Not a good sign. Now look at Oracle. EPS growth rates are sliding down from 26 percent to 18 to 16. Cash growth is sliding from 35 to 16 to 11 percent. Sales and equity slid, then bounced back up. So Oracle is kind of mixed. Not real clear what's going on, is it? Not what we want. We want it *obvious*. Maybe it's just a business recession. Maybe there's a new technology that's attacking them both. But who knows? You and I don't need to know. We just need to know they've got problems and we don't want to own companies with problems we don't understand. Scratch these two.

Here's General Motors compared with Harley-Davidson:

Company	ROIC			Sales			EPS			Equity			Cash		
	10	5	1	10	5	1	10	5	1	10	5	1	10	5	1
GM	3%	1%	1%	2%	2%	4%	13%	14%	27%	11%	15%	9%	-4%	-23%	23%
Harley-Davidson	16%	18%	18%	17%	15%	8%	23%	28%	20%	20%	17%	27%	33%	23%	74%

Note: All figures are yearly averages.

General Motors' EPS growth rate is awesome, but the sales growth rate is far below our 10-percent requirement. And equity growth is going the wrong way even while cash is bouncing up. Mixed signals again. Unclear what's up. Do you know where this firm is going to be in 20 years? Neither do I. Neither do the guys who are running it. Harley has mixed signals, too. Notice that their current sales growth is slipping off below our minimum. EPS is slipping, too. Watch out. Could it be that the boomers are done buying bikes, and the next generation doesn't want Dad's Harley? On a positive note, equity and cash growth rates are rising. Harley is not so obvious, either, is it?

Here's Whole Foods compared with Albertsons:

Company	ROIC			Sales			EPS			Equity			Cash		
	10	5	1	10	5	1	10	5	1	10	5	1	10	5	1
Whole Foods	7%	10%	12%	20%	23%	26%	42%	28%	26%	18%	21%	24%	32%	64%	-10%
Albertsons	9%	6%	6%	14%	2%	11%	6%	9%	-30%	9%	5%	0%	53%	5%	2%

Note: All figures are yearly averages.

Whole Foods' sales, EPS, and equity growth rates are stunning. EPS has slowed to the mid-20s, but that's still a great number (twice our 10-percent minimum). That's what we like to see. But the cash growth rate is down. We'd need to understand what's eating up their cash.

Albertsons, on the other hand, is getting killed across the board. If businesses were castles, Albertsons would be blown to bits. Every set of numbers except recent sales is headed south. And none is above the minimum. No question here which is the better choice.

Here's Dell compared with Gateway:

Company	ROIC			Sales			EPS			Equity			Cash		
	10	5	1	10	5	1	10	5	1	10	5	1	10	5	1
Dell	43%	43%	42%	29%	14%	20%	38%	21%	17%	29%	23%	30%	53%	6%	6%
Gateway	-10%	-50%	-113%	0%	-17%	6%	-35%	-115%	-17%	-16%	-37%	-15%	-23%	-28%	-53%

Note: All figures are yearly averages.

It's easy to find out answers to questions about what a company has been doing to eat up free cash. In the example of Whole Foods, I logged on to their website and listened to the replay of their quarterly message. The managers informed investors that they'd allocated a lot of cash to building new stores. So okay. We'll see the benefit of that down the road. I'll go into more detail about how to find answers to questions like these in a later chapter.

Dell's sales and equity growth rates are recovering, EPS is continuing to drop, and cash growth rate appears stuck at a weak number—6 percent. Dell has big numbers that seem to say it has a wide Moat, even if things have slowed down lately. Looking at Dell and Gateway, it's not hard to see which is the stronger, is it? (Answer: Dell.) (If you're not sure, start this chapter over again and read more slowly.)

If you were investigating Dell in the hopes of buying it someday, you'd discover that Dell spent half of its free cash on buying back its stock. Twelve billion dollars was paid to investors out of equity and cash to buy them out.

That's actually not a bad thing. If I owned Dell and thought the stock price was well below the Sticker Price (or fair value), I'd want to take the excess cash and buy the stock, too. Why? Because I'm getting $1 of value for fifty cents, and if other owners are willing to sell out cheap, that's good for me. I will own more of the pie, and I paid half price for it. Good deal. Oracle managers were doing the same thing with almost all of the Oracle free cash flow. Maybe the managers think their stock is a bargain. If it is, the buy-back benefits the remaining shareholders big time. Buffett loves companies that buy their stock back when it's cheap. However, if they buy it back when it's expensive, the maneuver works against the shareholders. Guess we have to know when a stock is cheap and when it's expensive to know if the company is being well managed. We'll get into that in a later chapter.

Remember this: When a company buys back its own stock when the stock is cheap, that's a good thing for us as owners. But when a company buys back its own stock at a high price, that's not so good. It may be investing in itself, but it's doing so in a spendthrift way.

WHERE TO GET THE BIG FIVE NUMBERS

Luckily, we don't have to go digging through long-winded and confusing annual reports anymore to get the information we need. (That's what I used to do!) Free sites like MSN Money and Yahoo! Finance do a fair job of getting us the numbers from which we can make a few choice calculations. MSN has ten-year numbers for sales, EPS, and book value per share (same thing as equity) but for cash the site shows only five years. It has return on capital (same as ROIC) for five years. Professional sites do it better, of course, but they charge for organizing the data because it saves time—and time, for a pro, is money. At first you may want to copy the data from MSN and make a chart like the Apollo one in this chapter, which has all the raw data organized from 1995 to 2004. This allows you to see four of the Big Five all in one place, and, from there, calculate growth rates quickly and easily. Later, when you gain more experience, all you have to do is look at the Big Five and the wonderful businesses just jump off the page.

A quick word about looking at accounting docs and numbers: No one approaches this task with relish (I certainly don't), so the best course is to focus on the *key* numbers and leave the rest. You'll find most of the data presented in the same general format—whether you're on MSN Money, Yahoo! Finance, or some other place. You'll locate a company's income statement (sometimes called profit and loss), balance sheet, and cash flow. The income statement presents numbers that reflect what a business made, what it cost the business, and what's left (and thus, sales and earnings). The balance sheet presents numbers that reflect what the business owns, what it owes, and what's left for the owners (and thus, equity).

And the cash flow shows numbers that reflect what cash came in, what cash went out, and what cash is left (and thus, free cash flow). So through these three views of a business we get to see the Big Five numbers and use them to evaluate our potential Rule #1 companies.

You may come across sites that use different terms or extra words that confound the process of extracting only what you need. For example, EPS numbers can be seen as "Diluted Normalized EPS" or just "Diluted EPS." But if you follow through the examples I use in this book, learning how to use MSN Money and Yahoo! Finance, you'll gain enough experience to pick up on how to navigate most sites (and read financial statements). With practice, you'll become a wizard at locating and manipulating the numbers no matter which site you're using, and no matter what fancy language it employs. (If you get stumped by a particular site's way of organizing and naming values, e-mail me.)

The truth is, most professional investors overanalyze. For us, the business will either *leap* out as a really good deal, or it won't. If it doesn't, we pass. If it does, we go on to the next step.

FINANCIAL STATEMENTS

Statements on companies are easy to find online. It takes a certain adjustment period to be able to read them and quickly extract the numbers you need (while forgetting the rest), but because they all follow the same general format, no matter what site you use, they're easy to become familiar with. Financial statements include the following documents:

- **Balance sheet:** includes a summary of assets (what the business owns), liabilities (what the business owes), and net worth (what's left over when you subtract liabilities from assets—also called equity) over a specified period of time. This is where you find equity and debt numbers.
- **Income statement:** includes a company's revenues (i.e., sales), expenses, and profits. Look here for sales and EPS numbers.

- **Cash flow (statement):** changes in cash from operating, investing, and financing activities. Here's where you find free cash and dividends paid.

NAVIGATING MSN MONEY

The first step to take in accessing a company's financials is to input its ticker symbol. At MSN Money, the box is marked "Symbol(s)" at the top of the screen (to the right, as of this writing) so that's where you'd enter "NKE" for Nike, for example. If you're wrong about the symbol, the program should either automatically figure out the correct symbol for you, or ask for some information so you can get the right symbol. Once MSN displays the screen with Nike's data, you'll see a column on the left-hand side (much like a margin) that lists links to information. Under "Research," go to "Financial Results." That's where you'll find the link to "Statements."

For ROIC, click on "Key Ratios" under "Financial Results," then click on "Investment Returns." ROIC is listed as "Return on Capital."

For equity numbers, refer to equity expressed as "Book Value per Share," which is under "Key Ratios" and then "10-Year Summary."

For EPS and sales numbers, go to "Financial Results," click on "Statements," and then click the drop-down box to "10-Year Summary."

For cash-flow numbers, call up the "Cash Flow" statement and refer to the very bottom line—"Free Cash Flow."

NAVIGATING YAHOO! FINANCE

Yahoo! is very useful for industry information, but carries only three years of financial data, which is not so helpful for the Four Ms. To get industry information go to www.yahoo.com, click on the "Finance" button on the top left. Scroll down and look at the menu in the left-hand margin. Click on "Industries" and the "Industry Center" page will appear.

For a complete list of industries, click on "Complete Industry List . . ." Every industry is listed under its major sector heading. Click any of these listings to see a summary of that industry. To see all the businesses in that industry, click on "Industry Browser." To see the best and worst in the industry, click on "Leaders and Laggards," and then select whatever criteria you want in the drop-down.

USING PROFESSIONAL SITES

If you use the sites professionals pay for, you can obtain even more sophisticated data. On my site (www.ruleoneinvestor.com), you can get links to such sites. Here are some examples:

- Investor's Business Daily: www.investors.com
- Zacks: www.zacks.com
- Morningstar: www.morningstar.com
- Success: www.success.investools.com

Generally speaking, the fancier and more info-packed the site, the more expensive it is to subscribe. You can do a lot, however, if not 99 percent, of Rule #1 work from free sites, and once you get comfortable with the evaluations, you'll feel better about paying for higher-quality (i.e., better-organized) data.

WHAT ABOUT DEBT?

I said at the beginning of this chapter that debt is more of an afterthought than one of the Big Five. When I teach people about these numbers, someone always asks me about debt, wondering why I *don't* consider it one of the Big Five. Here's what I have to say about that.

Businesses are just like families — they borrow when they want something now and don't want to wait. Most of us have borrowed to buy a car or a house because if we wait until we can pay cash, we might never reach the point of buying. Similarly, a business like Whole Foods, when it needs to build a new store, might borrow to pay for it. There's no problem with getting a loan. Everybody and every business does it. The problems start when you borrow so much that your monthly income must stay the same or even grow bigger or you won't be able to cover your loan payments. In a default situation, you have to sell the house (or the car, or whatever you borrowed the money for) to pay off the loan. Sometimes people borrow a lot, expecting they're going to get a better job (that is, they borrow based on "future income"), and then they lose their job. And they can't sell the house fast enough or they resort to credit cards and they have to declare bankruptcy to keep the debt collectors off their backs. And just as a family can borrow too much, getting into too much debt, so can a business.

When a business borrows more than it can handle with its income, the managers try to get out of the loans just like you do: They try to borrow more money from some other lender, or they sell assets to try to pay off the loans. Or they can sell a piece of the business and use that money to pay off the loans. But just as with you and me, about the time you really need the money, the banks won't lend you any and you can't sell a thing. Businesses can run into this problem, too. The managers borrow a bunch of money to build more stores and then the economy slows down, customers start to worry about their own money and spend less in the stores, and suddenly the business is in a serious cash crunch and can't make the payments on its loans that month. It can't sell its stores, and because it's in trouble, no one wants to buy a piece of the business. Uh-oh. And then they do what we do to keep the loan collectors at bay: They declare bankruptcy. When that happens, a lot of investors get a nasty surprise.

Rule #1 investors want investments that are certain to make money. To be certain we're going to make money, we have to have a predictable business. A business (or a family) that's carrying a lot of debt relative to its income has an unpredictable financial future. If there are any problems with the economy, a business with a lot of loans might be in big trouble, just as a family with a lot of loans might have big problems if the breadwinner loses his job and the income is cut down severely. We don't like unpredictability. Therefore we don't like a lot of debt in a business.

The right amount of debt is zero. But as I've said, lots of companies borrow for lots of good reasons, so let's just say that as long as a company can pay off its debt quickly, it's okay. Same with a family. Zero debt is best, but if you know you can pay off all your debt out of the money you save in one year, then your debt is probably manageable. Let's say the same for a business. If they can pay off their debt in one year of free cash flow, then the debt load is good. We'll set the maximum payoff time at three years. After that, we're not interested.

There are other ways to evaluate debt. We can see it as a percentage of the equity and the liabilities, or just as a percentage of the equity (the popular "debt/equity ratio"). But businesses can manipulate those ratios for lots of good and bad reasons. It's better to just know how long it would take to pay the debt off, and keep that number reasonably conservative. And that's what I'm going to show you how to do. As you're about to find out, all you need in terms of numbers is a company's total long-term debt and its current free cash flow. Obviously, those will be given in millions of dollars. If all you find are percentages listed for debt, try another site for financial data and hunt around on its financial statements for the long-term debt and current free cash flow numbers in dollars.

> **The Rule on Debt:** To determine whether a business's debt is reasonable, find out if it can pay off its debt within three years by dividing total long-term debt by current free cash flow.

Don't worry so much about short-term debt; long-term debt is what we want to watch out for, and you'll find it on the balance sheet as simply "Long Term Debt."

Let's look at a company that has some debt, and try to figure out if it's "acceptable debt" or just too much.

H&R Block has debt. Here are H&R Block's long-term debt and free cash flow for 2005.

Financial Statement	Balance Sheet	Cash Flow Statement	
Line Title:	Total long-term debt	Free cash flow	
Amount:	$923 million	$304 million	923/304 = 3

Let's ask ourselves, given this company's long-term debt and free cash flow, how long would it take it to pay off the debt? This is simple math: Divide $923 million by $304 million ($923 ÷ $304) and we get 3. H&R Block can pay off its debt with three years of free cash flow (barely). Therefore, H&R's debt is okay (barely).

While I don't consider debt the "sixth number" to evaluate, you'll want to consider debt when you're reviewing the financial strength of a business. Besides, you'll come across debt numbers when you're looking at the balance sheet and wonder what to do with them. Once you've said yes to the Five Numbers, go ahead and make sure the debt load is reasonable. Simply divide a company's total long-term debt by its current free cash flow.

In all likelihood, if all the Big Five are lined up and looking good, debt is under control. But if you do see a red flag in the debt area, search for a business with better numbers and *no* bad debt.

THE RULE AS APPLIED TO A FEW BUSINESSES IN 2000

We're almost ready to learn how to find rates of growth across the Big Five, select businesses that appear to be wonderful, and move on to calculate their Sticker Prices. But before getting out the calculators, I want to show you what happened when I applied the Rule #1 strategy in 2000 to this same group of stocks — Harley, GM, Dell, and Apollo. In 2000, The Rule determined I could buy Harley-Davidson and Apollo

Group, but not GM and Dell. (Remember, this decision was made in 2000, not 2005, so even though Apollo and Harley have had some iffy moments in recent years, in 2000 The Rule said to buy them.)

Here's how, as of 2005, the return on investment would have turned out in each case had I bought and just held the stock for those five years (keep in mind that you'll learn how to arrive at these dollar values in the upcoming chapters):

Harley: The Rule said buy it at $27. The experts thought it would continue to grow really fast and be worth $120 by 2005. In fact, things have not gone as well with Harley as the experts had hoped. Right after the year 2000 began, the United States slumped into a recession. A lot of jobs were lost and Harley-Davidson's earnings didn't grow even close to what the experts thought. In spite of that, by using The Rule, five years later this investment still produced a nice 100 percent return even though the stock was selling for half of the projected price for the year 2005. Half. And we *still* made good money.

General Motors: The Rule said not to buy General Motors in spite of the experts' conservative expectation that it would go up 50 percent in the next five years. The problem was that if the experts were right, the price of the stock in 2000 was well above its value for a Rule #1 investor. The Rule shows us that companies priced well above their value are the first to go down in a market downturn. That was certainly the case with GM. Priced at twice its value, the stock got hammered over those five years. Had I invested, instead of making 50 percent, the return on this investment would have been a loss of about 70 percent. The stock is now selling for about one-third the price it would have been selling for if the analysts were right. One-third.

One of the reasons The Rule is so important is that it won't leave you in a bad investment. Without The Rule, after five years of losing money on GM, the investor who's still holding the stock must see it go up 300 percent just to break even. A stock that goes up 300 percent over the next five years would have an annual return of 25 percent. The investors holding GM through a 70-percent loss must be praying that suddenly the company is going to grow magically at a rate that isn't being projected by either the company or the analysts. By sticking with this stock, those investors are living in dreamland.

(Dreamland is where a lot of amateur investors live who don't want to deal with reality and who don't understand The Rule. Rule #1 investors do not live in dreamland, ever. If a Rule #1 investor were given GM five years ago, I promise you he wouldn't be sitting on it through a 70-percent loss unless he became catatonic. Rule #1 investors have the tools and knowledge to see the reality of the business they have money in, and understand that there are better businesses out there for them to spend time and money owning.)

Dell: One of the best businesses in the world if you think you understand the high-tech hardware business. In 2000 the experts thought it would give an investor a 50-percent return by 2005, but the price the stock market wanted in 2000 was too high for a Rule #1 investor. Investors who paid it lost 20 percent of their money. Astonishingly, as you'll later see, if you bought the same stock in 2002 — instead of 2000 — based on the experts' projections in 2002, you would have doubled your money in just three years.

Apollo Group: This business was a solid Rule #1 investment that, based on expert projections, was expected to make us a huge 700-percent return by 2005. In fact, things worked out far better than expected, and by 2005 the stock had given Rule #1 investors a 900-percent return. It was an excellent Rule #1 buy in 2000, and even though its EPS and equity growth slowed in the last year, our overall rate of return over those five years was stellar.

So, based on expert analysis, Harley expected 400 percent and made 100 percent while GM expected 50 percent and made −70 percent. Dell expected 50 percent and made −20 percent, and Apollo Group expected 700 percent and made 900 percent. If risk and reward are as related as everyone thinks, then GM and Dell, with expected 50-percent "rewards," must have been less risky investments than Harley and Apollo Group, which projected 400 percent and 700 percent respectively. That didn't turn out to be true at all, did it? In fact, at the time, according to The Rule, the higher potential return investments in this case were the lower-risk investments. Rule #1 investors know through personal experience that in any stock market they're capable of finding very low-risk business investments that have very high potential rewards. And, conversely, all day, every day, the stock market offers up low-reward investments that have a great deal of risk associated with them.

Finally, a word about dividends . . .

DIVIDENDS

So far, our wonderful business is a business that has one of the five Moats, nice Big Five numbers, and little or no debt. That probably means that every year the business has leftover cash. Since we're thinking like business owners, we look at that leftover cash as ours. But the CEO gets to decide whether to give it to us or spend it to do a bunch of things like developing new products, increasing the numbers of salespeople out there selling, building stores, increasing the marketing budget to build our brand, and so on. Obviously, if he doesn't give it back to us, we want him to get a high return on the investment he's making with our money. As long as the ROIC is staying up there, he's probably doing a good job of investing our money. In that case we should prefer that he keep growing it rather than give it back to us, because if he gives it to us, we're just going to have to reinvest it in some other business that can grow it, and it's a lot simpler if he just keeps it.

But what happens if the CEO can't invest all of our money back in the business and get a good ROIC on it? What happens if he can only use some of it effectively to grow the business, but the rest of it won't speed up growth? That would mean he's either throwing part of our money away or just sitting on it. And those are bad things. We'd rather he not throw any of our money away. We'd rather he give that piece back to us, thank you, so we can put it into a business that can grow it. When the CEO gives us back a portion of our money, it's called a dividend. Whether a company pays dividends or not has nothing to do with whether it has a wide Moat. Some wide-Moat companies such as Procter & Gamble and Microsoft have decided they can't use the excess cash to grow any faster, so it gets paid out to the owners. Other wide-Moat businesses such as Starbucks think they can use every penny of earnings to grow, and so they don't ever pay a dividend. As Rule #1 investors, we don't exclude a business because it pays (or doesn't pay) a dividend.

Paying dividends is not an indication of slow growth or fast growth. It's just a choice being made by Management about how best to manage the owners' cash.

Many fast-growth companies do pay a dividend. Whether a company pays a dividend should have no bearing on how you apply Rule #1.

A dividend is neither good nor bad on its own. A good dividend is one that's paid out with money the CEO cannot efficiently allocate to growth. He thinks if he keeps the money, his ROIC is going to go down. We love CEOs who think like this, which is one of the reasons we watch ROIC. By giving the money to the owner, the CEO is allowing us to allocate that capital more efficiently. A bad dividend is one that's paid out with money the CEO could have used to grow the business. General Motors, for example, probably would have been better off reinvesting its precious cash into growing the business than allocating it to its shareholders in the form of a dividend it couldn't afford to pay.

Why would a CEO pay a dividend when he really shouldn't? Because it's politically correct to do so. Many people who own stocks think of

Consider this about dividends: Before the business can pay a dividend, it pays taxes on earnings that belong to the owners. About 35 percent in taxes. Out of the 65 percent left, the business can pay dividends. If it paid all of the earnings out to you, the owner, as dividends, you'd have to pay short-term gain taxes on the whole amount. All of it is taxed again at some rate, depending on Congess. That can leave you, the owner, with as little as 40 percent of the original earnings of your company. The government has confiscated the rest by double taxation. If you are paid dividends and get taxed at 60 percent of your earnings, it makes sense not to encourage dividends and to have the business pay only 35 percent tax even if the business is having trouble allocating the earnings efficiently. The result, then, of a government double taxation policy is to make American businesses less competitive against more efficiently run foreign corporations.

themselves as "investors" instead of owners, and as such they want the *appearance* of consistency. To an ignorant investor, a consistent dividend can provide the illusion that all is well, and that way the CEO gets to keep his job. That's what's been going on at General Motors.

The key to knowing your business has a Moat is to see it from the perspective of the Big Five plus debt. Guessing doesn't cut it for a Rule #1 investor. We like certainty that this is a wonderful business. If the business has one of the five Moats, and the Big Five plus debt look good, we go on to the next step. If not, we drop it off the list. Whether the business is paying dividends is irrelevant. When Whole Foods pays me a dividend, I typically just buy more Whole Foods stock. But if the price of that stock goes over the Sticker Price, I start looking for a better deal—which means I'm selling Whole Foods and saying good-bye to that dividend.

Now you're going to learn how to figure out the Big Five growth rates.

DIVIDENDS AND EQUITY GROWTH

Dividends are deducted from equity. Since most businesses pay dividends more or less as a constant percentage of the surplus, I haven't concerned myself with adding the dividends back to the equity before calculating the equity growth rate. However, occasionally a business will pay out a huge, one-time dividend—like Microsoft did a year ago when it paid more than $52 billion to its shareholders. In a case like that you have to add that big dividend to the equity and then calculate the growth rate. It's easy to see that there might have been a payout because you'll see the equity suddenly drop like a brick. Then just look at cash flow to see if there was a big payout that year. (Such payouts will also be seen in company news.)

Chapter 6

Calculate the Big Five

That which we persist in doing becomes easier, not that the task itself has become easier, but that our ability to perform it has improved.
—RALPH WALDO EMERSON (1803–1882)

I N CHAPTERS 4 and 5 we explored the Big Five numbers and debt, the telltale signs that a business will either grow our money or potentially betray us and cause us to violate Rule #1. When I introduced these numbers and showed you what they look like for a few companies, I simply gave you the data without involving you in much calculation. Now we're going to work with the Big Five so that we're comfortable finding growth *rates*. You're going to be good friends with these numbers by the time you've looked at just a few businesses, so you might as well get used to the idea that the Big Five, with some practice and a little patience, are going to be as easy for you to play with as 2 + 2 = 4. You can do that one, right? If not, don't worry, that's what computers are for. We don't actually have to do any of the math; we just pick the numbers we need to toss into the computer, and it'll do the rest. So let's get started.

GARMIN

We're going to compare two companies: Garmin (GRMN) and General Motors (GM). I'll take you step-by-step through calculating some of the various growth rates on Garmin and GM. The process is the same no matter which growth rates you're calculating, so for any rate that I don't show you how to do step-by-step, go ahead and try to perform the calculations once you're comfortable with this methodical procedure.

Garmin is the number-one GPS gear company for the worldwide market. It's a relatively new company in a new field. General Motors (GM) sells cars worldwide. They sell more cars worldwide than any competitor. GM is about five times larger than Garmin in market cap. GM is old, huge, famous, and American. Garmin is young and growing, but relatively unknown and Taiwanese.

GARMIN 1995–2004

Year	1995	1996	1997	1998	1999	2000	2001	2002	2003	2004
Sales*	$102	$136	$160	$169	$233	$345	$369	$465	$573	$763
EPS	0.26	0.26	0.41	0.35	0.64	1.05	1.05	1.32	1.64	1.89
Equity				136	195	365	454	602	750	936
Cash			37	28	16	58	103	149	140	130
ROIC					23%					22%

*Sales figures are in millions.

In the above chart, which is similar to the one we looked at in the previous chapter that revealed Apollo's numbers, I've collected all the numbers we need for arriving at growth rates. Remember, ROIC is always given as a percentage (you won't have to do any growth rate calculations among ROIC values). You can get most of these numbers from an online site like MSN Money by clicking on the "Stock" button and then finding the box where you can enter a stock symbol. Enter "GRMN" or "GM" and look for the financial statements. (Remember: Look for Income Statement, Balance Sheet, and Cash Flow.)

The first thing we do is check for consistency in the numbers just by looking at them. If I graphed the numbers, I'd want to see a nice steady, upward-trending line. Here's what Garmin's EPS numbers look like graphed:

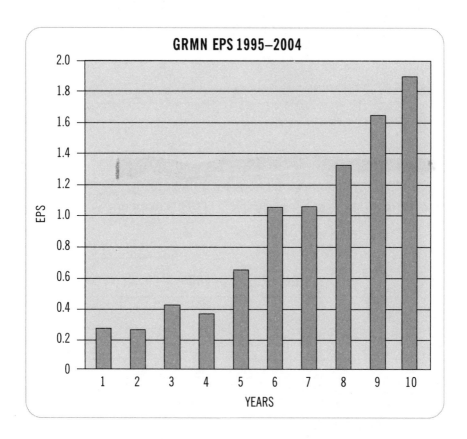

Pretty good. Steady and consistent. That's what we're looking for. You don't necessarily have to create a graph like the one I did here (for the purpose of giving you a visual). You can simply look at the numbers from 1995 to 2004 and notice they go up, not down.

Let's graph GM's numbers. To start, here's a chart of GM's numbers for the last ten years, starting with 1995:

GM 1995–2004

Year	1995	1996	1997	1998	1999	2000	2001	2002	2003	2004
Sales*	$164	$158	$166	$154	$167	$184	$177	$187	$186	$194
EPS	7.28	6.07	8.70	4.18	8.53	6.68	1.77	3.35	5.03	4.96
Equity	23	23	17	15	21	30	20	7	25	27
Cash	8	9	7	5	20	12	4	4	-3	5
ROIC					1%					0%

*Sales figures are in billions.

Again, first we look for consistency in the numbers. If I graphed the General Motors numbers, I'd hope for a nice steady, upward-trending line. Here's what I get when I graph GM's EPS numbers:

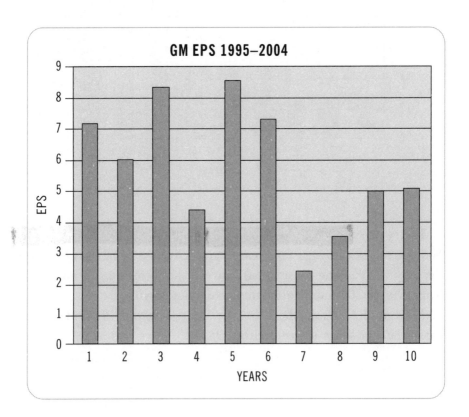

Not too pretty. Bouncing around all over the place. This isn't what we'd hoped for. We're looking for predictability. We want to have a high degree of certainty that this company is going to do well in the future. If it's bounced around in the past, we can't be very certain it won't bounce around in the future. All that bouncing means the numbers aren't doing what the management and the owners want the numbers to do. Something is going wrong a lot. We don't want to invest in companies where something's going wrong a lot. There are too many companies we can find where everything is going very well consistently.

Now let's figure out what the four growth rates are for these two businesses. There are four ways to do this:

1. Learn how to use Excel Rate calculations. If you feel like doing this, I put all the instructions on my website, www.ruleone investor.com. It's quite easy once you get used to it — but slow. (Once you do it once or twice, however, it becomes automatic.)

2. Learn how to use the Rule #1 calculators on my website. These calculators are as quick as a button but require a bit of practice. Just go on my site and follow the directions.

3. Learn how to do the calculations by hand (or in your head), which does become automatic once you do several rounds of practice. I'll take you through this process below.

4. Look up the growth-rate numbers on a stock data website. This is not only the fastest way to get this information, it's also the easiest — but you may not find all of the growth rates you want online. And the sites that do *all* of the fancy footwork are more expensive.

We're going to have to choose between paying for information and getting it for free. If we want it for free, however, we either learn how to derive growth rates from raw numbers ourselves or settle for five-year and one-year growth rates. Nobody does ten-year growth rates for free — yet. To illustrate the limitations of what a free website can provide, go to MSN Money and input "GRMN," click on "Financial Results," "Key Ratios," and then "Growth Rates." We find growth rates for EPS and sales only.

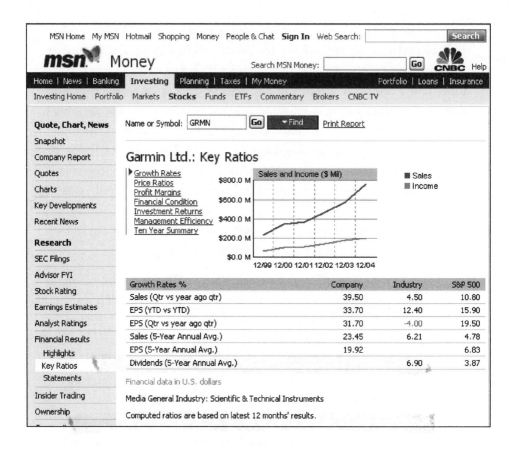

Notice that the five-year EPS growth rate was 19.92 percent, while last year's EPS growth rate was 33.7 percent. Also, the five-year sales growth rate was 23.45 percent while last year's sales growth rate was 39.5 percent. That's two out of our four, and it gives us only the five-year and one-year. It'd be nice to see the nine- or ten-year and the three-year rates, too. But this site can't give us those rates. We have to calculate equity and cash growth rates if we want them, as well as other growth rate periods for EPS and sales.

FIGURING GROWTH RATES IN YOUR HEAD

I'll take you through a few sample calculations you can do in your head (without the use of a programmed calculator like those on my website), and you can do the rest once you get the hang of this procedure. Notice the pattern that emerges in conducting these calculations. If you can do one growth-rate calculation, you can do them all. Let's start by figuring out Garmin's six-year equity growth rate. And start by having the raw numbers handy:

GARMIN EQUITY 1995–2004

Year	1995	1996	1997	1998	1999	2000	2001	2002	2003	2004
Equity				136	195	365	454	602	750	936

As you can see, Garmin's equity grows from 136 to 936 in six years. Ask yourself: How many times does 136 have to double to get to 936? First, we're going to round the 136 off to something we can double easily — say, 150. Then we're going to double it: 300. And we're going to keep doubling it until we get in the ballpark of 936, and while doing so, we're going to count each time we double it. So 150 to 300 is one double; 300 to 600 is two doubles; and 600 to 1,200 is three doubles — except that the equity didn't get to 1,200, so we don't quite have three doubles. Now, how many years did we just cover? Wasn't it six years? 1998 to 1999 is one year; then 1999 to 2000 is two; 2000 to 2001 is three; 2001 to 2002 is four; 2002 to 2003 is five; and 2003 to 2004 is six. Six years.

So, if Garmin doubled almost three times in six years, ask yourself: How many years did it take Garmin to double just *once*? Well, if we have a nice clean three doubles in six years, it's easy — two years to double once, another two to double again, and another two to double the third time. So, two years to double. Now here comes the trick: How many times does 2 go into 72? (This neat little trick is called the Rule of 72, and it's how we used to figure this math out before we got computers. The Rule of 72 is a universally accepted method for figuring out the growth rate if you know how many years it took to double the money once. My teacher taught me how it works, and I'm teaching you.) Two goes into 72 exactly 36 times, right? So Garmin's equity growth rate is probably a little less than that, since we didn't get an exact three doubles. So let's call it 30 percent. Cool, huh? No computer required.

THE RULE OF 72: BEHIND THE SCENES

It's wholly unnecessary for me to go into the mathematics behind why and how the Rule of 72 works. It's a can of worms you don't want me to open because it involves applied mathematics, logarithms, and a deep understanding of how annually compounded interest works. Put simply, it's called the Rule of 72 because at 10 percent, money doubles every 7.2 years and when you divide 7.2 by 10 percent, you get 72. This rule of thumb helps you compute when your money (or any unit of numbers) will double at a given interest (growth) rate. For example, if you want to know how long it'll take to double your money at 9-percent interest, divide 9 into 72 and get 8 years. You can also do the reverse, and solve for the interest (growth) rate. For example, if your money has to double in two years so you can buy your significant other a trip to Europe, you'll need 72 / 2 = 36 percent rate of return on your stash.

So the Rule of 72 is an approximation, but it's a remarkably accurate one we can use with confidence in our Rule #1 calculations.

Let's do cash. We want to see how free cash flow is growing. That's the cash left over after investing available cash in equipment, R&D, and so on. We'll do the seven-year growth rate (from 1997 to 2004):

GARMIN CASH 1997–2004

Year	1997	1998	1999	2000	2001	2002	2003	2004
Cash	37	28	16	58	103	149	140	130

Garmin's cash numbers go from 37 to 130 in seven years. Round 37 up to 40 to simplify the math. So 40 doubles to 80 for one double, 80 doubles to 160 for two doubles, and we're already over the 130. So call it not quite two doubles in seven years. That means it took Garmin 3.5 years to double once — maybe four, since we were a little short there. Now use the Rule of 72 and divide four into 72 for the growth rate: 72/4 = 18. The growth rate for Garmin's cash over the last seven years is 18 percent a year.

Now that we know how to do this, we can do Garmin's sales and EPS for nine years.

GARMIN SALES 1995–2004

Year	1995	1996	1997	1998	1999	2000	2001	2002	2003	2004
Sales	102	136	160	169	233	345	369	465	573	763
EPS	0.26	0.26	0.41	0.35	0.64	1.05	1.05	1.32	1.64	1.89

Sales went from 102 to 763, or, rounding, 100 to 800. Do the math: 100 to 200 is one double; 200 to 400 is two; and 400 to 800 is three doubles. So we have roughly three doubles in nine years. That's three years per double. Apply the Rule of 72: 72/3 = 24. So the nine-year average sales growth rate is about 24 percent.

EPS went from .26 to 1.89 in nine years. Start doubling: 25 to 50 is one; 50 to 100 is two; and 100 to 200 is three. So roughly three doubles on EPS, too. We already know the answer to this one: 72/3 = 24. Sales and EPS have about the same growth rate — 24 percent for the last nine years.

That's just a slice of Garmin's Big Five numbers. You can perform these calculations using different sets of numbers to get your averages for different periods of time. The reason it's best to look at these numbers over different periods of time is to see if there's a change for the worse. For example, if you were to run Garmin's equity numbers between 2001 and 2004, you'd find out that its three-year equity growth rate average is about 27 percent. If you did its one-year rate, you'd get 25 percent. Notice that the equity growth is slowing down a bit, but

it's still excellent—and way above our 10-percent minimum requirement for Big Five growth. That's huge for us because ultimately the
growth of *equity* in the company is what we want to see more than any
of the other growth numbers. That's because the growth of the Sticker
Price—the value of the business—is going to most closely follow the
growth of equity.

PRIORITY OF GROWTH RATES

Not all four growth rates bear the same weight, or share the
same level of importance. Although they all should be above
our 10-percent minimum, here's their order of importance,
starting with the most important:

1. Equity growth
2. EPS growth
3. Sales (or gross profit) growth
4. Cash flow growth

This means that when you have to refer to growth rates or derive other estimations from them, which we'll be doing shortly,
you should focus on equity and EPS growth first, and then
sales and cash flow. Equity and EPS growth say a lot about the
future of a company, and how certain we can be in *predicting*
that future, which is a cornerstone to Rule #1.

Ready to do GM? Same way exactly: See what growth rates you can
gather online without doing any work, and figure out the rest by performing the same calculations we just did above with Garmin. I'll run
the ten-year sales numbers on GM as an example:

GENERAL MOTORS SALES 1995–2004

Year	1995	1996	1997	1998	1999	2000	2001	2002	2003	2004
Sales*	$164	$158	$166	$154	$167	$184	$177	$187	$186	$194

*Sales figures are in billions.

Sales went from 164 to 194 in nine years. Start doubling: Oops! You can't! No doubles in nine years. That's a zero in my book. Ordinarily we'd be done with GM right about there. But you're just learning, so let's do another one. Let's try EPS:

GENERAL MOTORS EPS 1995–2004

Year	1995	1996	1997	1998	1999	2000	2001	2002	2003	2004
EPS	7.28	6.07	8.70	4.18	8.53	6.68	1.77	3.35	5.03	4.96

EPS went from roughly $7 to $5. Negative numbers? Forget it. Just put a zero for EPS growth for nine years. Equity went from 23 to 27. Forget it. And cash went from 8 to 5. Another zero. (FYI: By cleverly purchasing stock, GM's BVPS looks good even though equity hardly grew at all.) So, quick and dirty with the Rule of 72, and we get 0,0,0,0 for GM. You can look up five-year and one-year numbers for sales and EPS on MSN and see if GM has a heartbeat, because from the nine-year view, this business looks flat-lined, dead on arrival.

If you're stubborn enough to run all the growth numbers on GM to rest assured it's a bad investment, here's what you'd get:

- *Sales growth rates:* 9-year = **–4%**; 5-year = **–11%**; 3-year = **–8%**.
- *Equity growth rates:* 9-year = 2%; 5-year = 5%; 3-year = 11%.
- *Free cash flow growth rates:* 9-year = **–5%**; 5-year = **–24%**; 3-year = 8%

We really don't have to run the calculators at all to see if GM's growth rates are good enough for us, because over ten years none go up. And when you look at the five-year, three-year, and one-year numbers, they may show improvement, but they still aren't that exciting. GM's inconsistency across the board is enough for us to turn our heads away. We can't be certain where this business is headed.

CALCULATING ROIC

And now the last but most important single number: ROIC (as I mentioned in the previous chapter, I prioritize ROIC as *the* most important

If you like playing with numbers and getting it exact, visit my website and use my online calculators to figure these numbers out quickly. At www.ruleoneinvestor. com, click on "Rule #1 Calculators" to access a host of calculators:

- Sales Growth Rate Calculator
- EPS Growth Rate Calculator
- Equity (or book value per share) Growth Rate Calculator
- Cash Growth Rate Calculator
- ROIC Calculator
- Debt Calculator
- Sticker & MOS Calculator
- Return on Investment (ROI) Calculator

These calculators do all the math for you; all you need to provide are the raw numbers, which you can retrieve from financial statements on any financial data website. Simply follow the instructions on my site.

number of all). The Rule of 72 won't work on ROIC, but fortunately we can simply look it up on a financial site and be done with it!

Unlike growth rates, figuring out the ROIC on a company shouldn't be a task you have to do routinely, since you can simply reference it on a variety of websites. But I know that some of you want the behind-the-scenes view of ROIC. Here's what it boils down to:

$$\frac{net\ operating\ profit\ after\ tax}{equity\ +\ debt}$$

Net operating profit after tax is often shortened to NOPAT. To get NOPAT, start with net income from operations, but add back in any interest and depreciation expenses. Luckily, we don't have to do this entire calculation ourselves. (If you want to learn how to plug in the numbers from a financial statement to arrive at ROIC percentages for certain periods of time on a company, go to www.ruleoneinvestor.com, and I'll take you through the mechanics using my ROIC calculator. For the most part, however, you can rely on the ROIC numbers that are freely available on many sites.)

Focus on making sure the ROIC is at least above 10 percent, and that it shows consistency from year to year—hopefully in an upward trend. We can access Garmin's ROIC numbers easily online by going to MSN Money, then "Financial Results," "Key Ratios," and "Investment Returns." (ROIC is called Return on Capital at MSN.) The site gives us the five-year and one-year ROICs:

Five-year Return on Capital is 23 percent and the one-year is 22 percent.

You can look up GM and see it has 1 percent and 0 percent respectively. The owners of GM would be making more money putting their money in a one-month T-bill at 1 percent a year.

Obviously, you don't have to do much soul-searching to see the huge difference between a company like Garmin and a company like GM.

BIG FIVE SUMMARY

Drum roll. Here's the summary we've arrived at from running the numbers on Garmin and General Motors. If they weren't previously, the positive and negative aspects should now be blindingly obvious:

GARMIN

EPS				Sales				Equity			Cash			ROIC	
9	5	3	1	9	5	3	1	6	3	1	7	4	1	5	1
27%	26%	27%	27%	24%	26%	28%	25%	38%	27%	25%	20%	22%	-7%	23%	22%

GM

EPS				Sales				Equity				Cash				ROIC	
9	5	3	1	9	5	3	1	9	5	3	1	9	5	3	1	5	1
-4%	-10%	28%	-1%	-4%	-11%	-8%	-8%	2%	5%	11%	8%	-5%	-24%	8%	500%	1%	0%

General Motors' Big Five look bad. Something is way, way wrong in Detroit. If this business has a Moat, it sure doesn't show up in the numbers. While there's some improvement in the last three years, three years of even good numbers wouldn't be enough to show a Moat. Moats are about long-term protection. If the business we are looking at doesn't have good long-term and short-term Big Five numbers, it's too inconsistent to predict its future. We can pass, and devote our time to finding something we can rely on. GM is obviously a nay at this time for a Rule #1 investor.

Garmin's Big Five look solid. (Yes, you'll notice that Garmin's cash slipped in the past year, but that's okay. *One* mediocre year is not enough to bruise the entire strength of the other Big Five numbers — especially the average numbers over the long term. Cash is also the least important number of all.) Garmin's numbers show us that there's a

Moat of some sort at the company. Garmin has been building a strong brand Moat among consumers, and it may have some trade secrets in its corner, too. Assuming we understand the business and would be proud to own it, Garmin is a go to the next level of analysis.

HOW RELIABLE IS PAST GROWTH IN PREDICTING THE FUTURE?

One last thing before we move on: Just because the Big Five were good in the past doesn't always mean they'll be good in the future. Almost every business ends its long streak of great Big Five numbers at some point. Maybe it runs out of people to sell goods and services to, or maybe some competitor swims the Moat and starts attacking the castle. Maybe the entire industry becomes obsolete. Past growth rates alone are not good enough to predict the future. Which is why Rule #1 investors don't rely *only* on past growth rates to make a prediction.

Remember the first M: *Meaning.* If the business has no Meaning to you (i.e., you don't understand it), even the best Big Five numbers don't say anything. You can't invest your retirement money in *anything* you don't understand and has no Meaning to you on some level, okay? But in addition to protecting ourselves by understanding the business, we've got to run it through a few more critical tests to make sure that even if we do make a big mistake, we don't violate Rule #1.

Consistent growth rates and a solid ROIC allow us to put this business forward as a candidate for our approval. At least with good historical consistency we can hope for a steady future based on expectations that the business will continue to do what it's been doing. We can continue investigating Garmin because it has a stable past. In GM's case, it has a persistently bad past. Hoping that GM will stop doing what it's been doing and become a completely different business requires too much faith in GM's claim that it sees a bright future for itself.

In the early days, back in the 1980s, I got a lesson in how important it is to have numbers that back up the Moat. Identifying Moats can be a subjective process, which means inexperienced investors like me at the time can be sold a great story that makes it seem like the business has a

Moat when in fact it doesn't. I got sold on a story about what a terrific Secret Moat a certain company (that shall remain nameless) had. Their technology was trade-secret and totally over-my-head science, but it really made for a compelling and convincing story. The business allegedly had experienced management and fantastic scientists, and, best of all, it was out to change the world in a major way. Suffice it to say I completely bought into the buzz surrounding this business.

The lesson: Don't get sold a story! Good intentions and attention-grabbing details aren't enough to make a good Rule #1 investment, because there's nothing certain about a nice story. You have to go behind it and find the numbers to back it up. Only outstanding long-term Big Five numbers can provide the certainty you need to be sure you're not going to lose money. You can read fairy tales in every annual report, but you can't stop there.

This business that I bought into had problems with its technology, then it had problems with marketing and even problems with management, all of which were showing up in the numbers. But in the end, the power of following The Rule saved me. That investment turned out okay because even though the Big Five numbers weren't great, I'd gotten in with a huge *Margin of Safety,* which I'll explain later. For now, the lesson is to identify the Moat, and be certain that the Big Five are there to back up the story.

NOW TO THE PEOPLE RUNNING THE SHOW

If we've gotten this far, the CEO is going to be the final determining factor for whether we really want to own this company. The CEO determines the focus of the company, the happiness of people working there, and ultimately the ROI (return on investment) we're going to get when we buy the whole thing. CEOs who stick to their knitting and who focus on what they do well are the right CEOs for us. We've covered Meaning and Moat to a great extent, and the next chapter tells you how to find Mr. or Ms. Right, which brings us to our third M: *Management.*

Chapter 7

Bet on the Jockey

Do not hire a man who does your work for money, but him who does it for love of it.

— Henry David Thoreau (1817–1862)

REMEMBER WHAT we're doing: We're looking at stocks as businesses; we're looking for a wonderful business; and we're insisting we buy it at an attractive price. Having a wide Moat is a critical part of a wonderful business, because a wide-Moat business can recover from lots of disasters — even those created by bad management decisions. Still, it'd be nice to know that the people running the company really have their act together and thus deserve to run it — not that they got the top job because they were politically clever.

This brings us to the third M: *Management.*

We might have to settle for politicos to run the government, but we don't have to settle for those types to run our businesses. We can insist on people we respect, trust, admire, and otherwise wish were part of our family unit. The sad truth is, it isn't hard to be fooled by politicians and other crooks who are disguised as honest, hardworking businesspeople, but if you follow a few tips in this chapter, you'll have a good chance of spotting the self-involved, unethical, prevaricating phonies who inhabit the head offices at far too many companies.

What we're looking for is a leader. Someone who is going to take our company to the moon. Someone who lives and breathes this company. Someone who has a Big Audacious Goal that he wants to drive the business to achieve. If we get someone like that, who's honest with you about what's going on, we can sit back and watch miracles happen. If we get the wrong guy, we can easily get Enronned or WorldConned. The good news is the clues are easy to spot — and if we're not sure, we don't invest. Same as always.

HOW VENTURE CAPITALISTS GAMBLE SMARTLY

Venture capitalists invest in companies before the firms offer their stock to the general public. At one point I had about $20 million invested in venture capital deals. I stopped doing so much VC because it was hard work and risky. I don't like hard work, and you know I don't like risk. It's just so much easier and so much less risky to do Rule #1 investing than VC investing. The basic idea of VC investing is to find a potentially wonderful company, buy into it at an attractive price, and then keep it forever (or at least until you can sell it at the IPO). Sound familiar? See, the basic ideas of investing that Ben Graham taught 70 years ago apply to all kinds of investing, including VC investing.

The reason I'm mentioning venture capital here isn't so you can learn to be a venture capitalist. I want to teach you the single most critical aspect of venture capital–type investing: betting on the jockey.

VC investing is all about investing at such an early stage that you can't really be certain it's all going to work out. You can't look at the Big Five numbers and see consistency because there is no Big Five. The business isn't even selling anything yet. Worse, sometimes the business is so new and cutting-edge that there isn't even an industry to understand. Because of the lack of any sort of track record, my venture capitalist partners bet on the management team at least as much as they did on the business plan. Sometimes we spoke of betting on the jockey at least as much as on the horse. The reason you need to learn this as a business buyer is that in every business you buy, the CEO — the guy or gal who's guiding the business — determines whether you're being lied to now and whether you'll be lied to in the future. In the long run, knowing you're going to get the truth about the state of the business is almost as important as the business itself.

One of the main reasons I want to own a specific business is that I like and trust the people who run it. This is so important when investing during the early stages of a business that most venture capitalists put it right at the top of their list of essentials a business must have — a CEO they trust and with whom they want to work. If the company doesn't have a great CEO (many early-stage technology start-ups are run by a technology wizard who has no experience running a $50-million company), VCs hold up funding until a great CEO can be found to join the team. VCs aren't willing to bet on even the world's greatest technology unless they have faith in the person who's going to guide this business to success.

WHO ARE WE LOOKING FOR?

I love putting my money on a great jockey, a great CEO. There's nothing better for sleeping well at night than knowing that some honest, owner-oriented, and driven person is out there thinking about how to make me money.

Author and business researcher Jim Collins thinks so, too. In his book *Good to Great* (New York: HarperCollins, 2001), Collins maintains that the CEOs who move their companies into greatness (much to the benefit of the owners, obviously) are almost all what he calls "Level Five" leaders. Collins goes on to explain that a Level Five leader is one who channels his ego needs away from himself and into the larger goal of building a great company. A fully developed Level Five leader "builds enduring greatness through a paradoxical blend of personal humility and professional will." I'll paraphrase for you what I think are the most important qualities of a Level Five leader. It comes down to two:

1. Owner-oriented
2. Driven

AN OWNER-ORIENTED CEO

What exactly does "owner-oriented" mean, and how would we know if a particular CEO fits the bill? An owner-oriented CEO is one who has his personal interests directly aligned with the shareholders of the business — the owners.

Microsoft's Bill Gates and Steven Ballmer see themselves as owner-oriented, and run the company accordingly. Here's an excerpt from their 2002 shareholder letter:

"For the two of us, the vast majority of our individual net worth is invested in stock ownership of the business. Since Microsoft went public in 1986, we have never taken stock options, and we never will. We hope this provides further assurance that our personal interests are directly aligned with the long-term interests of all shareholders."

Mr. Gates and Mr. Ballmer are making an important point about being owner-oriented execs versus speculators. If the top officers get stock options, in effect they become speculators who benefit if the stock price goes up, even if it goes up only for a short time, during which they can exercise their options. This fact causes many executives to make bad long-term decisions benefiting the stock price in the short run. By not accepting stock options, Gates and Ballmer are saying, in effect, that as the company's top officers (and, of course, shareholding "owners"), they intend to run the business for the benefit of long-term owners like themselves. This outlook is very Rule #1 in its perspective (and probably lies at the heart of Mr. Gates's friendship with Mr. Buffett).

The idea that you—as an investor—are marrying the CEO isn't such a bad metaphor. Don't marry anyone unless you know and agree with how they're spending your money.

Warren Buffett clarifies this point when he describes how an owner-oriented CEO should run his business. As he said in his 2004 shareholder letter, "My message to [the CEOs] is simple: Run your business as if it were the only asset your family will own over the next 100 years."

Since talk is cheap, one of the ways we can tell if a CEO is walking the walk is to find out if he's telling us what, as owners, we need to know to be properly informed about our business.

TELL ME WHAT I NEED TO KNOW

It's tough for some CEOs to tell us owners what we need to know because they're afraid of looking bad or of creating a bigger problem by going public. As a result, we owners get these nice letters at the end of the year that never indicate a problem — and then we wake up one morning to discover there were indeed huge problems that had been mounting for a long time.

Can you really ever know if the people running the company are honest and telling you everything you need to know? Well, answer this: Can you ever really know if your spouse is cheating on you? Some of us would have answered "yes" to that question, only to find out later we were mistaken. On balance, it seems logical to conclude that a CEO *is* capable of breaching our trust and hiding important information if he wants to. The best we can do is to pick CEOs who *seem* to be acting as if the company were the only asset their family will own for the next 100 years.

Here's a great example of a CEO who is spelling it out. This is from Whole Foods' CEO John Mackey's 2002 letter to shareholders:

Q: What are the main challenges you see for 2003?
A: The biggest challenge for Whole Foods Market in 2003 will be to continue to improve our operations. We do not expect to sustain the excellent 10% comps we saw this year. The Harry's stores will have a negative impact as they enter our comp base at the beginning of the year, and we will be up against very tough comparisons. However, we are hopeful that when the economy rebounds, we will maintain our high transaction count and see further increases in our average basket size. In order to keep increasing our market share, we will have to continue to learn and improve faster than our competitors.

Our second-biggest challenge will be to increase the number of stores we have in development. Our stated real estate goal has been to add 15 to 20 new and acquired stores to our store base each year. We have not always been successful at meeting this goal, and the main reason has been that we have not been adding enough stores to our development pipeline. We take a very disciplined approach to real estate and are unwilling to sacrifice our high standards merely to achieve an arbitrary growth target. Nevertheless, it is important to our shareholders that we grow both through strong sales at existing stores and through adding square footage. Therefore, we must increase the number of stores that we have in development, while simultaneously maintaining our real estate discipline. To achieve this goal we have bolstered our real estate team and are devoting more resources to new store development.

Our third challenge is to successfully integrate the Harry's stores into the company. It is important that in 2003 we reverse the sales decline at Harry's. The store remodels and the further integration of our strong corporate culture will upgrade the quality of the customer shopping experience, and we hope to see positive comps before our second year of ownership is complete. One of the most exciting things about Whole Foods Market is that as successful as we have been, there are still so many areas of opportunity in which to improve.

Note that Mr. Mackey highlights the great question I always want an answer to: What kind of speed bumps are in the way next year? And he gives me the answer: He doesn't expect to sustain the 10-percent "comps"; he's got problems integrating Harry's stores (a chain that Whole Foods acquired); he's hoping for an economy rebound to help out; and he's gotta build more stores without hurting standards to keep guys like me happy.

This is an excerpt from Warren Buffett's 2004 letter to shareholders. It's representative of the tone of his letters for the last 20 years:

Last year, Berkshire's book-value gain of 10.5% fell short of the index's 10.9% return. Our lackluster performance was not due to any stumbles by the CEOs of our operating businesses: As always, they pulled more than their share of the load. My message to them is simple: Run your business as if it were the only asset your family will own over the next hundred years. Almost invariably they do just that and, after taking care of the needs of their business, send excess cash to Omaha for me to deploy.

I didn't do that job very well last year. My hope was to make several multibillion-dollar acquisitions that would add new and significant streams of earnings to the many we already have. But I struck out. Additionally, I found very few attractive securities to buy. Berkshire therefore ended the year with $43 billion of cash equivalents, not a happy position. Charlie and I will work to translate some of this hoard into more interesting assets during 2005, though we can't promise success.

He spells out what went wrong last year, whose fault it was, and what he's hoping to do in the current year. My kind of jockey.

DRIVEN

The second quality of a great CEO is that he or she is driven to change the world in some small and cool way, although a big and cool way is okay, too. I call the thing a CEO wants to make happen his BAG — Big Audacious Goal, which is an acronym originally coined by Collins. (He called it a BHAG, short for Big *Hairy* Audacious Goal.) CEOs who have a BAG use it to fire themselves up so much that they can't wait to come to work every day, even if they, like Buffett, Gates, and Mackey, are already rich. The BAG also tells everyone in the organization the most important thing to focus on every day. It becomes the company's vision, or at least the CEO hopes it does, and if the BAG is a good one, it can drive the business for years. The BAG doesn't have to be as world-changing as John Mackey's desire to have "Whole Food, Whole People, Whole World." Mr. Buffett seems to be driven quite nicely just by his audacious attempt to keep Berkshire Hathaway's returns in the plus-20-percent range.

Darwin Smith's BAG at Kimberly-Clark is another great example of a fighting jockey riding an outrageously difficult horse who managed to win the race. And the payoff was huge. When he arrived on the scene at Kimberly-Clark as its leader in 1971, the Neenah, Wisconsin–based company was already nearly 100 years old. He wanted to turn his company into the best paper products business in the world (think toilet paper, tissues, diapers, paper towels — the practical materials we see and use every day in washrooms, workplaces, hotels, and our own homes . . . and yes, they're the makers of Kleenex). The only obstacle stopping him was the giant Procter & Gamble, which also made consumer products. It took Mr. Smith a while, but during his 20-year tenure as CEO, he inspired Kimberly-Clark to climb the mountain and he made the business owners millions.

When Steve Jobs started Apple Computer, his BAG was to fight the evil empire of IBM with inventions that people could use without a manual. His BAG challenge to Apple was to make the goods "cool" for the consumer. His vision of "cool" resulted in the Apple, the Lisa (computer), the Macintosh, the NeXT, the iPod, and, at Pixar, movies like *Toy Story, Finding Nemo,* and *The Incredibles.* The guy is worth more than a billion dollars and he still goes to work every day because he's driven by his BAG. As investors, we gotta love really smart rich guys out there who're killing themselves and making us rich in the process.

FIND THE BAG

So how do you know if the CEO has a BAG that's going to drive him or her? Put it like this: If they aren't in your face telling you what the BAG is, they probably don't have one. They probably just have mission statements. Lots of companies have mission statements that sound as if they have a big goal. But a BAG isn't about a mission statement. It's what's driving the CEO. If the CEO isn't driven, the company's mission statement can be hot air. (As you'll find out below, an effective way to detect hot air is to compare a company's numbers — its growth rates and ROIC — with what the CEO says in his letters to shareholders. At the end of this chapter I'll call your attention to some particularly egregious examples of hot-air-blowing.)

How do you know if a CEO is driven? You go online and Google the CEO's name. *Fast Company, Business Week, Forbes, Fortune,* and the *Wall Street Journal* have charged reporters with the task of digging up stories on CEOs. Learning who these corporate chieftains are and how they run a business is what these reporters are all about. And the beauty of this is that you can get all these stories with a mouse click. Think about that. You have — at your fingertips — an all-star reconnaissance team that's already put together all the information about this CEO you'll ever need to decide if he or she is the kind of person you want to invest with.

While many, if not most, articles tend to be "puff pieces," you can get a lot of clues from a well-researched article. When Jim Collins was doing his research for *Good to Great,* one of his research methodologies was to read the articles written on CEOs with an eye for terms like "humble" and "self-effacing." He found that great CEOs usually negated their own contributions and gave praise and credit to others. The difference between a CEO who is in it for himself and one who is in it for the BAG is often detectable even in a complimentary article.

Once you've read the articles, read his or her annual letters to shareholders on company websites. Again, you're looking for a CEO who's telling you what you need to know. They usually put their BAG in their letters, too. After you read the articles and letters, you have to decide whether it's all talk or whether they're walking the walk. If you'd be proud to own the business, you understand the business, and the Big Five numbers point to a great Moat, you're in a pretty good position to make an informed decision about whether the CEO is Level Five or not.

But I have two more little tricks that can help: (1) checking out insider trading activity and (2) considering the CEO's compensation.

Let an online search engine like Google do the heavy lifting and pull up articles on your jockey. Read to find out all you ever wanted to know about a company's CEO. You can also try the following websites:

- www.forbes.com
- www.businessweek.com
- www.fortune.com
- www.fastcompany.com
- www.wsj.com

INSIDER TRADING

Remember, if the CEO is Level Five, she should be treating this business as if it were the only asset her family will own over the next 100 years. So here's a question: If it's her only asset for 100 years, why would she sell off pieces of it unless she had to? When a CEO (or anyone in the company who has access to nonpublic information about the company) buys or sells stock in her own company, it is called "insider trading." You'll see it listed among the data available on financial websites. At MSN Money, for example, it's listed under "Research."

Insider trading is legal if the CEO notifies the Securities and Exchange Commission (SEC) that she's doing it within 48 hours of the sale. Insider trading is one of the great tip-offs that something good or bad is about to happen, the reason being that a CEO often knows months in advance what's going to happen, and if she's not in for the long run, she's liable to cut her losses and sell her stock. Or if something truly wonderful is about to happen to the company, she'll move in and buy up stock in preparation for reeling in great returns.

Warren Buffett is an extreme case when it comes to CEO insider trading. To my knowledge, in 40 years of investing, Mr. Buffett has never sold a single share of Berkshire Hathaway stock.

Other CEOs are not so attached. Just before Enron crashed from $60 to $0, the chairman, CEO, and CFO were all unloading their shares of Enron stock—even while they were telling their employees to buy more.

Mr. Buffett *does* sell his stock in other companies, and when he does, you'd better be heading for the hills, too.

The sale of stock by company officials isn't always a red flag. For example, Bill Gates sells Microsoft stock to fund various charities and other investments. So does John Mackey at Whole Foods. But if you look at the total amount of stock they own, you can see that the vast majority of their personal wealth is invested in the business, just as with Mr. Buffett.

There isn't a perfect way to gauge when some insider sales are *too many* insider sales. You have to use common sense. If most of a company's executives are unloading more than 30 percent of their stock all at once, that's probably not a good sign. As I've said, common sense. I once considered buying into a famous financial business until I noticed that the chairman of the board and the CEO were unloading more than 50 percent of their shares. I didn't buy, and later the company's stock price dropped like a brick. You'll read that there are lots of reasons why people sell their stock, but if everyone is doing it, get a clue. And you'll also read that there's only one reason execs buy stock: because it's going to go up. But that's not true, either. Lots of times, company officials will buy stock just to show their support. They'll even go so far as to try to shore up a stock drop, especially if the business is relatively small and a few strategic purchases would impact the price. But when insiders are mortgaging their children to buy stock at full retail, that's a serious clue that something good is about to happen.

A good "insider trading" website shows the shares being sold and the total shares owned, but not all sites share this information. MSN, for example, reveals how many shares an officer still owns ("Remaining Shares") if you click on "Insider Trading" while on a company's stock information page, and then click on any officer's name. You'll also see how much a certain recent sale of stock was worth. At Yahoo! Finance, click on "Insider Roster" while on the main stock page of a company, and you'll get the number of shares owned by the major shareholders. Then click on "Insider Transactions" to see who's selling or buying. Vickers (www.vickers-stock.com) does a better job all in one place, but it's a subscription site. Check around to other sites and see what you can find (some may offer free trial periods).

I'll talk more about insider trading in a later chapter, where I show you how to access this information alongside the other tools you'll find online. For now, just note that sudden buying or selling by the CEO might signal that he or she has decided the 100 years are over.

LOOKING AT THE CEO'S COMPENSATION

Another way to evaluate whether Management is on our side is to view the compensation paid to the CEO. Virtually every CEO who works for Mr. Buffett (an exemplar I keep going back to) is a multimillionaire. So why do they go to work and work hard? The same reason Mr. Buffett does, the same reason Bill Gates does — because they love doing what they do. It isn't about the money, although they certainly expect to be well paid for doing good work; it's about the challenge of making their business successful. Steve Jobs came back to Apple Computer in 1997 and accepted a salary of $1 per year, working without receiving either stock or options — just so he could put the baby he'd created (the one "politician-style CEOs" were destroying) back on track. Once he returned Apple to the spotlight, he started taking more compensation. Mr. Buffett works for $100,000 a year. Beyond that honorarium, his compensation is exactly the same as that which is received by his shareholders — i.e., whatever the appreciation is of Berkshire Hathaway in a given year. I love this kind of CEO because he's on my side.

> Where do we find the CEO's salary listed? In annual reports. So we go to the business's website, download its latest annual report, and go to the table of contents. Look for "Executive Compensation" (try "Part III"). We can also get to these annual reports on both Yahoo! Finance and MSN by clicking on "SEC Filings" and then selecting "10-K" (the annual report); if you subscribe to Edgar Online, it comes right up.

Unfortunately, there's another kind of CEO out there: one who wouldn't get up to go to work in the morning if he didn't have his outrageous perks and a cozy deal with the board of directors to get paid an enormous amount of money. These CEOs aren't running businesses with clearly defined BAGs in mind (because they don't have any). They aren't running businesses because they love it. They aren't corporate patriots like Buffett, Jobs, and Gates — leaders who love their businesses. They're mercenaries. Fast guns for hire. And just like actual mercenaries, their loyalty to the cause goes about as deep as the depth of their paychecks. If the business is in real trouble, their chief concern will be escaping with a pile of gold. Recent corporate debacles such as those involving Tyco, Enron, and WorldCom have in common massive overcompensation deals for the companies' top executives.

Because I see myself as the sole owner of any business I own a piece of, I view the money these CEOs take as coming straight out of my pocket—and I don't like it. To a Rule #1 investor, these CEOs—and the boards of directors that support them—are out-of-control mercenaries who deserve nothing but contempt and termination. Throwing the bums out is, of course, not so easy. Many of these scoundrels have put in place a "poison pill"—a contract between the board of directors and the company's top executives that guarantees an insane payoff if the owners (i.e., shareholders) ever sell against their wishes. These selfish deals make it incredibly difficult for the owners to do anything other than stand by and be taken advantage of. The following are all actual cases (names withheld) of rape performed by mercenary CEOs and unethical boards within the last few years:

From 2000 to 2004, one CEO's compensation was $40 million while the owners were wiped out. Another group of owners lost 80 percent of their equity and still were forced by the board to pay the CEO more than $20 million for hitting one quarter's target. The value of another business dropped 40 percent, but the board paid out more than $70 million to the CEO for the fine job he did. Another huge business lost 70 percent of its value and a large piece of its market to overseas competition over the last five years and still paid its CEO more than $40 million. It would be one thing if the business were stuck in a contract and *had* to pay this out, even after firing the guy. But these people were paid these insane amounts as *bonuses* for good work well done! How crazy is that?

The primary fault does not lie with the CEO. He is who he is. The main problem is with the boards of directors, who are paid, principally, to put the right guy in the top position and compensate him or her in a way that encourages the CEO to act in the best interests of the owners. Boards have had a hard time doing that lately. Many have long ago forgotten who the owners are. Perhaps that's why they call us "shareholders" as opposed to owners, to keep from reminding us that we actually own the business.

We're not going to buy any business if we don't like the Management enough. Simple as that. And one of the main reasons to dislike Management is if they're getting overpaid. One key way Management gets overpaid, for example, is with stock options. Stock options don't cost the manager anything. They're an award from the business, giving the manager the right to buy company stock at a set price at some time in the future. The idea in awarding stock options is to incentivize the manager to drive up the stock price to make the options worth something.

Let's take an example: Say I want to hire Mr. Slick to be my CEO, and the stock price is at $30 a share. I give Slick an option to buy 1 million shares of the business at $30. If he can get the stock to go up to $40, he'll make $10 million. He has no downside risk since he didn't pay anything for the options. (Those options will, of course, also come with a nice fat paycheck, since he can't be certain he can make the stock go up, other things in the world being influential.) Nice deal. Especially since Slick knows that 4 percent inflation might move the stock up to $40 in seven years if he does nothing but maintain the status quo. Sweet. Except for the owners, us. We get screwed. A million-share piece of our pie went to this guy for nothing. Our "return" means nothing if it only keeps pace with inflation.

The worst part of the options craziness taking place in unscrupulous companies is that, until recently, this expense to the owners wasn't even called an expense. The CEOs got the options, and the business didn't have to take a hit to the bottom line. Only the owners took the hit, in the form of a loss of a piece of what they owned. But if that isn't a loss, what is? As of this writing, Congress is looking at passing a law that forces businesses to expense option grants so the money isn't just slipped out of the back pocket of the owners without the business reporting it as an expense. The reason many businesses don't want to report this dilution as an expense is that it'll make their short-term earnings look bad compared with the year before, when they didn't have to take that expense. They complain to their congressman, who owes them for donating money to his campaign . . . the CEOs wave

ADVANCED RULE #1 ANALYSIS

A business's annual report is required to disclose options deals to owners. Look in the index to the financial statements under the heading "Notes to the Consolidated Financial Statements." Simply scroll down to near the end of the notes and you'll find a section called "Stock Options." That's where you can read about how a business structures its options. This level of evaluating a business is more for *advanced* Rule #1 investors, however. As a beginner, don't feel as if you need to understand options and how they *should* be structured within a company. At a basic level, check to see if the business structures a logical and appropriate "strike price" (the fixed price at which a company official who owns options can buy the stock during a set period). It should reflect success for owners. And, second, see if the company enforces a ban on the CEO quickly disposing of any shares purchased through options, thereby helping to ensure that the CEO sees the world as a long-term owner. Your goal in conducting this type of analysis is to filter out any business being run by a bunch of mercenaries who're in it for the quick buck.

checks . . . and, son-of-a-gun, the law gets hung up. Here's what Mr. Buffett has to say about that:

"The accomplices in perpetuating this absurdity have been many members of Congress who have defied the arguments put forth by all Big Four auditors, all members of the Financial Accounting Standards Board and virtually all investment professionals."

A standard for expensing options is supposed to have been adopted by all companies by 2006. This new standard may eliminate one of the biggest scams perpetrated by boards and CEOs against unsuspecting (and unwatchful) owners.

So what does a Rule #1 investor make of all this when looking for a wonderful business that's, by definition, run by a wonderful CEO?

Read the annual reports. Ask yourself: Is the CEO being compensated as an owner or as a mercenary? If he's being compensated with a reasonable salary and perks (and you can figure out "reasonable" as well as I can) and has a stock or option position in the business that lets *him* make a reasonable amount of money when *we* do, then fine. If it's otherwise, why own something that can bite you when you aren't looking?

By the way, to see how things *should* work, check out the way Whole Foods is set up for executive pay all the way down to its cashiers, and you'll see what's possible if the guys on top aren't in it solely for the money.

APPEARANCE VS. REALITY

As I've already mentioned, a great way to spot a shady management team and/or CEO is to find a gaping disconnect between the hard-core numbers — specifically the Big Five — and what the CEO is peddling about the state and fate of the company. You can trust numbers more than what issues from the mouth of an overpaid company executive.

DANGER ZONE!

The red flags exist if you search for them. And it's not too difficult to distinguish between integrity and fluff. If you know that a company had a bad year, evidenced in its numbers and how much stakeholders lost, check out what the CEO had to say about it in his annual letter to shareholders. If he doesn't admit to mistakes and not only highlights the challenges ahead but explains what he intends to do about them, you're staring at a questionable jockey who doesn't know how to ride the horse. Don't get on that horse with him.

In doing my homework for this book and searching for illuminating examples of poorly managed companies, I came across an article by

Michael Brush titled "The Five Most Outrageously Overpaid CEOs" (posted August 24, 2005, at www.moneycental.msn.com), which covered five CEOs who took huge paydays while the business owners suffered. Curious, I checked to see what these CEOs wrote in their letters to shareholders while they were losing money hand over fist. Were there any signs? Did their letters reflect what was going on?

I couldn't possibly give you better examples of what to watch out for when you're evaluating CEOs. If your CEO writes like these guys, you'd best know the business and watch it like a hawk because these guys are experts at hiding the truth from the owners. (I do, however, have a better feeling about one of these guys than the article suggests, as you'll see.) I'll summarize here what I learned, but I encourage you to check out these letters yourself so you know what I'm talking about. All you have to do is log on to each company's website and access its annual reports (they all post annual reports, usually under "Investor Relations").

Ciena (CIEN): Ciena, a company that specializes in fiberoptic communication networks, is run by Gary Smith, who took more than $41 million in pay while his shareholders lost more than two-thirds of their book value per share and more than 90 percent of their stock value from 2001 to 2004. Look up Ciena's annual reports online and read Mr. Smith's letters. Remember that the ideal CEO writes Buffett-style — taking blame for the failures of the business, and telling the owners what they need to know to evaluate his performance and the future of the business. At the end of 2002, a year during which Ciena lost $1.5 billion, Mr. Smith's letter didn't get around to mentioning the apocalyptic loss. If you were an owner of Ciena, wouldn't you expect your manager at least to note that you lost a few bucks and tell you what went wrong? Instead, Mr. Smith tells the owners how well he set the business up for success to come in the following year. In the next year, 2003, sales went down, Ciena lost another $386 million, and another 20 percent of owners' equity disappeared, which means either Mr. Smith was not able to judge how his business was doing at the end of 2002 or he didn't want to tell the owners the truth. Since his CEO letter wasn't written until well into the 2003 fiscal year, you can make your own judgment.

Read these letters. This is the kind of "it's all good from here on out" language to watch out for. If the business is having trouble, the CEO had better spell out what happened, take responsibility, and tell you how he's going to fix it — just like anyone who works for you who screws up the job. No big secret here, is there? If we're looking for honest CEOs who know they're working for us, we'd better see something of that in their letters to us over the years. If we don't see it, we don't invest, because guys who won't tell you the truth can easily be running the next Enron and WorldCom disasters — either because they're liars or because they're clueless. Either way, we're outta there.

Sanmina-SCI (SANM): This company provides electronics manufacturing services. Its CEO, Jure Sola, likes to use phrases like "met the ongoing challenge," "unyielding in its commitment," "continued to optimize," "made significant progress," "our customer-focused strategy," and "we are excited about the future." This type of letter gives me the creeps. Sanmina-SCI is growing shareholder value at about 2 percent a year — about as good as your savings account. Return on capital (ROIC) is −12 percent for five years. They haven't made any money since 2001.

Wouldn't you think he'd mention that things haven't been going so well? It's not as if the owners didn't notice the market price of the stock dropped from $60 to $5 since 2001. Sheesh. Seems like the owners might expect some kind of explanation other than it's been "the worst technology downturn in history." Uh, Jure, the last two years have been pretty good for other tech companies. Maybe you should start taking some responsibility instead of blaming the market. But instead, you took home a nice $19-million bonus. Why you accepted that compensation should be in the letter, too.

Sun Microsystems (SUNW): Sun is run by its founder, Scott McNealy. To his credit, his letters reflect more of the owner point of view than that of a politician running a business. Sun's price-per-share drop from $65 to $4 and its loss of about one-third of the equity since 2001 was a shock to the owners. Of course, McNealy is a very big owner himself so he was pretty shocked, too, no doubt. Here's what I like: McNealy admits in one of his letters that he didn't do what he hoped to do and Sun lost money. He goes on to tell the owners about a big negative issue — the perception in the market that Sun systems are too costly. Then he explains what he's doing to fix that. And he emphasizes he won't tolerate unethical business behavior. While anyone can write that, I get the feeling that Scott means it. All in all, this is a much better letter to the owners than we usually see in struggling businesses. Read Scott's 2002–2004 letters to get an idea of how a good, honest, owner-oriented CEO writes when things are going bad.

Albertsons (ABS): Albertsons, a supermarket chain, is managed by Larry Johnston. Earnings per share haven't grown at all — zero, in ten years. Equity growth has been flat for five years. This company feels like it's treading water about 15 miles from shore with no life preserver. It might be getting ready to just sink quietly under. That bleak assessment comes just from looking at the numbers. However, reading Mr. Johnston's letters to the owners — letters that are supposed to let the owners know how it's going with their money — you get the distinct impression that Mr. Johnston, far from treading water, is sitting in the cockpit of a 50-foot racing boat, ready to take on the world. He uses phrases like "in the midst of an exciting transformation!" "passion to win," and "new energy."

If 2002 was "one of the most demanding years in business history" when "some companies stumbled, most struggled and more than a few failed," Mr. Johnston was proud to lead a "solid business performance" and "one of the largest restructurings in retailing history." One of the tricks of the CEO letter-writing trade that I see repeatedly is listing facts that "prove" what a great job the CEO did last year. Hey, guys, the facts are right there on the ROIC, sales, EPS, equity, and cash lines in black and white. We're not stupid anymore, so in the future don't bother telling us about how "the average shopping basket size improved" or how "customer service scores improved steadily" or how, in Phoenix, "total market share accelerated between 10 percent and 130 percent." If you had a bad year and you think you're going to have another one, just tell us straight up. We own the business you run, okay? Start treating us with a little respect. Oh, and while you're at it, Larry, would you mind putting in the next letter how your leadership was worth $76 million while the business lost 40 percent of its value?

Bristol-Myers Squibb (BMY): Peter Dolan manages this big pharmaceutical company. Since he took over in 2001, the market price for BMY has dropped by 50 percent, and yet he took home $41 million. He earned that, in part, by doing a $2-billion deal with ImClone for a drug that the FDA turned down just a couple of months later. Ooops. There goes two bil. Guess that's worth a bonus. Oh, and then in the fall of 2004 he decided he'd better have the company change its previously reported financials to reflect reality a little better. Always love to see a business I own restate its numbers, don't you?

Under Dolan's leadership, sales have gone nowhere for four years. EPS has been flat for four years. Debt has grown by over 600 percent in the last four years. Equity growth, the best indicator of growth in long-term value, has averaged 3 percent per year for the last four years. And here we go again with the CEO's hype phrases: "In addition to delivering solid financial performance," "we met other key objectives," and then he goes on to hype the new products. That's it. That's all the owners get. No apology about taking $41 million of their money for doing . . . what?

The conclusion: With the exception of Scott McNealy, these CEOs have failed miserably in their fiduciary responsibility to the owners of the business to tell them the truth about what's going on — and that, for a Rule #1 investor, is enough to keep us from getting involved. The guy or gal who runs things is critical. You don't get a great company without a great CEO. Don't fall for CEO jargon and hype phrases. The numbers don't lie and if a CEO isn't explaining what happened candidly in his letter to the owners, how can you trust him? And if you can't trust him, you can't buy that business.

FIRST, BE SURE YOU'RE RIGHT

Now that we've learned how to spot a wonderful company from a financial and Management standpoint, we're at the point where we must decide if it's really a business we want to own. I've already mentioned in previous chapters how you must consider your core values when you decide to buy a business. It's an important part of Rule #1 investing, and it'll ultimately help you narrow down your choices when it comes to buying a few choice businesses. It's up to you to make sure the company is trying to do what you want it to do. If you wouldn't change its focus, fine. But if you *would,* then strictly from your perspective the company isn't owner-oriented, and you shouldn't invest in it.

When I was a little kid, Davy Crockett was my hero. (For the young folks unfamiliar with this show, *Davy Crockett* was a hit television show that ran in the mid-1950s. I was glued to our black-and-white TV set.) In every single episode, Davy would remind us that his motto was "First be sure you're right and then go ahead." Well, as a Rule #1 investor, I can appreciate the Davy Crockett motto. If I'm not sure, I don't do nothin'. Just sit in cash until I can find one I'm sure about. If, on the other hand, I think this business is truly wonderful, then I'll go ahead to the final M: *Margin of Safety.*

Chapter 8

Demand a Margin of Safety

A cynic is someone who knows the price of everything and the value of nothing.

—OSCAR WILDE (1854–1900)

W E'RE ALREADY up to the fourth M: *Margin of Safety* (MOS). It's what defines our "attractive price," and as you'll see in this chapter, it begins by first getting a correct Sticker Price on a given business. We'll be calculating Sticker Prices in the next chapter. Here, I want you to focus solely on the concept of a Margin of Safety, which is critical to Rule #1 and all too often forgotten.

THE CRAZINESS OF EMT . . . AND THE MARKETS

Earlier in this book I mentioned Professor Burton Malkiel. His work at Princeton University was seminal in the Efficient Market Theory, or EMT, which states that stocks are priced according to value. In 1972 he proved to the satisfaction of the Ivy League intellectual community that even Warren Buffett could not get higher returns on his investing than a monkey randomly picking stocks. Probably this came as a significant surprise to Mr. Buffett. Prior to the release of Malkiel's book, Mr. Buffett had been under the impression his rate of return for the previous 16 years of 29 percent per year was due to the superior investing strategy taught by his mentor, Benjamin Graham, and based on the idea that the stock market occasionally misprices stocks. In fact, Professor Malkiel argues that Mr. Buffett's success was simply a statistical aberration, akin to a long streak of coin tosses coming up heads — unusual but certainly to be expected in any large statistical sample of a random system.

As I pointed out in the first chapter, Malkiel's book on Efficient Market Theory, *A Random Walk Down Wall Street,* is still sold today. In fact, it's in its eighth edition and unrepentant in its support of EMT. But take a look at what Professor Malkiel said during an interview with Geoff Colvin, a co-anchor for *Wall Street Week with FORTUNE,* a financial news analysis television program. The interview was broadcast on June 20, 2003:

BURTON MALKIEL: I'm the guy who said that a blindfolded chimpanzee throwing darts at the stock pages could select stocks as well as the experts.

COLVIN: Why is it so? Why is it that nobody can reliably, consistently beat the market?

MALKIEL: I think there are a couple of reasons. One, our markets are really for the most part extraordinarily efficient. When information arises about a particular company or about the economy, people pounce on that information right away, so that by the time you and I hear the news, it's already reflected in the price. . . .

COLVIN: Now, a lot of people have said that the great bubble of the late nineties, when stocks went sky-high for no identifiable reason and then in early 2000 plunged for no identifiable reason, shows that the efficient markets idea is bunk.

MALKIEL: In the long term, I think that they are generally efficient. Though I'll admit *they do go crazy from time to time.*

For the entire interview go to http://www.pbs.org/wsw/tvprogram/malkiel_interview.html.

So this is what the professor of Efficient Market Theory says: "In the long term, I think that they are generally efficient. Though I'll admit they do go crazy from time to time." And here is what Ben

Graham said about 50 years earlier: "In the short run the stock market is a voting machine but in the long run it's a weighing machine." This is Warren Buffett: "The basic ideas of investing are to look at stocks as businesses, use market fluctuations to your advantage and seek a Margin of Safety. That's what Ben Graham taught us. A hundred years from now they will still be the cornerstones of investing." In other words, after only 30 years of being dead wrong and while still not admitting it like a man, Professor Malkiel is now spouting the exact philosophy of investing that Mr. Buffett and Mr. Graham have been using successfully for 80 years. The only difference is that Mr. Malkiel continues to maintain that no one can successfully use the fact that "they do go crazy from time to time" to make money. Mr. Buffett, Mr. Graham, and thousands of other successful investors do use these "crazy" times when the market is mispricing stocks as an opportunity to make a lot of money. And so will we.

The analogy: One afternoon at a prestigious university, an economics professor who believes stocks are always priced correctly is walking down a path with a graduate student, when they both see a $100 bill on the ground. The student starts to bend to pick it up, and the professor says, "No, don't bother. If it were really a $100 bill, it wouldn't be there."

THE STICKER PRICE

The practical application of Rule #1 investing is this: Buy $1 of value for 50 cents. This is possible because sometimes the value of a business we want to buy is not equal to the price it's selling for. It is critical to our job of buying businesses that we understand this. *Price* is what the market is getting for the business today. *Value* is what it's worth. Recall what I said in Chapter 2: Sometimes the price of a thing is not always equal to its value. When you're in the market to buy a new car, for example, you should know what your potential new car is worth before you step into a dealership and ask about its price.

Because Rule #1 investing is essentially just a shopping trip for something on sale, critical to Rule #1 investors is understanding that we *must* know what an item — or business — is worth. Let's take the car-buying example further. While on Park Avenue in New York City, I saw a brand-new Maserati Quattroporte in the dealer's window. That's a beautiful car. Seriously. So I went in and asked one of the sales reps what the sticker price was on the car. She told me $101,000 to $115,000, depending on the options.

By then I was sitting in the driver's seat, playing with the buttons on the dash. I asked her, "How much for this one?" She told me it was a six-month wait, that they were fetching somewhere between $120,000 and $145,000. I excused myself and escaped.

Still curious, I went to eBay and found one on sale for (only) $145,000. The New York dealer I'd spoken to hadn't been kidding! The sticker price was $106,000. That first dealer and another on eBay wanted $145,000. Why? Because there was a big demand. Hey, welcome to America. Some buyers are willing to pay that price because they have more money than they know what to do with. The money is there. They want the car. They pay the $145,000 even if the price is above the sticker by 40 percent.

I don't pay sticker price for anything, so I'm not buying that car. I might even be in love with that Maserati, but I've got to take care of my money so my money will take care of me. That means not blowing it just because I can't wait a while. You and I both know that the over-sticker price isn't going to last long. Soon enough, that Maserati will be available to me at sticker and then, at some point, below sticker.

We're going to buy businesses in a similar fashion. First we're going to find a few businesses we love and that meet our criteria thus far, then we're going to be very patient and wait until we get the chance to buy them below Sticker Price. Contrast that with the way your average mutual fund manager operates. He pays Sticker or above Sticker most of the time. He does it because it's not his money. He also does it because a part of him actually believed his professors in B-school who taught him EMT, which says that everything always sells for Sticker Price. And he does it because it's his job to buy something with your money in some reasonable amount of time after you give it to him.

If he doesn't buy anything for two or three years because he's waiting patiently for one of those moments when the markets go crazy and he can buy some great big companies at wonderful prices with those billions you all have given him, then you — the mutual fund investor — aren't going to be very happy. He's taken your money under his management for two years, and given you a zero rate of return. This is unlikely to happen, because your fund manager knows he's evaluated on his performance during the last year or so — not the past decade — so he's not about to take your money and leave it outside the market for two or three years. He's going to buy something with it right away, which is particularly easy for him if he took Professor Malkiel's course at Princeton, where he learned that the market always prices everything according to its value. To your fund manager, the secret to successful investing is knowing something about a company before anyone else, and if that isn't possible, being comfortable that whatever price he's paying isn't out of line with the value he's getting, even if it seems absurd. Oh, and it did seem absurd from time to time in the late 1990s. A lot of fund managers were buying stocks as absurdly priced as that Maserati.

Here's a great example: At the end of 1999, Yahoo! was at a split-adjusted price of $118. That price could be the Sticker Price of Yahoo! only if the growth rate of the company exceeded 70 percent a year for the next 15 years. That kind of growth would have been amazing, but if Yahoo! did grow that fast, it would, in 15 years, have been worth 1.5 trillion dollars — significantly larger than Exxon will be at that time, and Exxon is the biggest company in the world. If you accepted that scenario, then you were counting on Yahoo!'s receiving in the year 2014 significantly more advertising revenue than Exxon gets from selling oil. If that couldn't happen (hint, hint), then the price your fund manager was paying for Yahoo! was absurdly high — so high that it would take more than 20 years just to get your money back under almost any other scenario. (At its highest trade, Yahoo! went for $118.75 per share at the beginning of 2000; by late August of 2002, that same stock was selling for a mere $4.50. At *that* price, Yahoo! was a steal if you understood the company — and I didn't — and since then it's up about 900 percent.)

Yahoo! was not alone in the insanity.

If your fund manager bought Coke in 1998 at $85 per share and if Coke kept growing at the rate it'd been growing for years, it would take you until after the year 2025 just to break even. More than 25 years of zero return.

What were the institutional fund managers thinking? They were thinking that although the prices of these companies were completely insane (or, as Alan Greenspan put it, "irrationally exuberant"), they were *forced* to buy them by . . . YOU! By 1998, investors were rapidly moving their money out of conservative mutual funds and into the funds that were producing 20 to 30 percent rates of return.

Fund managers, in addition to being smart people, have a honed survival instinct. They get a significant portion of their income by attracting more investors. If you and your investor brethren take your money away, their income goes down. In addition, if their fund rate of return stays significantly below other funds, they get fired. So what were they thinking? They were thinking it's better to continue working and receive that nice fat $1-million-per-year income for one or two more years, even at the risk of losing all your money, than to get fired today because you took your money and went to some other fund manager who would be more aggressive with it.

That's what they were thinking then. And that's what they are still thinking *now.* Today, right now, your fund manager is trying to find a stock that will go up a lot within the next few weeks so his overall rate of return will look great compared to his peers and the S&P 500. Do you really think he's looking farther down the line than that? Wake up and smell the coffee, guys.

Here's my point: We're going to have to admit that sometimes the market prices stocks, as Malkiel puts it, "crazy." Sometimes this crazy refers to very high prices, and sometimes this crazy refers to very low prices. Guess which kind of crazy *we're* interested in? Actually, as business buyers, we're interested in both kinds of crazy. We're going to use these regular market fluctuations as opportunities to both buy and sell. We load up the truck when prices drop significantly below Sticker Price, and we sell the truckload when prices go above the Sticker Price.

The single most important determinant of the money we get in the future is the price we pay today. Is the price *at* the Sticker, *above* the

Sticker, or *below* the Sticker? We can figure out what the Sticker Price is, but we can't control the price being charged for the business. That's up to our partner, Mr. Market.

MEET MR. MARKET

The idea that the market is our partner came from Ben Graham. And like many of Graham's insights about investing, this concept is immediately obvious and profound (at least it should be). Mr. Market is an incredibly agreeable partner. At any time he's willing to make a deal happen. If we want to buy a business, he'll sell it to us. If we want to sell a business, he'll buy it from us. Awesome! The catch: Mr. Market gets to name the price.

This catch would give us no particular advantage in making great investments if it weren't for the fact that Mr. Market is bipolar. Our partner goes through gigantic mood swings from the highest euphoria to the lowest depression. Most of the time Mr. Market is taking his meds, and on most days he's pretty lucid and rational about the prices he sells and buys at. That means most of the time the price of a business is pretty close to its value. But sometimes he can get so insanely optimistic that he prices everything insanely high. On other days Mr. Market can get so depressed that, unlike Annie, he's convinced the sun will *not* come up tomorrow. On those days he feels there's never going to be a good day again for any of these businesses. And he prices them so low that it's as if he's giving them no value at all. Crazy or not, his mood that day sets the prices.

Obviously, even if it's not very fair to take advantage of this massive emotional handicap, we prefer to *buy* from Mr. Market when he's severely depressed and we want to *sell* to Mr. Market when he's irrationally exuberant. It's kind of a shame to take advantage of someone who's emotionally unbalanced, but then again, he doesn't seem to mind. He's been bipolar for so long that he just thinks it's normal. He honestly doesn't think he's mispricing anything, even if one day the price is $100 per share and just a few months later it's $10 per share. And if you ask the professors who study Mr. Market, they'll tell you the guy is fine — they'll tell you that his behavior is completely rational and give you all kinds of reasons why the price of that company was rationally $100 and then rationally $10! I guess when the keepers of the loony bin are loony, everybody is "normal."

Let's go back to the Maserati. If our Maserati dealer was also a manic-depressive, he might price the car one month at $145,000 and a year later at $50,000. If we pay $145,000 and then sell the car a few weeks later, we're going to lose money. But if we could get that same car for $50,000, even if we aren't professional car dealers, we're sure to make money even if we have to sell it tomorrow. See what a huge difference price makes?

A *big* part of the secret of getting rich buying businesses is knowing what they're worth. And, equally important, what they're *not* worth.

By knowing that (1) price is not value; and (2) Mr. Market is going to price stocks crazy from time to time, we know that if we can properly value every business we are interested in buying, all we have to do is be patient and wait for Mr. Market to bring it to us at the right price — the price where making money is certain.

Some investors think that great companies don't go on sale, and they're usually right. But usually right isn't the same as *always* right. Here are a few recent examples of mistakes Mr. Market made in pricing great businesses (don't worry about how I arrived at these Sticker Prices, since I'll soon be showing you, step-by-step, how to calculate these easily on any company):

2000 Apollo (APOL): The Big Five were consistent and looking great. Sales growing at 35%; EPS growing at 35%; equity growing at 36%; cash growing at 30%; ROIC 18%. Historical growth 35%. Analysts estimating 25%. Assuming the analysts were correct, Sticker conservatively at $40. Mr. Market couldn't believe his own analysts, I guess. Mr. Market's price: $10. By May 2005 Mr. Market's price: $79. Five-year compounded return is 52% per year.

2003 Walgreens (WAG): Sales growing at 15%; EPS growing at 17%; equity growing at 15%; cash growing at 50% . . . all consistent. ROIC: 15%. Assuming the analysts were correct about its future growth, a

Sticker of $44. Available from Mr. Market at $27. Why? Scared away from retail by recession. May 2005 price: $45, or 29% compounded for two years.

2000 Bed Bath & Beyond (BBBY): Sales, EPS, equity, and cash flow all growing at 25%. ROIC at 19%. Sticker $40. Mr. Market dumping it for $12. Why? Market meltdown started and took BBBY with it. May 2005 price: $40. Compounded ROI for 5 years: 27%.

2000 Starbucks (SBUX): Sales, EPS, equity, and cash flow growing at 24%. ROIC at 10%. Assuming the analysts were correct about its future growth, Sticker $60. Mr. Market selling it for $14. May 2005 price: $56, or 32% compounded ROI for 5 years.

2001 Dell (DELL): Sales, EPS, equity, and cash flow growing at 35%. ROIC 40%. Assuming the analysts were correct about its future growth, Sticker $70. Mr. Market panics out of tech stocks. All of them. Selling Dell for $20. Go figure. May 2005 price: $40, or four years compounded at 19%.

2000 Toll Brothers (TOL, a home-building company): Sales, EPS, equity, and cash flow growing at 18%. ROIC at 12%. Assuming the analysts were correct about its future growth, Sticker $25. Mr. Market was selling real estate cheap: $9. May 2005 price: $90. Compounded 5 year ROI: 58% per year.

Collectively the average return in 2005 on these was 30 percent per year. If you invested $10,000 into this basket of stocks in the year 2000, your basket was worth $37,000 in 2005. Meanwhile the S&P averaged minus 2 percent and the same $10,000 invested in a broad market fund was worth $9,000. In 15 years it's possible that the $37,000 will be worth $2 million at this rate, while the $10,000 invested in the mutual fund is going to be worth $10,000.

MARGIN OF SAFETY

The secret to making a fantastic rate of return on our business buying is to be sure we're getting a dollar of value for only 50 cents. First we determine the value — the Sticker Price. Then we determine the Margin-of-Safety price — the MOS, which is half of Sticker. If we've done a good job of determining the Sticker, we're going to make a lot of money. If we've done a bad job, we have an MOS and we're going to get outta there without violating Rule #1. Cool!

Because we're not geniuses and we're not perfect, it's incredibly important to get an MOS on every business we buy, no matter what kind of business it is. If I don't get an MOS Price, I don't buy. C'mon! If a genius like Buffett insists on an MOS, don't you think we should, too? These three critical words — Margin of Safety — are going to make you millions of dollars when you do it right. And they'll keep you from losing money when things don't go as planned.

> Getting a Margin-of-Safety Price on any business is just one step in the process of making successful Rule #1 investment decisions. Remember: You have to do an entire analysis through the Four Ms before taking the leap and buying any business. You'll violate Rule #1 if you simply seek MOS Prices on businesses that have no Meaning to you, that don't have a Moat with great Big Five numbers, or that don't have strong Management.

Let's return to the year 2000 and check out a few stocks. If the Sticker Price for Harley was $50 in 2000, the MOS Price was $25. If you got that price, you should have loaded up the truck with Harley! If the Sticker Price for General Motors was $33, the MOS Price for GM was $17. That's a long way away from the $77 it was selling for in 2000, but a lot closer to the $26 that it was at in 2005. In 2000, Dell's Sticker was $40, its MOS Price was $20, and it was selling for $40, so we weren't buying. Not that the price wasn't fair. It was actually priced pretty close to its value, right? In a situation like that, a stock stays on our watch list because the price isn't cheap enough for us yet. We want certainty. The only way we're going to get it is to buy $1 for 50 cents. A year later it was selling for $20. Perseverance pays off. Apollo had a Sticker Price of $40 with an MOS Price of $20. Since Mr. Market was asking for $10, we got a pretty spectacular deal.

> To experienced investors who are wondering if this is "value investing," my answer is no, this is Rule #1 investing. Here's why Rule #1 investing is different from value investing: Value investing is all about buying businesses no one wants. Mr. Buffett calls such a business a "cigar butt" business—the idea being there might be one more puff in it. We're not looking for a "cigar butt" business. We're looking for a "Maserati" business that has gone on sale. As I've said, we find a wonderful business, know what it's worth, and then just wait for Mr. Market to get emotional and hand it to us at an attractive price. It's called Rule #1 investing. Get used to it!

MOS will not only make you money, it will keep you from losing it in a bubble. In 2000, JDS Uniphase, Oracle, Microsoft, Apple, Intel, and virtually every other NASDAQ stock that crashed were priced way over their Sticker Prices. Coke, Disney, and Gillette were also priced way over Sticker. Telecom stocks? Priced way over Sticker. Knowing the Sticker and MOS Price keeps you from buying businesses that are too expensive — and that, my friends, will save you a lot of grief.

By now you're probably clamoring to know how to determine the value — the Sticker Price — of a business. We'll get to that, and then you'll be able to find your MOS Price.

APPLYING MOS TO OTHER INVESTMENTS

You can take the principle of MOS and apply it to all kinds of investing. If you are a Rule #1 real estate investor, you aren't buying real estate in adherence to the "greater fool" theory of real estate speculation (where you hope a greater fool will come along in a year or two who'll pay more than you paid!). You're buying real estate as a business, and you're doing it with a big MOS. Just because I ranted about real estate investments in the first chapter (as compared with buying businesses) doesn't mean you can't invest in real estate. Most of us, at some point, buy property. And you can apply Rule #1 elements to that endeavor to maximize your return. In fact, seeing how you can get an MOS Price in the real estate world can crystallize the concept.

For example, I once bought 55 acres of raw land from a farmer in Iowa. The land was on the edge of a small, growing town, but it wasn't included in the town limits and it didn't have a sewer hookup. I got the land for $5,000 per acre — about two times the going price of farmland, but one-fifth the value of similar land across the street that was subdivided and hooked up to the city sewer and water. I brought in the water and sewer from a mile away (because they wouldn't let me just hook up across the street!), put in a road, subdivided the 55 acres into one- to three-acre parcels, and then, with major help from friends in the real estate business, sold off the whole thing in small pieces at an average price of $25,000 per acre.

The difference between my cost, including development cost, and the post-development retail price per acre represented my Margin of Safety. It translated to an MOS of about $12,000 per acre. I could drop my lot price in half if I had to, and still come out even. So why don't we do that same thing when we consider buying a business?

The real estate entrepreneur who drives into a good neighborhood and spots a rundown home requiring a lot of elbow grease to fix up (but not much real skill or money) — we're talking tasks such as roof-fixing, fence-painting, lawn-cutting, and weed-pulling — is creating a wonderful Margin of Safety with his sweat. Because once he's finished, the redone house has a new value and the difference between the price he paid for the rundown house and the new value is his MOS. If housing starts to go flat in his area, he can lower his price, sell the house, and still make a profit. Those who bought hoping for a bigger fool will be losing their money.

GETTING OUT

If we've done our work well, we'll buy a wonderful business at an attractive price. Following our purchase of the business, it usually doesn't take that long for Mr. Market to see his mistake and re-price the business upward toward the Sticker Price. And as we'll see a bit later on, when it gets to the Sticker Price, it's a signal to get out (sell the business).

Before we get into the details of getting out, though, let's get more into the details of getting in. So far, we have a wonderful business and we're learning how to know what an attractive price is. Let's do some calculating in the next chapter to determine values, Sticker Prices, and Margin-of-Safety Prices.

Chapter 9

Calculate the Sticker Price

In mathematics you don't understand things. You just get used to them.
—Johann von Neumann (1903–1957)

T HE STICKER PRICE has a lot of other names in the financial community, including "intrinsic value," "fair value," and simply "retail price." The label we give it doesn't matter. Call it whatever you want; I'm calling it the Sticker Price. Remember what Sticker refers to: the price of a business that's fair—that's neither overpriced nor underpriced. It's what the market *should* be selling it for (but often doesn't).

Labels aside, what's most important about the Sticker Price is that we get it right. The essence of Rule #1 investing is buying stocks as if they were businesses, and businesses are not pieces of paper. They also aren't like tangible goods (remember the car example?). Businesses have employees, buildings, and machinery that all come together to sell a product and make money. The Sticker Price of a business is more than the value of its parts. The major part of a business's value is the money it's going to make *in the future* for its owners. No one knows exactly what that amount will be; therefore, no one knows *exactly* what the Sticker Price should be. However, figuring out the Sticker Price is something Ben Graham made his specialty. He taught the technique to Warren Buffett, who then modified it some and taught it to other investors — either personally or through his letters and speeches. And my teacher, the Wolf, taught the process to me. I've modified it a bit to fit today's ordinary, individual investor, and now I call it Rule #1 investing.

Part of your learning curve in becoming an expert Rule #1 investor will be becoming proficient at figuring out Sticker Prices. The math is basic and becomes quite repetitive and automatic once you've done it a few times. Your first encounter with running the numbers may feel a bit overwhelming, but take it slow and steady. Reread sections. Keep in mind that I'm giving you the 1-2-3s to arriving at Sticker Prices *without* a calculator just so you'll know what's going on behind the calculators you'll come to use for speed, convenience, and greater accuracy. You'll soon be able to run the numbers on any company—and probably get so used to the routine you'll be able to just glance at a bunch of numbers and immediately know what they mean without having to do *any* math in your head.

The key to the Rule #1 method of finding the Sticker Price is, as I said, to buy businesses — not stocks — and build in layers of protection when we buy them. These layers are what we've been learning so far in this book. The first layer is the necessity of understanding what being in this business *Means* well enough so you know it's a durable business. Second, make sure it has a wide *Moat* so you know you can make a reasonable prediction about the future from its past Big Five numbers. Third, make sure you're in love with the *Manager* so you know he or she will act like a long-term owner. And the fourth layer—maybe the most important—is to buy with a huge *Margin of Safety* so that if anything goes wrong, you won't get burned. These layers are the Four Ms. We're going to finish the fourth M, Margin of Safety, or MOS, in this chapter. To do that, we have to calculate the right Sticker Price.

Arriving at the right Sticker Price entails knowing four numbers — ones that will be used to make a few critical calculations. Let me first map out and explain what numbers I'm talking about—and then I'll teach you how to figure out the Sticker Price from there.

I'm going to take you through the process of arriving at a realistic Sticker Price without using a calculator. You may prefer to do this without playing with numbers in your head. For those of you who feel that way (and believe me, I understand), I had some friends build Rule #1 Sticker Price calculators and put them on my website. If you want, you can go to www.ruleoneinvestor.com and use the calculators while you're reading this chapter. After every step in the Sticker calculation process here (where you do the calculations on paper or in your head), I list the step-by-step process to use with my calculators. And for those of you who prefer to work directly with Excel formulas, those are on my website, too.

FINDING THE STICKER PRICE

To find the Sticker Price, we need four numbers handy:

1. Current EPS
2. Estimated (future) EPS growth rate
3. Estimated future PE
4. Minimum acceptable rate of return from this investment

Why these numbers? The Sticker Price is calculated by knowing the amount of money a business is going to make in the future. The amount of money a business makes is called earnings (or profits), and the most accurate way earnings are reported to owners is called earnings per share, or EPS. So what we really want to know to get started is what the EPS is going to be in the future. In particular, we want to know what the EPS is going to be in ten years. And to figure out the *future* EPS, we need two numbers: the current EPS and the estimated (future) EPS growth rate. By growing the current EPS at the estimated EPS growth rate for ten years, we can obtain the future EPS ten years from now.

Once we know the future EPS, we can figure out what its future market price is going to be in ten years, too. That part's easy. Mr.

Market prices businesses by some multiple of their EPS. This multiple is called the PE (price/earnings) ratio, or just "PE." We find out the best future PE to use — which I'll soon teach you how to do — and then multiply that number times the future EPS to arrive at the future market price for the business in ten years.

> The Sticker Price of any business is based on its *future* EPS and *future* PE. In other words, if we can figure out what a company's future EPS and PE numbers are going to be in, say, ten years, we can multiply those two numbers together and determine its future price in ten years and then, from that, work backwards to determine its Sticker Price today.

It's just common sense that if we know what the market price of the business will be in ten years — if we have a crystal ball and can see what destiny has in store — it's easy to decide what to pay for the business today. All we have to know is what our minimum acceptable rate of return is per year. *You* should know this already; for Rule #1 investors, our minimum acceptable rate of return is 15 percent. With that knowledge and the future market price, we can figure out the all-important Sticker Price.

1. Current EPS

We don't have to do any fancy calculations to get the current EPS, which is reported on most financial websites and easy to obtain. You'll find it's also called the "TTM EPS," short for the Trailing Twelve Months EPS. In fact, you'll see "ttm" a lot on financial sites, referring to data measured during the last four fiscal quarters. On MSN, the current EPS data sheet looks like this:

MSN Home   My MSN   Hotmail   Shopping

msn Money

Home | News | Banking | **Investing** | Planning | Taxes | My Money

Investing Home   Portfolio   Markets   **Stocks**   Funds   ETFs   Commentary   Brokers   CNBC TV

Quote, Chart, News

Snapshot

Company Report

Quotes

Charts

Key Developments

Recent News

Research

SEC Filings

Advisor FYI

Stock Rating

Earnings Estimates

Analyst Ratings

Financial Results

Insider Trading

Ownership

Community

Guided Research

Research Wizard

Name or Symbol: WFMI   Go   ▾Find   Print Report

Whole Foods Market, Inc.: Company Report

Financials

	Last 12 Months	5 Year Growth
Sales	4.5 Bil	18.9%
Income	160.1 Mil	NA
fyi Dividend Rate	1.00	NA
Dividend Yield	0.70%	0.10%

More Financials - as of 06/2005

Fundamental Data

Debt/Equity Ratio	0.01
Gross Margin	30.20%
Net Profit Margin	3.50%
Total Shares Outstanding	67.3 Mil
Market Capitalization	9.08 Bil
Earnings/Share	2.35
Stock**Scouter** Rating	8

Earnings Estimates

Qtr(9/05) EPS Estimate	0.53
FY(9/05) EPS Estimate	2.47

2. Estimated EPS Growth Rate

We get the second number, the estimated EPS growth rate, from the work we've already done: the Big Five numbers (the core of Chapter 6). It makes sense that to predict the *future* EPS growth rate on a business, we have to look at *historical* growth rates to base our decisions. Now here's the tricky part that won't make sense at first: Of the four growth-rate numbers in the Big Five that tell us the historical growth rate for a business, the one that best points to future EPS growth is actually *not*

The Sticker Price process in a nutshell:

1. Grow the current EPS at the estimated EPS growth rate for ten years to obtain the future EPS.
2. Multiply the future EPS by the future PE (the calculation of which I'll describe) to obtain the future market price.
3. Shrink the future market price by the minimum acceptable rate of return per year to obtain the Sticker Price.

Rule #1 uses ten years for the future for two simple reasons:

1. The 10-10 Rule: We never buy a business for ten minutes if we aren't willing to hold it for ten years.
2. Practicality: Twenty years is too far into the future to do any sort of reasonable predictions, and five years is too short for a long-term hold.

So ten works best.

the historical EPS growth rate, but rather historical *equity* growth rate. I know this sounds confusing and counterintuitive, but lock into your brains that the single most important number for choosing a business's estimated *future EPS growth rate* is its past *equity growth rate* — and not necessarily its past EPS growth rate. Why?

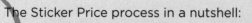

It's because a history of growing equity shows that the business has been able to create more and more surplus cash each year. Such growth of surplus cash is what makes a business valuable to the owner, because the real value of a business is just all the money you can collect from it over the years. Think about it for a second: If the Laundromat you just paid $100,000 for doesn't produce surplus cash, what do you get out of owning it besides free starch in your shirts? Nothing. Zero. Because all the earnings per share are getting plowed back into the business to keep the doors open. If that keeps up forever, you're never going to see a dime out of this deal, are you? On the other hand, if this Laundromat that you paid $100,000 for produces $20,000 in surplus cash this year, that means the equity grows by that much. The value of the business obviously increases with the increase in the value of the equity; a business that's growing its cash surplus at 20 percent a year has more cash for the owner each year. That's why Warren Buffett says in his 2004 chairman's letter that the best proxy for the growth of intrinsic value (Sticker Price) is the growth of equity.

> I hinted in Chapter 6 that equity growth in a company is what we want to see more than any of the other three growth numbers (EPS, sales, and cash). Why? The growth of the Sticker Price—the value of a business—most closely follows the growth of equity because a growing equity comes from growing surplus cash . . . and surplus cash is what makes a business valuable. Which is why we give a priority to equity growth numbers when we're estimating the future growth rate.

While we're going to give a priority to equity (knowing that it's the best indicator of future growth), we still review all our growth rates to find the best number for the estimated EPS growth rate. What we're looking for is consistency and a reasonable growth rate number that the business can sustain. But remember, if the number you decide on isn't fairly obvious, if you feel yourself making a big guess based on a lot of scrambled numbers, then this isn't a business to own. Especially as a beginner, you need to be patient and wait for a really obvious one to come along.

Since the estimated growth rate of a business is such an important number, we'd like a second opinion. Wouldn't it be nice to know what the average professional analyst thinks the rate of growth will be? At least every quarter, professional analysts make their best guess on the growth rate of a business for the next five years. This is important information for investors, so it's tracked on most financial research websites. Most get this information from one source: Zacks, a service that tallies up the estimates from the pros. You can go to Zacks (www.zacks.com) directly and pay to see the range of estimates on a company. Or you can get the analysts' *average* (i.e., not an entire range from different analysts) estimates from your favorite research site. MSN Money calls this number—which, you'll note, is based on earnings rather than equity (our ideal growth indicator)—the "earnings estimate" and it looks like this:

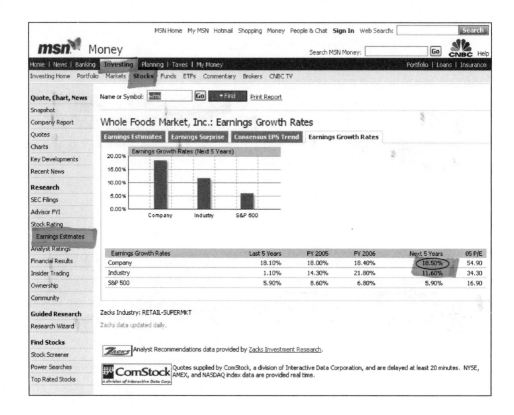

Our job is to compare what we've decided is the business's historical growth rate with the professional estimate of future growth. If those two numbers are not similar (say, for example, the analysts project a business to grow much faster in the future than it has in the past), then we need to decide which of the two numbers we trust the most for purposes of calculating the future price of the business. At first we'll use the lower, more conservative number. So if the historical growth rate is lower than what the analysts are predicting for future growth, we'll go with the historical rate. If the analysts are projecting a slower growth rate than our historical growth rate, we'll use their number. Later, when you have more experience, you can use the higher number if you feel it's justified.

Some of you might be thinking that the analysts can be way off. Or that historical growth might not accurately predict future growth. Right on both counts. In fact, some businesses, especially those that are reasonably new, can have terrible historical growth rates (or barely any at all), and yet the analysts predict wonderful future growth. These businesses automatically get disqualified from Rule #1 analysis. They can, however, become part of what I call a "Risky Biz" portfolio—where you accept more risk because you think these businesses will perform a lot differently than they have in the past.

For example, I bought a bunch of Google shares for the Risky Biz part of my portfolio (a part that I cap off at 10 percent of my holdings) because its price was incredibly cheap if either the analysts or the historical growth rates were to hold true. But, as you know, there's no way I can predict Google will be in business in 10 or 20 years; therefore it's disqualified as a solid Rule #1 investment. I'll discuss Risky Biz investments later, and give you some rules to live by if you really want to accept the risk. You shouldn't ever allocate more than 10 percent of your portfolio to Risky Biz holdings. For now, stick to the Rule #1 basics and focus only on businesses that qualify as true Rule #1 companies—ones that have solid and consistent Big Five numbers.

3. Estimated Future PE

Once we have the estimated (future) EPS growth rate, which we'll call the Rule #1 Growth Rate—again, based on either historical growth rates or what the analysts predict — the next thing we need to know is what multiple of EPS we should assign a given company ten years from now to determine its value ten years from now. We need to provide a multiple (called the "PE" or "PE ratio") to change the earnings-per-share number into a *price*-per-share number. For example, if this business is earning $1 per share ten years from now, its correct price per share may be anywhere from $5 to $50 depending on what future PE we multiply the future EPS with.

Businesses almost never sell for just one times their current EPS, or a PE of 1. That's way too cheap because the seller is getting only what he would have gotten in one year anyway. For example, if the current EPS of a business you own is $1, would you sell it for $1 per share? Only if you thought the business was going to go broke almost immediately! Otherwise, you know you're going to get that dollar anyway. You don't need to sell to get the dollar. You might be willing to take $5 or $10 for your $1 of EPS, but not $1. That is, you might sell it for a 5 PE or a 10 PE, but not for a 1 PE.

Mr. Market operates just like that: If Mr. Market thinks a business is going to grow really fast, he gives it a high PE, like 50. If he thinks it isn't going to grow much, he gives it a really low PE, like 5. The PE is all about what Mr. Market thinks about the future. Lots of times Mr. Market isn't thinking — he's reacting emotionally. When he does that, he can put the PE way too high or way too low. We are, of course, hoping he'll put the PE way too low when we're buying and then way too high so we can sell for lots more than we expected. But when it comes to deciding what to pay for a business, we're going to use a PE that makes sense — not too high, not too low. Like Goldilocks, we want the PE to be "just right."

A quick rule of thumb for figuring the PE is to double the Rule #1 growth rate. Thus, if we think a company is going to grow its earnings at 8 percent for the next ten years, then we can expect to see a PE of around 16 about ten years from now (assuming it will continue that rate of growth). We'll call this the default PE. If we don't have anything else to go on, we'll use the default PE. But, of course, we do have something else to go on — we have the historical PE. Every good business has earn-

Ah, the seemingly important "PE ratio." You're probably surprised I haven't mentioned PE ratios until now, when so many other financial guys like to spout about them frequently. Before you get all confused about PE ratios, let's keep it simple. Remember: We're figuring out the price of a given stock ten years from now, so we can work backwards from that number to get our Sticker Price today. Every stock has a price, right? And every stock we're going to look at has earnings, right? Well, a PE ratio is just the price divided by the earnings. Here's the formula for those of you who like math:

$$PE \times EPS = Price$$
$$or$$
$$PE = Price\ /\ EPS$$

For example: Assume Starbucks today has a current PE of 42 and an EPS of $1. What's the price of Starbucks today?

$$42 \times \$1 = \$42$$

Correctamundo. The PE ratio indicates how much we're willing to pay for a dollar's worth of a company's earnings. Be careful not to fuss over the PE ratio too much. We're simply using it as a plug-in tool for figuring the Sticker Price. Other than that, we don't care what the PE is.

ings per share, and every good business has a price per share, so every good business has a PE. We can look up the historical PE and see how that compares with the default PE.

Take a look at this list of Rule #1 candidate companies and their PEs in relation to their estimated EPS growth rates from the analysts in 2005:

	Estimated EPS Growth Rate	Current PE
Starbucks	22	42
Apollo Group	24	76
Dell	15	31
Costco	12	22
Automated Data Processing	12	26
Paychex	16	34
Whole Foods Markets	19	44
Chicos	24	43
Anheuser Busch	9	17
Microsoft	11	25
Merck	7	13
Pfizer	9	23

Notice how these companies' PEs are roughly twice their estimated EPS growth rate? This is common enough with Rule #1 businesses that we're going to use it as a rough-cut way to approximate a PE number we need to determine a Sticker Price.

If the historical and default PEs are not the same, we'll use the lower of the two when making calculations. You can find any company's average historical PE on any financial website. At MSN Money it looks like the screen shown at the top of page 157.

Example: If our default PE is 48 for Garmin (GRMN) because we estimate the future growth at 24 percent a year and $2 \times 24 = 48$, but the company's average historical PE is 23 (my best guess upon looking at this chart and seeing a high of 35.3 and a low of 12.1), we'd use 23 for the future PE, not 48.

The chart on the bottom of page 157 depicts four examples of companies with their historical and projected growth rates and PEs. Note that the "Rule #1 growth rates" are the lower of either the analysts' projections or the historical rates. The default PEs are then determined by

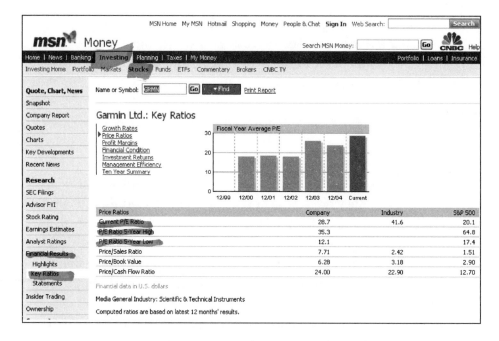

simply doubling our Rule #1 growth rates. And we get our "Rule #1 PEs" by picking the lower of either the historical PE or the default PE. These examples are from the year 2000.

Company	Analysts' growth rate	Historical (equity) growth rate	Rule #1 growth rate	Default PE	Historical PE	Rule #1 PE
Harley-Davidson (HDI)	24%	24%	24%	24 × 2 = 48	46	46
General Motors (GM)	10%	6%	6%	6 × 2 = 12	15	12
Dell Computers (DELL)	20%	17%	17%	17 × 2 = 34	40	34
Apollo Group (APOL)	20%	35%	20%	20 × 2 = 40	45	40

Again, the Rule #1 growth rate is just the lower of what the analysts think of our estimate based on the historical growth rates. The Rule #1 PE is just the lower of the default PE or the historical PE. Once we have our Rule #1 estimated growth rate and PE, we can proceed.

4. Minimum Acceptable Rate of Return

The Rule #1 minimum rate of return is 15 percent per year. The Sticker Price is the maximum amount we can pay and still get that 15-percent return on our money over the next ten years. In other words, the value of the business to us is the price that, if our projections are correct—and everything works out perfectly—will give us a compounded 15-percent annual return for the next ten years. Of course, things almost never work out perfectly and we're going to insist on a big Margin of Safety below Sticker Price.

Fifteen percent isn't a number plucked out of the blue; it's a figure that I use as my target rate of return because it's high enough to cover reasonable inflation, taxation on the gains someday when I take the money, and the risk of giving my money to someone else. And it's not so high that I can't find wonderful businesses at prices that'll give me a good return. It's what my teacher, the Wolf, taught me (and it's rumored to be the default rate of return Mr. Buffett uses). Put simply, 15 percent is a pretty good rate of return for what we're doing, and if you get it for lots of years, you're going to get rich for sure. Write that down in your brain: 15 percent is our minimum acceptable return per year. Anything that looks like it's going to pay us less, we don't buy.

The Rule #1 minimum return is 15 percent per year. Don't accept anything less!

THE RULE OF 72

Now that we know the four numbers we need to calculate the Sticker Price, here's how we do the calculations in our heads. The first thing we need to find out is the EPS ten years from now. The current EPS and the estimated EPS growth rate are used to calculate the EPS in ten years. Take your time reading the following so you won't get lost: *The EPS growth rate will double the current EPS in some number of years. We need to know how many years it takes to double the current EPS if it grows at the EPS growth rate.* The Rule of 72 tells us the number of years it's going to take to double the current EPS. We just divide the estimated EPS growth rate into 72 and the number we get is the number of years it takes to double.

Let's say our current EPS is $1 and we estimate the EPS growth rate to be 24 percent. The Rule of 72 says to divide 72 by 24; well, 24 goes into 72 three times. So, if it grows at 24 percent per year, every three years our $1 will double.

> The exact number of years it takes to double once at 24 percent growth rate is 3.2, which is to say that the Rule of 72 is very accurate around 10 percent but gets less accurate the farther from 10 percent we go. However, for our purposes, the Rule of 72 is close enough since we shouldn't be buying anything that's marginal anyway.

Since we're trying to find out what the EPS will be in ten years, how many doubles will we expect to happen? Well, we just figured out by the Rule of 72 that the EPS will double once every three years, so in ten years it will double about three times. I say "about" because the Rule of 72 is an approximation, so we don't have to get all perfect about using it. But it'll work for us just fine, and it has the advantage of letting us do the numbers in our heads.

So, we know we can expect three doubles in ten years at a 24 percent EPS growth rate. Let's do the math: $1 doubles to $2 in the first three years; $2 doubles to $4 in the second set of three years; and $4 doubles to $8 in the third set of three years. Thus, we'd expect the future EPS (in ten years) to be something like $8 per share. Congratulations, you just did the hardest math you need to do in Rule

#1 investing. Now all you have to do is repeat similar calculations using different numbers. And if you don't want to go through these routines, you can rely on my calculators to do the job for you.

FROM FUTURE EPS TO FUTURE MARKET PRICE

Once we know the EPS in ten years, we can figure out the price of the business per share in ten years — the future market price — by using a PE, a multiple of earnings. Simply multiply the future EPS by the future PE. Let's say we expect Mr. Market to use a 40 PE, since the historical PE of 40 was lower than the default PE of 48 (the default PE being simply double the Rule #1 growth rate, or 24 percent times two). That means the future market price ten years from now will be about $320 (40 PE times $8 EPS).

FROM FUTURE MARKET PRICE TO
STICKER PRICE

We can figure out what the business's Sticker Price is today by utilizing our future market price. Again we'll use the Rule of 72.

We know our minimum acceptable rate of return is 15 percent. By the Rule of 72, 15 percent doubles our money about every five years (72 divided by 15 is roughly 5). So we can expect, at our minimum acceptable rate of return of 15 percent, to double our money twice (ten years divided by five equals two doubles). That means we get only two doubles from the Sticker Price to the future market price. If we double $1 to $2 and then double $2 to $4, we have two doubles. You might notice one more pattern: $1 is one-fourth of $4. So if we know our future market price, we can just divide by four to get the Sticker Price. We can do that every time because 15 percent is always our minimum acceptable rate of return (it's a constant) and one-fourth of the future market price always gives us the correct Sticker Price if we want a 15-percent return. Clever.

Let's go back to our example. If we expect the business to be fetching $320 per share in ten years, we can just divide by four to get the Sticker Price: $320 divided by 4 is $80. If I want at least a 15-percent compounded rate of return for the next ten years, I need to buy this business for $80 or less per share today.

> Assuming 15-percent returns, the Sticker Price today is always going to be about a quarter of the Market Price ten years from now. This is because any price, growing at 15 percent a year, doubles according to the Rule of 72 approximately every five years or twice in ten years. Two doublings equal one quadrupling. And to reverse it, just divide that future market price by four.

STICKER TO MOS

Don't forget: We never pay the Sticker Price. We always want to buy a dollar of value for fifty cents. We always, always, always want a big Margin of Safety—a big MOS. To get a big MOS, we want to buy this business for 50 percent off the Sticker. We want this thing when it's on sale big-time. In our example, we know the Sticker Price is $80, and we can easily figure out what half of $80 is. The "on-sale" price we want to pay for this business, the MOS Price, is $40. If we can buy this wonderful business for $40 a share, we have one heck of a nice cushion to make our minimum 15 percent on a business we expect to sell in ten years for $320.

Let's take a real-world example.

HARLEY'S STICKER PRICE, MOS PRICE, AND ROI

You guys know I love motorcycles in general and Harleys in particular. I've owned up to ten Harleys at a time, although I'm down to just one these days. I love cruising across a vast desert with the wind blowing through my thinning hair.

I've been to the Sturgis Harley rally lots of times (lo and behold, it's in Sturgis, South Dakota). Every year, bands come that were popular in the seventies, and the guys in the band are getting older. Recently the lead singer for one band, who's getting up there in years, got up on stage in front of 100,000 bikers and said, "It's just great to be able to play to you guys because Sturgis is the only place in America where it's cool to be old, fat, and bald!"

Because of all the years and miles I've put on Harleys, the business has a lot of *Meaning* to me. It has a heck of a brand *Moat,* and its numbers, as we've seen, back it up big time. The biz is still managed by family members, and the *Management* treats this business like the American icon it's become — as if they expected to own it for the next 100 years. Those three Ms tell me this is a wonderful business *for me* to own. (Remember, just because this might be a wonderful business for me doesn't mean it's a wonderful business for you. Maybe you hate motorcycles and think they should be banned from highways. Maybe you haven't a clue as to why Harleys are so popular or what makes a great bike. Don't buy a business just because someone else is buying. Buy businesses that are wonderful to *you,* okay?)

Let's travel back to a few years ago and pretend we're in the early part of 2000. The stock market has become "irrationally exuberant." Prices are simply off the chart for almost every business I'm interested in, so I'm wondering where I'm going to put my money. I'm going to let you climb into my head at that time early in the year 2000 as I analyzed Harley-Davidson.

I need to know what price to pay for Harley at the beginning of 2000 that'll get me my 15-percent return, minimum, for the next ten years. How the heck does a Harley-riding river guide figure that?

Ready? Just like baking a cake, we need to get the ingredients all out here on the counter. The ingredients for this cake are not eggs, flour, sugar, and milk. They are (1) the current EPS, (2) the (future) EPS growth rate, (3) the future PE, and (4) our minimum rate of return. Now let's mix them up to get a decent estimate of the future market price of the stock ten years from now. With that number, we can find the price we need to pay today to make our 15 percent—the Sticker Price.

Okay, in early 2000 Harley had a current EPS of 89 cents. Good. First ingredient on the counter—89 cents for current earnings per share.

Next, figure out the (future) EPS growth rate. I'm going to get this number from either the historical growth rate or the analysts' projected growth rate, whichever is lower. Of course, at this point in my research, I had already figured out the Big Five numbers and checked the debt, so all I had to do to get the historical growth rate of the business was to review those numbers. Here are the four growth rates in order of importance: equity 24 percent, EPS 25 percent, sales 24 percent, cash 35 percent. You know I'm going to go right to equity because I want to use that as my indicator for long-term projections of growth. But I want confirmation from EPS and sales — the next most important numbers. In this case they're aligned closely with the equity growth rate. The cash growth rate, on the other hand, strikes me: 35 percent per year growth rate for cash is a huge number. It doubles the cash in the business in just a bit over two years (I figured that out quickly by dividing 35 into 72). I doubt even Harley can keep that up for a long time. Too high for the real world. Equity is growing at 24 percent, which means it's doubling every three years. (Can you guess where I got that? Right. Rule of 72.) I don't know if 24 percent growth is sustainable for Harley, but it's certainly historically accurate, so I'm going to use it. Thus my historical growth rate is 24 percent. Time to check what the experts have to say about it.

I look up Harley (ticker symbol HDI) on a financial research site and discover that the analysts are estimating a 24-percent growth rate for the next five years. Guess they see the same numbers I do. So not much to decide: 24 percent it is. You gotta love it when it's that obvious.

Now I can use the Rule of 72 to get the number of years it takes to double the EPS once if it grows at 24 percent. Answer: three (72 divided by 24). So every three years Harley will double its EPS. In ten years it'll double a little more than three times (because $3 \times 3 = 9$, which is close to 10). Okay. Now I can figure out the EPS in ten years.

I start with the current EPS — $0.89. Round that to $0.90 because I'm bad at math. Ninety doubles once to 180; 180 doubles to 360; 360 doubles to 720. Even I can do that and it tells me my expected EPS in ten years is a bit higher than $7.20. I'll use $7.50. (And right about here, all my engineer-type students are groaning about being sloppy. So quit groaning and get out your slide rules or calculators or go to www.ruleoneinvestor.com and use mine and figure it exactly and be happy. I can do that, too. The exact number for future EPS is $7.65.)

Back to the inside of my head. I've got $7.50 for the future EPS in ten years. Now I need the future PE. If the default PE is simply double the growth rate, the default PE is 48. That's way up there, so I'm going to take a look at the historical PE. I look it up and see it's 46. Way up there, too, but at least it confirms the default. So 46 it is. And that's all I need to figure the price of the business, per share, ten years from now. I multiply the future EPS of $7.50 times the future PE of 46 ($7.50 × 46$) and get . . . Sheesh. I gotta get out a calculator for that one. Answer: $345. Now I know that $345 is my best guess for what this business will sell for, per share, ten years from the year 2000. Time to figure out what to pay for it right now — i.e., the Sticker Price. (Notice I haven't even looked at the actual market price yet because the current market price doesn't matter. I don't care, yet, what Mr. Market wants for the business any more than I care what some car dealer wants for a new car I'm thinking of buying. First I want to know what I should pay.)

That's really easy. Since I'm selling the business in ten years for $345 a share, I'm going to divide 345 by four and get $86. (Again, for you engineers who like it perfect, the exact answer is $86.97, so ha! I was almost perfect in my head.)

So I figure that in early 2000 Harley's Sticker is $86 a share. If I buy it for $86, I'm likely to make 15 percent a year for the next ten years. Of course, that assumes everything goes as planned, which is a naïve expectation, don't you think? I need a nice big Margin of Safety. Remember, I want to buy $1 of value for 50 cents. If I've got $86 of value, then I want to buy it for $43. My MOS Price — the price I'll pay if I can get it — is $43. Done. Finally, it's time to look at the actual market price and see if I'm going to be buying this business right away or not.

If doing the math in your head or on paper isn't your cup of tea, you can perform the Sticker Price and MOS calculations on my website with my Sticker & MOS Calculator. The computer will do all the figuring for you. All you have to do is plug in the numbers. Here are the steps you take:

1. Click on the Sticker & MOS Calculator.
2. In the box labeled EPS, input .89.
3. In the box labeled "Growth Rate," input 24.
4. The box labeled "PE" has 48 in it. That's higher than Harley's historical PE of 46, so change it to 46.
5. The box labeled ROI has 15%. Leave it; this is our Rule #1 minimum rate of return.
6. The box labeled "Years" has "10" in it. Since we're doing a long-term valuation, we'll leave that one at 10.
7. Click "Calculate" and it tells us the following:
   a. The future stock price is $351.86.
   b. The exact Sticker Price is $86.97.
   c. The exact MOS Price is $43.49.

RIDING HARLEY FROM 2000 TO 2005

Now we'd look to see what Mr. Market is doing with the price of Harley today. Is he overly excited or is he freaking out? If he's pricing this business well below Sticker, he's freaking out. Well, Harley is selling for $29 (in the year 2000). Guess he's freaking out, huh? He's got it priced a whole lot below Sticker. Heck, he's got it priced well below MOS! That's good for us if we're a Harley buyer. Imagine, if we can make 15 percent buying it at $86, what can we make if we buy it at $29?

That's an exciting question, isn't it? And immediately I start doing my favorite pie-in-the-sky calculation in my head. What is my rate of return if I buy Harley tomorrow at $29 a share and everything goes according to plan and I sell it in ten years for $345? I ask myself the question this way: If I buy it for $29 and ten years later sell it for $345, how many times did my $29 double? Because of my math skills, I round the $29 to $30 and start doubling in my head: 30 to 60, 60 to 120, 120 to 240, 240 to 480. Oops. $480's too high. And the previous double, $240, is too low. $345 is about in the middle, so I've got roughly 3.5 doubles in ten years. That's a double every . . . uh, 10 divided by 3.5 is . . . uhhh . . . a bit less than every three years. I already know by the Rule of 72 that doubling every three years is 24 percent a year (72 divided by 3 is 24). So a bit less than three years means a bit more than 24 percent. Maybe 26 percent? Something like that. (See the "Cheat Sheet" below.)

Whatever—it's a *huge* number! My rate of return, instead of 15 percent, could be 26 percent. Sweet. (And, once again, if this sort of rough work bothers you, just use the calculators and you'll discover that my rough in-my-head calculation was *almost* on the money. My return on investment [ROI] would actually be 28 percent. Crazy fantastic!)

"CHEAT SHEET" TABLE FOR THE RULE OF 72	
Approximate years to double once	Growth rate
2	36%
3	24%
4	18%
5	15%
6	12%
7	10%
8	9%
9	8%
10	7%

Buying substantially below a big MOS is a very good thing because you'll get richer a lot faster by making 28 percent a year than by making 15 percent per year. How much faster? If you have $50,000 right now and get 15 percent on it, you'll be a millionaire in 21 years. Not bad. But if you rake in 28 percent per year, you'll be a millionaire in 12 years, about half of the time, and you get an extra nine years of living rich.

How much can $50,000 in Harley priced at $29 give us in ten years? Perform the following step-by-step calculations using my ROI calculator:

1. Open the ROI Calculator.
2. In the box labeled "Years" input the number of years before you are going to cash out—in this case, 10.
3. In the box labeled "$ Invested," input $50,000, assuming we're investing $50,000.
4. In the box labeled "Buying Price," input $29, which is the stock price of Harley in 2000.
5. In the box labeled "Selling Price," input the estimated future stock price from above—in this case, $345.
6. Click "Calculate," and it tells us the following:
   a. The percent ROI is 28 percent compounded for 10 years.
   b. The dollar ROI is $600,000 in 10 years.
   c. The time to get to $1,000,000 is 12 years.

Harley at $29 in 2000 was a heck of a deal. And that's exactly what we're looking for—a fantastic deal, because we have a huge upside with a huge Margin of Safety in case all doesn't continue to go great. All we have to do is be able to see it when Mr. Market offers it up to us on one of his bad days!

So, did Harley do as expected? Not exactly. Harley hit the skids a bit with the 2000–2003 recession, then performed even worse in 2005. The stock went up from $29, but peaked at $60, then, at this writing, was $50 per share in June 2005. At this point, assuming we bought and held through all of this stormy weather (a not-so-good idea, as you'll soon see), our rate of return on our investment in Harley would be . . . let's go back in my head . . .

How many years since I made the original investment? About five. What was the original money I put in? Let's say $100,000. What was the price I paid? $29. And what did I sell it for? Let's say $58 for round numbers. (And again, buying and holding a business in this market isn't necessary to make a very nice rate of return, so you can suppose correctly that I didn't buy and hold.)

How many times did $29 double by the time it got to $58? Twenty-nine doubled once is 58. One double. And how long to double once? Five years. By the Rule of 72, if I double once in five years I'm making a 15-percent-per-year rate of return. But again, for my engineer friends who like it perfect, your calculator will conclude that I actually got a 14.9-percent-per-year return.

Not the 28 percent I was hoping for at all. On the other hand, 15 percent a year right through one of the worst stock market drops in history is pretty decent compared to the average mutual fund losing 50 percent.

The power of a big Margin of Safety is that you can ride through major changes in a business, economy, and stock market and still not get burned.

The power of Rule #1 for getting rich is illustrated by the following scenario. Let's assume you made a mistake and left your $100,000 with a fund manager five years ago and now you have $50,000 instead of $200,000. If you started right now making 15 percent a year, how long before you'd make a million dollars? Twenty-one more years. Losing money just kills your rate of return. One bad five-year stretch, and instead of having a 15-percent rate of return, you have a 9-percent return . . . and instead of retiring with $1 million in 2016, you get to retire (assuming no more mistakes) in 2031.

To find out how much return we could get on Harley between 2000 and 2005:

1. Get out the ROI Calculator again.
2. In the box labeled "Years," plug in the number of years: 5.
3. In the box labeled "$ Invested," input $100,000, our original investment.
4. In the box labeled "Buying Price," input $29, our original purchase price.
5. In the box labeled "Selling Price," input the current stock prices—in this case $58.
6. Click "Calculate" and it tells us the following:
   a. The percent ROI is 15 percent compounded for five years.
   b. The dollar ROI is $200,000 in five years.
   c. The time to turn that $100,000 into $1 million at this rate is 16 years. Eleven years to go.

GENERAL MOTORS' STICKER PRICE, MOS PRICE, AND ROI

If you performed the same calculations on General Motors, again assuming we're looking to buy it in the year 2000, here's what you'd find: 1999 EPS at $8.53; estimated EPS growth rate at 6 percent (I arrived at 6 percent given the comparison between the historical rates and what the analysts were saying. The four growth rate numbers looked like this: equity at 6 percent, sales at 0 percent, EPS at 3 percent, and cash at 3 percent. The analysts were hoping for better, so I placed GM at the equity growth rate for the future—6 percent); future PE at 12; and minimum acceptable rate of return is our standard 15 percent. Based on these numbers, we get the following outcomes:

a. future stock price (in 2010): $183
b. Sticker Price in (2000): $45
c. MOS Price: $22

The problem: GM was selling in 2000 for $73 a share — almost double the Sticker Price. If you pay $200,000 for a $100,000 Maserati, you're not going to make money when you sell that car, no matter how great a car it is. You're going to lose. Same thing here with GM.

And, if you calculate the return on a $100,000 investment in GM over ten years, assuming you bought it in 2000 for $73 and sold it in 2010 for $183, you discover the following:

a. The percent ROI is 10 percent compounded for ten years.
b. The dollar ROI is $250,000 in ten years.
c. The time to get to $1,000,000 is 24 years (or twice the 12 years you appeared to need when you were looking at Harley in 2000, and remember, the Harley grubstake example was only $50,000, not $100,000; see a few pages back).

This assumes everything goes as planned! And as you know, just as with Harley, things didn't go as planned for GM — not by a long shot. If I had violated Rule #1 and bought GM for $73 a share in early 2000, I would have been in for a rude surprise: GM fell to $25. That would've been a loss of two-thirds of the money I invested. And since, as a Rule #1 investor, I focus and do not invest in more than a few businesses at any one time, a loss like that would punch a big hole in the rest of my investing returns. Thus, children, we play by The Rule or we get spanked.

> *Never, ever pay the Sticker Price — or more — for a business.*

WHEN TO BUY

Once we have our Sticker Price and our MOS, we know what price we should pay for the business. It's a wonderful business, and when it becomes available at an attractive MOS Price, we are prepared to buy it. There are a few more considerations we have to deal with, however, before we actually start investing our hard-earned money.

Knowing when to get in is one consideration, but we should also know what price we'd *sell* it for. Read on.

A question that comes my way a lot goes something like this: "GM pays a dividend, so why can't I consider that a positive for GM—especially when you consider I get to add that dividend to my ROI and let it all grow and compound together?" Here's how I answer this question (notice how I didn't include the dividend in the ROI calculations for GM):

A friend of mine just had a birthday party. I was asked to pick up her friend, an 83-year-old woman, and bring her to the party. When I arrived at the nursing home, she took my arm and steadied herself on the way to my car. On the way over to the party, we talked about investing. She believes in finding great businesses that pay a consistent dividend. GM is one she owns.

A lot of investors buy stocks, not businesses, and expect a consistent dividend return from the stock and the heck with anything else. That's why GM borrows money to pay dividends: to keep up the charade that everything is fine. And thus an 83-year-old woman continues to believe the illusion that everything must be fine with GM since it wouldn't be paying a dividend otherwise. I just smiled, nodded, and drove her to the party, where she had a great time.

Just remember what I said earlier in this book: Rule #1 isn't about dividends one way or the other. Rule #1 investors can't be suckered or paid off. We're about owning something wonderful. And we're about buying that wonderful business at an attractive price. If the wonderful business pays dividends or reinvests the surplus, either way is good for us. But it has to be wonderful . . . and it has to be at an attractive price. Period.

Chapter 10

Know the Right Time to Sell

The right time to sell a company is never.

—WARREN BUFFETT (1930–)

As MR. BUFFETT says, the right time to sell a business — *in theory* — is never. So the perfect business to buy is one we never have to sell. That's our ultimate objective: to buy a company so wonderful at a price so attractive that we never, ever sell it. It continues to make us rich. That, my friends, is Rule #1 nirvana. Approaching Rule #1 methodology with this idea in mind is part of the process, just as is buying a business as if you were going to buy the whole thing. You want to assume you're never going to sell your wonderful company. And while it's true you can't realize a gain until you sell, and your riches may all be "on paper," that's okay. The conceptual exercise of thinking you're never going to sell is an important one for the Rule #1 investor. It prevents you from falling into the trap of being an ordinary speculator in the market. In other words, it reinforces the tenets of Rule #1.

Of course, it doesn't often happen that you can hold on to a wonderful company forever. Not all companies stay wonderful. Even Mr. Buffett sells businesses from time to time. Over the years he's bought and sold hundreds. He may buy with the hope of never selling, but since he's a Rule #1 investor, he probably also buys with a Margin of Safety and therefore a way out without losing money if things don't go well. The businesses he buys stock in and actually holds forever are few and far between. Even Coke, a business he said he'd never sell, led him to regret that he *didn't* sell it in 1999 when Mr. Market was pricing Coke insanely high.

But still, the goal of every Rule #1 investment is to never sell. Don't lose sight of this concept, since it's part of the mindset you must adopt for purposes of finding and buying wonderful companies.

> "Our huge positions add to the difficulty of our nimbly dancing in and out of holdings. Nevertheless, I can be properly criticized for merely clucking about nosebleed valuations during the Bubble rather than acting on my views. Though I said at the time that certain of the stocks we held were priced ahead of themselves, I underestimated just how severe the overvaluation was. I talked when I should have walked."
> —Warren Buffett's "Chairman's Letter," February 28, 2005

THE INCREDIBLE ADVANTAGE OF NEVER SELLING

There is a reason that the richest people in the world are business owners: Businesses grow our money much faster than anything else, because we don't have to find a new place to reinvest our annual gains. If we're making 15 percent per year returns from a wonderful company, where else can we get that rate of return? What better place to put our money than a company that returns to us 15 percent or more a year? There is no better alternative, which is why leaving the gains from our investment *in* our investment (rather than cashing out) is critical to becoming very, very rich. This is true whether we're retired or not.

Being able to reinvest our annual gains and compound money continually at 15 percent or more a year in a wonderful company is incredibly important to a Rule #1 investor. It means that, theoretically at least, we have to pick only a few wonderful businesses, buy them at attractive prices, and we're done. We're certain to get rich. The money pouring in will do all the work for us from then on.

Keep in mind that our definition of a wonderful business includes the notion of Moat, which further includes the notion of predictability. If the business becomes unpredictable, perhaps the Moat has been breached. In that case, the business, by Rule #1 definition, is no longer wonderful and we sell it.

It's true, the richest people in the world got their money, almost without exception, from businesses that grew their fortunes. On Forbes's 2004 list of the richest people in the world, the first real-estate mogul doesn't make his appearance until number 34, and the next one, Donald Trump, doesn't show up until number 78. Everybody else on the list grew their money from businesses. The top ten built their fortunes in such areas as technology (Microsoft and Oracle, numbers 1 and 5 respectively), mass retail (Wal-Mart, numbers 6–10), grocery (number 3), oil and gas (number 4), investing (Warren Buffett at number 2), etc. The power of a business to compound money is, in the words of Albert Einstein (who was especially referring to compounding rates of return), "the most powerful force in the world."

Let's say, for example, we buy Apollo Group in 2000 at an attractive price; in this case, $10 per share. By the end of 2004, Apollo Group had grown its earnings by well over 300 percent and we hadn't taken any of the money out (i.e., our gains) to use elsewhere. We left it all in the business and continued to compound our money at well over 15 percent per year. By 2020, if Apollo can keep the growth going, our reinvested earnings will have grown 7,000 percent.

At that point, let's say we decide to retire. The year is 2020, and assuming Apollo Group is still as consistent and predictable as ever, we can sell the business we paid $10 per share for in 2000 for about $1,000 per share — a 25-percent-per-year rate of return. If we had put $10,000 into Apollo Group in 2000, we now have $1,000,000. One *million*. Is it better to cash out and take that $1 million to live on in retirement? Or should we do something else with that money?

What's the best — most secure — way to retire?

Can a stock price really go from $10 a share to $1,000? Businesses rarely allow their stock prices to run up to $1,000 per share. Berkshire Hathaway, the *Washington Post,* and a few others do, but not many, because the higher stock price makes it more difficult to find buyers (most people are intimidated by the thought of paying that much for a single share). Berkshire Hathaway Class A shares are currently priced at over $80,000 per share. Mr. Buffett leaves it up there intentionally to help prevent a lot of trading in the stock.

What most businesses do to keep their stock prices south of $80 is, at a point when the price is soaring to triple digits and beyond, give every shareholder two new shares for each original share, the value of each new share being half the original. For example, if the stock price is $100 a share and you give me two $50 shares to replace my one $100 share, I've still got $100 worth of stock, but now I have two shares trading at $50 each. This is called a *stock split,* and it's done all the time. So, ten years from now, we might not have one share worth $1,000. More likely, for each of our original shares we'll have 50 shares worth $20 each for a total of $1,000 of value for our original $10 investment.

If, at any time along this 20-year investment journey, Apollo becomes less than wonderful or massively overpriced, we'll sell it and stay out of it until the situation is rectified. Our money, in that case, will be invested in some other wonderful business that we can find at an attractive price. So, although I write about staying for 20 years in one business, in reality few businesses make it 20 years without becoming un-wonderful along the way. Nonetheless, for a Rule #1 investor, the compounding numbers work out the same whether we're talking about one business for 20 years or serial businesses for 20 years.

If 25 percent average annual returns for 20 years sounds like a high rate of return, get used to it. It's Mr. Buffett's average for the last 50 years, and we, as small Rule #1 investors, have major advantages over Mr. Buffett that more than make up for our lack of genius. While we shouldn't expect 25 percent a year for 20 years, don't count on *not* getting it. It can happen to you, and you'd hate to let yourself down.

Need some proof? Consider the following true stories of wonderful companies whose stock prices (per share, split-adjusted) exploded:

- Walgreens: 50 cents to $48 (1978 to 2002)
- Wal-Mart: 20 cents to $64 (1975 to 2000)
- Dell: 4 cents to $42 (1989 to 1999)
- Amgen: 10 cents to $72 (1985 to 2001)

These (and more) all grew at 25 percent a year average for 20 years or longer. In the last ten years, Apollo Group ($1 to $80), Whole Foods ($6 to $120), Toll Brothers ($4 to $48), Urban Outfitters ($1 to $50), Chicos Fashions (20 cents to $35), Bed Bath & Beyond ($3 to $46), and more have done 25 percent or better. Ten thousand dollars invested in any or all of the first group (from Walgreens to Amgen) is now worth well over $1 million. Ten thousand dollars invested in any or all of the second group (from Apollo to Bed Bath & Beyond) is now worth over $100,000 through one of the worst stock drops in history.

TWO WAYS TO RETIRE

We can go about this retirement in two different ways: We can sell all of our stock in Apollo (worth about $1 million) and use that to finish paying off our mortgages, traveling the world, and visiting our children; or we can keep our money in the company and skim what we need from the top to live during retirement. Which way is better?

Scenario 1: Sell all of Apollo. When we sell the stock, we'll pay long-term gains tax on the million and end up with roughly $850,000. Then I suppose we might invest in a government bond at 4 percent and we'll have $30,000 per year after tax to live on.

This is how someone *not* tuned in to Rule #1 would retire.

Since *we* play by The Rule, we know we can invest our retirement money without fearing loss, so why would we sell 100 percent of Apollo

Group as long as it continues to be wonderful and priced by Mr. Market at or below Sticker? Why not keep the million dollars growing at 15 percent and live on the annual gains? Apollo's stock is going to go up with its equity growth, and its equity is going up at 15 percent a year, so at the end of the year, the value of our Apollo Group stock will, in theory at least, have appreciated 15 percent. Where else can you get 15 percent or more? Certainly not in a government bond!

Obviously, this assumes Mr. Market is rational, which, as we know, he isn't all the time. In the real market in any given year, the price of Apollo stock could be far above or below the 15-percent increase we expected. For a retiree, those ups and downs could create an emotional rollercoaster. I'll show you how to solve that problem in the next chapter. For now, however, let's assume Mr. Market does get it right enough for this example to be true on average.

Scenario 2: Sell only what we need for living, and keep Apollo compounding our money. At the beginning of that year, we had $1 million of Apollo Group stock and it continued to grow at 15 percent, so by the end of the year we have $1.15 million of Apollo Group stock. If we sell just those gains from that year, or $150,000 worth of stock, and pay long-term gains tax of 15 percent, we have $128,000 after tax to live on.

Two scenarios set up with the same amount of money, yet two entirely different outcomes. With the exact same amount of retirement money at the start ($1 million in stock), a Rule #1 investor is living on $10,000 a month while another millionaire (who cashed out of Apollo and bought a T-note) is trying to get by on $2,500 a month.

This little compounding example highlights one of the great and wonderful benefits of Rule #1 investing: After a few years, our wonderful Rule #1 business is compounding all of our money—including our gains—over the years at such an enormous rate that, even starting with a small amount of capital, we'll be able to live very well off our investments in a very short time.

Think of the advantage that gives us over owning a real estate apartment complex. After I pay all the management costs of the apartment complex, the maintenance costs, insurance, and the mortgage, the money I have left over is mine to spend—the equivalent of earnings in a business. But I can't reinvest this money in this apartment complex very easily. I have to go find another real estate investment that's just as good as the first one. And I have to do that with all the gains I'm making. On the other hand, a wonderful business will reinvest my earnings for me and give me back an ever-growing return on my investment.

Can you imagine just sitting there retired and watching a $10,000 investment you made 20 years ago handing you $150,000 per year with zero work on your part?

Nirvana in retirement.

In a perfect world we might find nirvana, but in this world businesses tend to have problems reinvesting our money at a high ROIC, as competitors learn how to cross the Moat, entire industries get wiped out by new inventions, and wars and economic crises can crash the market for long stretches. And so nirvana with just one wonderful business is a hoped-for but seldom-achieved ideal. What do we do?

The answer: Sell.

Yes, sometimes it's time to sell. But when?

WHEN TO SELL

There are two times to sell:

1. When the business has ceased to be wonderful
2. When the market price is above the Sticker Price

1. The Business Has Ceased to Be Wonderful

A business is "wonderful" in Rule #1 terms because we want to own it, we understand it, it has a consistent, predictably durable Moat, and Level Five Management. Wonderful businesses by definition tend to stay wonderful. In other words, something big has to change or they'll just keep being wonderful forever. There are only two reasons a business can change from wonderful to not wonderful: (1) an Outside Attack, and/or (2) an Inside Traitor.

The Outside Attack comes from a competitor who's crossed the Moat and is tearing down the castle. That can happen because either our Management team didn't defend the Moat or a competitor made our products obsolete. Similar to what happened to the typewriter when word processing emerged. Similar to when railroads couldn't compete with airplanes. Similar to when DVDs wiped out video, CDs wiped out records and tapes, and online downloading wiped out brick-and-mortar music stores. Successful Outside Attacks happen all the time, which is one of the big reasons we have to understand the business we own and why we insist on a durable Moat — a Moat that, by definition, is easily defended against an Outside Attack.

The Inside Traitor is less obvious. The Inside Traitor is a CEO who's gone from being on your side to being on *his* side. This is common because CEOs of successful businesses often love growing the business more than they love doing what's right for the owners.

In the real world, over time the cost of growth goes up for every business. The CEO then can't reinvest our earnings into the business with the same nice ROIC we've been getting. He pays for more advertising, but not as many new customers come to the store. At this point, as owners, we'd prefer he give us the money. If he'd just do that, we'd be happy because we can invest it in a different, faster-growing business.

But our CEO might not see it that way. Instead he might think, "Hey, how great would it be to take that excess cash and, instead of giving it back to the owners, use it to buy up all these other businesses." For a lot of CEOs, buying businesses and building an empire are much more fun than playing golf. We should have been given that excess cash to reinvest in a business that can grow at 15 percent a year. Instead, our Inside Traitor CEO ripped us off to look good to his buddies.

The Outside Attack and Inside Traitor problems both show up in the Big Five numbers. If the Big Five are no longer good enough to warrant holding on to the business, sell it.

2. The Market Price Is Above the Sticker Price

This is a problem we love to have. We buy a business like Apollo Group in 2000, when Mr. Market is in love with technology and underpricing simple educational businesses. We get a 75-percent discount off Sticker. We're set. The business continues its growing ways and finally

Mr. Market begins to realize he made a mistake in pricing this one, so the price starts going up and up and up and up. Within four years the price of the company is above its Sticker.

Now what? The company is still growing really well. Sales, EPS, equity, and cash are all growing steadily. ROIC is still high and steady. Shouldn't we just keep it? Isn't the right amount of time to hold a stock forever?

Apollo Group continues to be a good example, so let's refer to it: In 2004 Apollo Group was priced at $95 per share. We bought it at $10 four years earlier when the Sticker Price was $40 and the MOS was $20. What is its Sticker now (in 2004)?

It's been growing so we have to recalculate Sticker. Again, like baking a cake, we have to pull together the ingredients. Here are the ingredients we need to collect from a financial website:

- EPS, 2004 TTM (trailing 12 months): $.90
- Analysts' average estimated EPS growth rate: 23%
- Historical PE: 62
- Market Price: $95

Now that we have the ingredients we need, we finalize the EPS growth rate by looking at the Big Five numbers. When I do that, I see that the analysts' estimate of 23 percent growth looks good. That means three doubles in ten years (72 divided by 23). Since the EPS is at .90, three doubles means it'll be $7 or so in ten years (.90 to 1.80, 1.80 to 3.60, 3.60 to 7.20). The historical PE is way high, so we'll use the Rule #1 default PE of two times the growth rate: $2 \times 23 = 46$. This makes the future price $320 or so. And since Sticker Price is always one-quarter of future price (a mathematical relationship dictated by the ten-year interval involved and our desire to reap a 15-percent-a-year return), Sticker Price is $80.

That's the quick and rough way to do this.

Obviously, if we want to get this as accurate as we can, we can do the calculations with an Excel spreadsheet or use the calculators on my website built for exactly these problems. But lots of really good investors don't use computers to figure this math out. It's become routine and automatic for them, and they can quickly eye a batch of raw numbers and know instantly what they mean. To paraphrase Warren Buffett, if it doesn't jump out at you that this is a super deal, then it's too close to call.

Are you noticing that these Apollo numbers are the same numbers we saw for Harley-Davidson in 2000? Just a coincidence? Not really. Fast-growing businesses can hover around the 24-percent range and by splitting their stock over and over they keep their EPS down in the $1 range. Lots of businesses do this, and because they do it, these numbers become a kind of comfort zone for big investors.

 On my website you can calculate Apollo's future price and today's Sticker and MOS by performing the following steps:

1. Open the "Sticker & MOS Calculator."
2. In the box labeled "EPS," input $.90
3. In the box labeled "Growth Rate," input 23%.
4. In the box labeled "PE," input 46 (since double the growth rate is less than the historical PE).
5. In the box labeled "Years," leave 10.
6. In the box labeled "Minimum Acceptable Rate of Return," leave 15%.
7. Click "Calculate" and we get the following results:
   a. Future value per share in 10 years is $360.
   b. Sticker Price today is $89.
   c. MOS Price today is $45.

The Sticker Price today is $89, but the market price today is $95 ("today," of course, being 2004). Apollo Group is priced above the Sticker and way, way above the MOS Price of $45.

Often, especially in this market, about the time a business is priced close to its Sticker is when the big guys (the institutional investors) start to take their profits off the table. They can do these calculations, too, you know. All it takes for them to run for the hills is some problem: a negative analyst report, bad press, government regulators taking a look, bad sector news, a missed projection, or maybe they're just in a funky mood and start taking profits off the table. Don't attempt to understand their thinking or why they decide to sell. It could be anything or nothing at all, and then, like lemmings off a cliff, the other institutional guys start selling, too. For us, this means that from this point onward, we're looking for a better opportunity for our money—one with a lot bigger MOS.

On the other hand, it's a shame to have done all that work getting to know Apollo Group and then say good-bye. Instead, after we sell it, we're going to keep Apollo Group on our Watch List. If it becomes attractive again in price (and still meets all four Ms), we may buy it again.

> A Watch List is just a group of stocks we're watching. When Mr. Market prices a business on our Watch List, completing our Four M criteria, we make a move and buy it! And if we have to sell that wonderful company at a later date, we put it back on our Watch List, where, assuming it continues to pass our Four M test, we can buy it back again when the price is right.

If the price goes down to where we get a big MOS again, we can buy Apollo back and ride it up. In fact, the reason I'm using Apollo Group as an example is that its price trajectory permitted exactly that. The stock price dropped from $95 in mid-2004 to $65 by November 2004. But should we have bought it back again at that price (remember that the MOS Price we calculated for Apollo was $45)? This is a key question: When should we buy back a stock that's below the Sticker Price? If we need a 50-percent Margin of Safety to buy it in the first place, can we rebuy with a smaller (narrower) MOS? The answer to that question is yes.

THE ONE EXCEPTION TO THE MOS PRICE

All things being equal between two businesses, I wouldn't choose to buy a business with a 30-percent Margin of Safety if I can buy just as good a business with a 50-percent Margin of Safety. Obviously, I'd buy the one where my money is going to get the biggest compounded rate of return. But at the moment Apollo is available with a 30-percent MOS, what other businesses are available that meet the four Ms? In the real world, there aren't a lot of wonderful businesses out there selling with a 50-percent Margin of Safety that really do have Meaning to me, whose Management I love, and that have a wide Moat. It's possible that for the whole time Apollo is available at a 30-percent discount, there may be nothing else I can buy on my Watch List that's as good a deal as that.

Once you've been buying and selling a business for some time, you'll find that you start to become much more comfortable investing in it than in something new you don't know as well. I find myself coming back to the same businesses over and over again when Mr. Market prices them below their value: Apollo Group, Chicos Fashions, Whole Foods, Harley-Davidson, and a handful of others are amazing businesses, best of class in every way, and Mr. Market is capable of pricing them at some kind of Margin of Safety whenever there's a hiccup in their upward growth.

As Rule #1 investors, we gotta love that. So answer this: Isn't it better to have our money working in wonderful businesses that we understand, even if the Margin of Safety isn't as big as we'd like? (Answer: Yes!) But only if we bought in originally with the full 50-percent MOS. If we did that, then in effect we're buying back in with gains we've made from the business price moving upward. That gives us the extra cushion. Don't use this exception to the MOS requirement as an excuse to buy businesses that don't have the full MOS. You can get in trouble doing that.

Having said all that, I'll give you a guideline I use for rebuying a business. Once we've gotten in at a great discount (our true MOS at 50 percent off Sticker), once we've been proven right and it's gone up to its Sticker Price, once we're buying the business back with gains from previous purchases, I'll buy back in when it drops to 20 percent below the Sticker Price. Great businesses have 20-percent price changes all the time. Harley-Davidson got up to its Sticker of $50 by January 2002, so I was out. Then it dropped more than 20 percent below Sticker by January 2003. Time to play with Harley again. Then, by 2004, it ran up to $62, right at the Sticker Price (and I got out again), and then it dropped to $45, more than 20 percent below Sticker again. Time to get into Harley yet again, and as of this writing Harley is at $52. I'll keep getting in as long as Harley is making reasonable progress (15 percent or better annualized rate of return as always) toward the Sticker. The actual progress Harley's made using this approach has been almost 40 percent per year. That's what can happen when you find a great Rule #1 business and know when to get in and when to get out. (If you're thinking that the tax consequences of getting in and out are something to consider, hold that thought. I'll delve into the tax issue later and prove to you that fearing Mr. Taxman shouldn't dissuade a Rule #1 investor from jumping in and out of a business.)

Actually, this in-and-out activity is pretty much a self-correcting process. As our wonderful business is available at a less and less attractive price, other wonderful businesses are going to become available and we're naturally going to shift our capital toward the highest potential rate of return with the lowest potential risk.

> If you're finding yourself buying back into a business you previously owned, but are now accepting it with a lower MOS Price, consider this a wake-up call to start searching for better bargains on businesses you love. Once you sell a company that's not so wonderful anymore, don't obsess over it as it sits on your Watch List, hoping you can buy it back as soon as possible. Make an active effort to find other wonderful companies that pass the Four M test. Do your homework. Don't get lazy. And, most important, don't lose sight of being a true Rule #1 investor. Get back in the game so you can make money work for you.

ELIMINATING DOUBT

This method of selling when the market price reaches our Sticker Price, and then buying back in at a lower price — but potentially with a narrower Margin of Safety — does require that we have faith in our ability to nail the correct Sticker Price from the start. And, lacking faith, we can easily start to guess, hope, and wish. "Is this business *really* priced at Sticker Price? Are the analysts *right* about the growth rate? What if I change the PE just a little? Should I wait a little longer and hold on to this business?"

In other words, like Mr. Market, we start to get emotional, which is bad for a Rule #1 investor. We have to have a better way of confirming our decisions and feeling comfortable about our moves.

In the next chapter, we'll learn to use tools that take the emotion out of investing, protecting us from our own inevitable mistakes.

Chapter 11

Grab the Stick

Chance fights ever on the side of the prudent.

—EURIPIDES (484–406 B.C.)

EVEN AFTER doing a good job of finding a business that passes the Four M test — one that has *Meaning* to us, that has a wide *Moat*, that has great *Management*, and that you can buy today with a big *Margin of Safety* — is it still possible we could make a mistake and violate The Rule? Of course. And even if we did everything totally right and didn't make a mistake, couldn't the stock price go down in the short run and cause us to lose money?

If those thoughts didn't occur to you already, believe me, when you start to do Rule #1 investing with real money, you'll hear in your head, "Did I make a mistake, and what do I do if this business goes down in price?" We need a solution to this problem.

SOLUTION #1: PRETEND

You bought a business and the price started going down the day after you bought it. And it is still going down with no sign of relenting. In case you've never experienced this, investors who have gone through it tell me this is not fun. (Okay, I admit it, I've goofed and experienced this, too.) One way to deal with this is to say to yourself that even though the stock has gone down in price, as long as you don't sell it you haven't really lost any money. In other words, just pretend you're not losing money and therefore not violating Rule #1. Right? Wrong. Big-time wrong. Escaping-from-reality wrong.

Imagine you're right about the business and its value but in spite of your brilliance, Mr. Market has managed to get even more depressed about the future, and now the company's stock is selling for less than what you paid last month. You say to yourself that you haven't lost money because you haven't sold it. But if you went to your banker and showed him your assets to get a loan and you said this business is worth what you paid for it last month, your banker would laugh at you. And throw you out.

He'd tell you your business is worth what Mr. Market is paying for it that day, not what you think it's worth or what you wish it were worth or what you paid for it last month. If Mr. Market is paying less than what you paid for it, as far as your banker is concerned, you lost money and your net worth has gone down. Therefore, neither you nor I can pretend we're not losing money if the market is telling us our business is worth less than what we paid for it. Because losing money, even in the short term, is a gross violation of The Rule, we must solve this problem some other way than just pretending it doesn't exist.

SOLUTION #2: MAKE UP THE DIFFERENCE

The second way to deal with this problem is the way Warren Buffett does it. He doesn't pretend he isn't losing money. Instead, he fills the hole by making more money in some other short-term investment than he lost in the Rule #1 business. This is a good trick if you can do it, and Mr. Buffett is smart enough that he can. He's not only one of the world's best long-term investors; he's also one of the world's best short-term investors. He's made billions in short-term investments like bonds, silver, currencies, and takeover arbitrage.

Can you and I do that? Takeovers and commodity and currency trading are actually a lot of fun and we certainly can do those, but that's the subject of another book. I'm assuming not every student of Rule #1 wants to get into this enough to be out there in the market as a trader. On the other hand, I'm also assuming that every single reader wants to not lose money. Since making up the difference with very clever short-term trading is a more advanced technique and requires more time and more training, we need another possibility.

SOLUTION #3: DON'T LOSE MONEY IN THE FIRST PLACE

There's a story about a student who'd been training in a monastery for many years to be a monk. One day his teacher came into his cell carrying a gnarly walking cane and said, "You've done well, my son. You have only one last test to pass. I will return in one day. If you pass the test you will become a monk and join our order as a brother. If you fail it, I'll beat you senseless with this stick." Before the student could ask what the test was, the monk walked out and locked the door. The student had nothing to do but sit in his cell and ponder his final test.

The next day his teacher returned carrying the stick and said, "Well?" And before he could say another word, the student leaped to his feet and grabbed the stick. The teacher smiled and said, "Welcome, brother."

Our third choice is to grab the stick.

GRABBING THE STICK

At this point you're like the student in the story. You've learned quite a lot about what makes a business wonderful. Still, no matter how much you know, Mr. Market can still beat you with a stick by making your wonderful company's price go down. Now I'm going to show you how to take away Mr. Market's stick. Until just a few years ago, this was not possible without a great deal of work. Today the small and insignificant investor has an enormous advantage over any of the big investors in the market, and I'm going to show you how to exploit that advantage to take away Mr. Market's ability to beat us by dropping the price of our business. But first you have to understand what makes a stock price go up and down.

When I ask people, "What makes a stock price go up?" they tell me stocks go up because interest rates go down. Or stocks go up because the company has higher earnings. Or stocks go up because they hired a better CEO. Or stocks go up because the dollar went up against the yen. Or a million other reasons, all of which are wrong.

Stocks go up for one reason and only one: They go up only because more money wants to buy than wants to sell. As I stated clearly in Chapter 1, today, of the $17 trillion in the United States stock markets, over $14 trillion is from pension funds, banking funds, insurance funds, and mutual funds. As a group, these are known as the institutional funds. They're usually quite large — typically investing over $1 billion. So, as a group, they *are* Mr. Market. They control the price of any stock they're investing in. If they put more money in, the price goes up. If they take their money out, the price goes down.

What all this means for you is that even a business that's on sale for 50 percent below its Sticker Price *could go down some more* in the short run if the fund managers keep selling it, *even though, rationally, it shouldn't*. Please remember that Mr. Market isn't rational all the time. As Ben Graham taught us, in the long run the market is a weighing machine giving us the correct weight (price) for every company. But in the short run the market is a voting machine that's fully capable of casting votes based on emotion and not reason, giving us the wrong voting result (price) for *any* company. What's more, institutional fund managers act nothing like owners of companies. They don't buy with the long-term success of businesses in mind. They only really care about the short-term success of their businesses — how much they can make in the current quarter.

The reason Mr. Buffett must take short-term losses in his long-term businesses if they go down in price is that he cannot easily get out of a business he has billions invested in. Recall what he said in the 2004 letter to shareholders: *Our huge positions add to the difficulty of our nimbly dancing in and out of holdings as valuations swing.*

If Mr. Buffett can't "nimbly" get in and out, how long does it take for other big guys? Amazingly, the average size of a trade on the New York Stock Exchange in 2005 was 345 shares! (Source: Mohammed Hadi, "Tracking the Number," *Wall Street Journal*, June 10, 2005.) That's

👉 The price of a stock isn't altered one penny by world events, higher earnings, firing a CEO, losing a patent, or anything else. Events themselves don't change the stock price; institutional money moving into and out of the market *in response to* these events is what changes stock prices. Think of events that appear to affect stock prices as proximate causes—the signals that bring about change. None of these events matters in the short-run price of the stock because the only thing that changes the stock price today is what the institutional fund managers as a whole do. If they sell, the price goes down. Obviously, these proximate events can and do affect the decision by the institutional fund managers to buy or sell the stock, but in the end the price of that stock goes up or down only because of increased or decreased institutional investing.

FYI: Part of the reason the stock market has surged in the past 25 years is that fund managers (the movers and shakers of the institutional funds) through the 1980s and 1990s had more money coming in from retirement accounts than anyone in the history of the stock market had ever seen. The managers had to invest it in *something.* They poured in that 401k money and stocks went up. (Big surprise there.) They went up because there was more money chasing stocks than ever before.

about $5,000. Not all that big, is it? Can you imagine how long it takes to buy or sell $2 billion when you do it in $5,000 chunks? That's 400,000 trades. Let's say I own 10 million shares of XYZ Company. At 345 shares per sale, it's going to take me 30,000 separate trades to get out. That could take weeks to execute without causing undue alarm in the market. But if I try to sell in a few big trades, other fund managers will see all the extra selling and they'll panic, start selling, and the price will drop so fast it could wipe out the profits I'm trying to hang on to by getting out in the first place.

Let me use an analogy so you can see the problem these big guys have. Imagine you're sitting in the middle of a packed theater. You smell smoke. Do you run for the exit, or do you quietly make your way to the door? Obviously, if you start running and others smell smoke, too, you could set off a panic and never get out. So you don't do that. You try walking quietly, taking as much time as you need to get to the door. But others smell smoke, and no matter that you're only walking, they get up and start walking, too. As more and more people try to leave, the exits get jammed and nobody gets out without being burned.

That's exactly what happened with Enron. When it was priced at $60, there were about 500 funds investing billions in it. Some fund managers started smelling smoke and headed for the door. Quietly. In an orderly way. And the stock responded to this quiet selling by sliding slowly over the next four months from $60 to $30. No panic. No gaps down. Just steady, quiet selling. And all 500 funds still had money in the stock, although some had less than when it was at $60. But now there was a lot of money headed for the door, and some of the fund managers started worrying they weren't going to get their funds all the way out. And the smell of something wrong was getting stronger. The selling became less quiet and the stock price dropped in one month from $30 to $9, but there were still 500 funds invested because it was getting harder and harder to find big buyers for all those blocks of stock. And then there was a full-on stampede for the exit by all 500, and in one night the price dropped from $9 to $0. And no one got out whole. Now there are still about 500 funds waiting for the bankruptcy court to sort through the burned building for any loose change.

TOOLS

So what do we do? We first recognize that we're not geniuses. We're river guides and homemakers and business managers and teachers and lawyers and candlestick makers. Second, we recognize that we're not big. We're little. We, unlike Mr. Buffett, have no trouble at all "nimbly dancing in and out." We should exploit our size advantage.

It takes a typical fund manager about six to twelve weeks to get fully invested in a stock or to get completely out. But how long does it take you and me to buy all of any business we want? About eight seconds. And nothing happens to the price. And we can get out in eight seconds, too, without affecting the price. Considering that the price of a stock goes up because the fund managers buy in with massive amounts of money, and similarly the price of a stock goes down when they sell out, how cool would it be if we could see them *moving* the money? Then we could get right in front of them as they begin to make their moves.

Think about that for a second. If they're going to take six weeks to quietly buy enough stock in this business, all the while driving the price up, what if we could see them doing that? Would that give us an advantage? The answer is YES!

Ready for this? Geniuses actually built a set of tools that track the flow of money in and out of every stock, mutual fund, and index fund in the market. Those tools were built for the pros. (Did you actually think anybody would bother to build such tools for the little guy with $5,000 to invest? Nobody even wants to be your broker if all you have is $5,000!) But, surprise, surprise, the Internet came along and all of a sudden *we* have access to professional tools, too. And here's the big shocker: You and I — the little guys — can use these tools far better than the big guys can. Ready to learn?

I'm going to select three carefully chosen computer programs that watch every trade in the business we're interested in. These are what I call my "Three Tools," but they aren't such a great secret. Almost every professional uses these Tools in some form or another, if only to check out what's going on with his competition. They're available on almost every online broker's website for free. If your broker's site doesn't have them, you can find them on Yahoo! Finance or MSN Money.

What these Tools do is tell everybody when the big guys are buying IN or selling OUT of any business. That's because the big guys are more than 80 percent of the market. (If they were only 15 percent, as they were back in the 1950s, this wouldn't be so effective. But since they control the market and move slowly compared to us, these Tools give us plenty of advance warning when something is changing in the flow of money in or out of any Rule #1 stock.)

These Tools are great for two reasons:

1. They lower our risk of losing money.
2. They eliminate ERI.

What the heck is ERI? It's my Emotional Rule of Investing, which says:

If you buy this business, immediately after you buy it, the price will go down, down, down.
But if you don't buy it, the price will go up, up, up until you do buy it . . . at which time the price will then go down, down, down.

Just as online insurance quotes and car buying guides like Edmunds.com have changed the world of insurance and car buying forever by giving us consumers—the little guys—insider knowledge about how much we should spend on insurance and a car (new or used), so, too, these investing tools have changed the way we make sense of the market, offering us an advantage we never had before. What these tools do is allow us to make smart decisions about our investments—and get ahead of the game in many ways, even if we're up against an entire industry filled with self-serving "experts." As Levitt and Dubner so eloquently state in their book *Freakonomics,* the raw power of information is enormous: "Information is a beacon, a cudgel, an olive branch, a deterrent, depending on who wields it and how." As a group, stockbrokers and fund managers previously derived their power mostly from hoarding information—keeping it from us or making us believe we couldn't understand it. God bless the Internet! Once that information fell through the Internet and into our hands, we suddenly had a few chips to play with, and much of the financial pros' advantage had disappeared. As Levitt and Dubner put it, the Internet "has vastly shrunk the gap between the experts and the public." That's good for us, and luckily it doesn't take a genius to understand how to use these tools, either.

You may have to download or register for advanced Tools on MSN Money and Yahoo! Finance. For example, at MSN you must download (for free) its "Advanced Investor's Toolbox," which is easy to do and gives you immediate access to more than just one type of Tool. Once you've got MSN's deluxe investing Tools working on your computer, when you click on "Charts" on the left-hand menu bar, you'll be able to pull up all of the Three Tools that I'll cover in the next chapter. (At Yahoo!, the Tools are also found under "Charts" on the left-hand menu. You may also need to create an ID and a password to maximize what you can see. This is all free.)

While onstage at the Cow Palace, the arena near San Francisco, I was talking about the institutional investors and the magic wand they could wave over the market. After explaining how they have more than 80 percent of the money in the market, and therefore control the prices of all stocks, I asked the audience a rhetorical question: "So who makes the market go down?" The answer, of course, is that it takes big money to make a stock go down, so it's the institutional investors who control the stock price. But a guy in the front row said, "I do. Whatever I buy goes down. It must be me." This is ERI.

We must get rid of ERI, because we must be willing to invest when others are afraid. And we must be willing to sell when everyone is telling us it can't go down. In other words, as a general principle, Rule #1 investors buy when others are fearful and sell when others are greedy. If you get caught up in ERI, no matter how wonderful the business is, if you're a novice investor (heck, maybe even more so if you're an experienced investor), you're going to second-guess yourself and stay out when you should get in, and get in when you should get out.

The Four Ms all by themselves give us a checklist to follow that gets us a long way toward eliminating ERI. If we understand the business and can get it at a great price, we've eliminated all the rational excuses not to buy a given company. Now we just have to eliminate the irrational excuses, the emotional excuses. The ERI. And I do that with my Three Tools.

In the next chapter, I'll show you how to use those Tools to determine when to get in and when to get out. Or, in other words, when to grab the stick.

 Points to remember:

1. Big investors (the ones who control the pension funds, insurance funds, mutual funds, and so on) control the market but have to turn slowly, like big cruise ships. Their movements are so huge that they're easy to see.
2. Little investors (you and I) can turn quickly like Wave Runners. Our movements are fast and small, so that we're invisible.
3. Tools tell us Wave Runners the direction the cruise ships are turning so we can get ahead of them in their path, and also see when they're turning so much that they can't turn back—and have left a big (destructive) wake in their path. The Three Tools keep us out of that wake so we don't lose money!

Chapter 12

The Three Tools

Any sufficiently advanced technology is indistinguishable from magic.
—ARTHUR C. CLARKE (1917–), FROM *PROFILES OF THE FUTURE,* 1961
(CLARKE'S THIRD LAW)

THREE TOOLS in particular are very useful once we've identified a wonderful business that passes all Four Ms and we want to buy. These Tools help us have the courage to "grab the stick" from Mr. Market, which is a good thing because we don't want Mr. Market to beat us. We much prefer to sleep well at night knowing our money is safe and that we aren't going to lose it because of being too afraid to get out (or get in).

I'm not married to the specific set of Tools I'm about to introduce to you, but these are the ones that work best for me. Also, they're readily available for free at sites like MSN Money, Yahoo! Finance, or on your broker's website. I'll warn you up front that you probably won't find exactly the same charts as you'll see in this chapter (that is, don't go looking for replicas of the charts used for illustration purposes here).

These Tools will look a little different depending on where you're getting them, but you can get the general idea of how you're supposed to use the Tools from the examples I'll present. Once you understand the Tools (some refer to them as "technical indicators") and become familiar with what you're looking at, it won't make a difference how one site's Tools compare to another's. Try not to be intimidated by their technical appearance, and for now don't bother trying to understand their underpinnings. All that's required is that you learn how to *translate* the signals — to know whether the Tools say "buy" or "sell." Interpreting them will quickly become second nature, much as you read different kinds of books. First, though, you must learn to read.

> When you reach a red or green light while driving, do you sit and ponder how those lights turn red or green? No, you know one means go and one means stop, and you follow the command—no questions asked. That's how I want you to approach these technical Tools. Learn how to read the signals to make a move; don't get sidetracked trying to dope out how the signals are generated.

If you grow accustomed to reading one site's Tools, feel free to stay with them. The key is to use a set of Tools you can rely on so that Mr. Market doesn't get a chance to use his stick.

THE POWER OF THE TOOLS

In the previous chapter, when I started talking about the power of these Tools, you may have gotten the impression they've only recently been available. In actuality, they've been around for quite some time, and they're what saved me from sinking with everyone else in 2000 and beyond. But not until the migration of a host of financial research data to the Internet did the functionality of the Tools become what it needed to be for the ordinary small investor. The key for the little guy is we no longer have to do the math. The computer does it for us and then plots the graph derived from the math in a split second, something that used to take hours. Instead of having to calculate the changes created by the day's trading and applying them to a graph of a given stock, and then repeat those calculations and graphing tasks for every business we're interested in, today all of that's done for us automatically. All we have to do is know how to read what the Tools say.

I never bothered to use these kinds of Tools until about eight years ago, when I shifted to doing everything online. A friend said I ought to try them out, so I took a class and really liked what I learned. I didn't see much difference in 1998, but then again, everything I bought was going straight up. In August 1999, these Tools signaled me to get out of the market, the market dropped, and I didn't lose any money. I thought that was pretty nifty. Then, in October 1999, the Tools signaled that the big guys were getting back into my businesses, and I jumped back in with them and sat back in astonishment as the market went straight up in spite of the dire warnings of computer collapses and Armageddon coming on January 1, 2000. No way would I have had the nerve to be in the market with all those warnings except with Tools that told me clearly the big guys were moving their money into my businesses. Then, in March 2000, the Tools signaled that the big guys were getting out again. Big time. So I sold off everything and watched in amazement as the whole market started to drop like a brick. When you've been through as big a drop as we went through in 2000–2003 and didn't lose any money while everyone else was getting slaughtered, you become a believer. These Tools are an invaluable aid for the little guy who's doing Rule #1 investing.

A student of mine asked me, "Doesn't my fund manager have these Tools, too, and if he does and they're so good, why did he lose half my money from 2000 to 2003?" Good question. Sure, your fund manager has these Tools. They were built for *him*, remember? (As I said in the previous chapter, don't think for one minute these awesome Tools were built for you and me. Get real! What's ironic—and surprising to fund managers—is that the small novice investor can use these Tools better than the pros.)

The problem for your fund manager is one we've already explored: He's moving so much money around that he *is* the Tools. It takes millions of dollars moving in one predominant direction to change the Tools to where they'll say "buy" or "sell." But your fund manager is moving millions, if not billions, and in doing so changes the signals that the Tools give off. It's very hard to watch these Tools for signals to get in or get out if you're the one creating the signals! If your fund manager starts getting in (and remember, it can take your fund manager weeks to buy in), the signals change. But if he waits until the Tools tell him to get in, then it's too late because it's going to take him too long to move that much money. By the time he gets all the way in, the other big guys who started first and created the change in the Tools will be selling and taking their profits.

If you have any doubt about this, you can see how it works firsthand by putting $50,000 into a micro stock—something that trades 50,000 shares a day at 10 cents a share. Go buy 500,000 shares and see what happens to the signals these Tools give off. You'll see every Tool shout "BUY!" as you start to buy your shares, and then you'll see the price skyrocket from 10 cents to 15 cents to 20 cents before you even get going! By the time you're done buying, the price might be 80 cents. Looks great until you start to sell. Again, you'll see that you're changing the Tools, except now they shout "SELL!" to the rest of the world, and suddenly there are no buyers and the price of the stock will drop all the way to 3 cents before you get out, *if* you get out at all. Do this just once and you'll appreciate just how hard it is for a fund manager to invest billions and why, with the exception of Rule #1 guys, almost no one beats the market for 20 years or more.

Okay, so let's see what the Tools are and how to use them. And let's take them one at a time.

MACD

The first Tool in our kit is the MACD — moving average convergence divergence. Quite a mouthful, eh? Developed by an economist, Dr. Gerald Appel, the MACD is probably the most consistent indicator of significant trend changes in a stock, and it's certainly the most commonly used technical indicator in the world. Essentially, what it does is look at several price average changes over time, generally in the short term. It shows us when momentum pressure is getting stronger either upward or

> The MACD is the combination of two moving averages—a fast one and a slow one—and how they interact (how they converge and diverge).

downward—like a gauge on a fire hose. Since most of the money in the market is institutional, in effect the MACD shows us when the big guys are sneaking in or sneaking out.

Using the MACD—learning how to read it for the sole purpose of knowing whether to buy or sell—is a lot simpler than understanding the mechanics behind it. The MACD uses moving averages (MAs). A moving average is the average of the price over some time period. Every day after the closing prices are in, the moving average is recalculated. If we're using a ten-day moving average, the average price over the last ten trading days is calculated and plotted on a chart as the latest point on the continuous ten-day moving-average line. (Most MACDs use an exponential moving average to get a smoother line that takes out unnecessary bounces up and down. These are called EMAs: exponential moving averages. More weight is given to more-recent data on an EMA than on an MA.)

The MACD uses three EMAs: a slow EMA, a fast EMA, and the "trigger" EMA. Dr. Appel's research determined that the best slow (or long time period) EMA is the 26-day EMA, and the best fast (or shorter time period) EMA is the 12-day EMA. His MACD computer program calculates the two moving averages exponentially and then calculates the difference between the two. This number is the MACD plot point for that day. That alone, however, is not enough. In addition, he found that when he plotted the 12-26 MACD for the day against the nine-day EMA, the two lines crossed on occasion. His research showed that when the MACD crossed above the nine-day EMA, the stock was very likely to continue to go up in price, and when it crossed below the stock price, it was likely to continue to go down. He called this crossing point the *trigger point.* It's called that because when the MACD line crosses the nine-day EMA line, the crossing triggers a "buy" or "sell" signal for us. Thomas Aspray added a histogram (representation of frequency distri-

bution) to the MACD that shows the crossing in terms of valleys, which become mountains at the zero line so we can more
easily see the trigger point coming. I have grown fond of one
of Dr. Appel's revisions to the 12-26-9 MACD, which is the
slightly faster and more responsive model—the "8-17-9" MACD.
MSN defaults to the 12-26-9, as do most sites, but since I'm
searching for stocks that are going to move up rapidly in price,
this more responsive MACD captures more of the upward
moves and makes me more money.

As I just mentioned, I think of the MACD as similar to a gauge on a
water hose that tells us the pressure in the hose. If the pressure is going
up, someone is pushing more water into the hose. If the pressure is
going down, someone is turning off the water. Just like that, if the
MACD "gauge" is moving up, someone big is pushing more money into
the stock, and if the MACD "gauge" is going down, someone big (or
many big someones) is taking a lot of money out of this stock. Here's a
picture of a typical MACD chart:

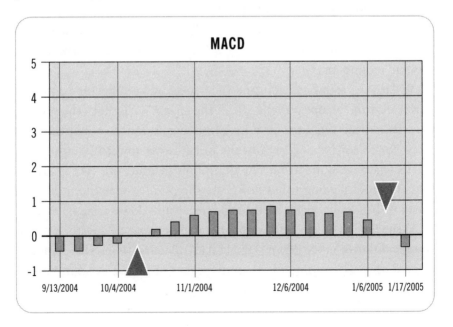

You can buy charts that are easier to read than this, but this one is free from MSN, so we'll use it. First, let me explain what you're looking at (refer to the box on pages 200–201) for a brief explanation of how an MACD works).

The chart on page 201 covers the period from September 13, 2004, to January 17, 2005, about four months. The line at number 0 is called the *trigger line*. The chart looks like a histogram valley below the trigger line, and a histogram mountain above the trigger line. The valley and the mountain are histograms graphing the 8–17-day MACD against the 9-day trigger line. The triangles point to the time when the MACD crosses the 9-day EMA, or trigger line. This chart reveals that moment graphed as a histogram showing a trigger for buying or selling.

On most MACD charts, you'll also see the MACD as a line and the trigger as a line. When the two lines cross, that's also the trigger point. On those charts the lines cross at the same time as the valley turns into a mountain. You don't need both, since they say the same thing, but some investors like the crossing-lines view, and others like the mountain-and-valley view. Below the trigger line and parallel to it is the timeline, which is why you see dates. I don't use the numbers above and below the trigger line. They're used for more complex analyses than we need. You need to know how to read this chart for purposes of one thing only: spotting where the money is going — in or out of this business. And all that requires is that you be able to spot the shifts between valleys and mountains.

What's the significance of the valley beginning to become a mountain (I inserted an upright triangle at the spot)? Well, that's the precise point when the big guys have been moving so much money *into* the stock for so long that a significant price move upward is imminent. That's when we want to buy. At that point in time, our risk is lowest that the stock's going to go down. At the point where the mountain starts to become a valley (I inserted an upside-down triangle at that spot) the big guys have made enough movement *out* of the stock that a significant price move down is likely. And of course when that happens our risk that we're going to lose money goes up, so we get out. Simple enough.

Beginning of a mountain, time to buy.
Beginning of a valley, time to sell.

Here's the catch: When consulting an MACD chart on a website, you'll find there's more than one way to look at it. You can, for example, change the settings on the chart so it plots the mountains and the valleys more quickly or more slowly. Think of it like changing the pressure gauge on that water hose. You can make it more or less sensitive to changes in pressure.

To imitate how I like to view an MACD chart, you need to configure the MACD in a particular way, namely by plugging in three specific numbers. Understand that you can use any MACD with whatever numbers it already has in it by default, but the signals change if you change the numbers. If you want to use these Tools the way I do, you need to program them just a bit differently from most defaults. Find the place on the website where you can change the defaults. At MSN Money, if you select MACD and click the "Settings" bar, it looks like this:

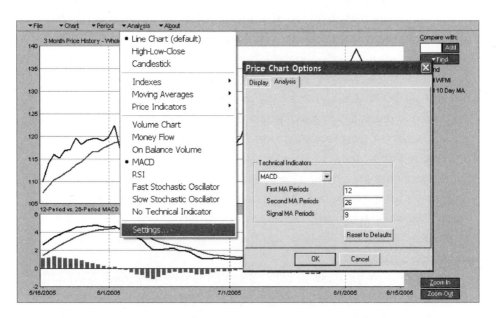

Now you can change the settings from 12-26-9 to 8-17-9. When you change those numbers, it makes the "gauge" more sensitive. I prefer it like that because I don't mind getting in or out and then reversing myself a couple of days later if it switches and heads in the other direction. It's up to you how you use these Tools. Believe me, there are lots of opinions among experts about how to manipulate them. If you want to get into technical trading, you can take lots of classes and buy sporty proprietary software. But for our purpose of getting a solid foundation in Rule #1 investing, the way I'm showing you here is going to work just fine.

Of course, we don't use just one Tool. We want *multiple* confirmations that the big guys are getting in or getting out. Hence, more backup Tools.

Can you find the Tools? If you're having a hard time finding them at either MSN or Yahoo!, it may be a result of not having downloaded an application that's totally free but that your computer needs to run for you to access and view all the financial data. If, for example, when you input a ticker symbol on MSN Money, click on "Charts" on the left-hand menu, and don't see the ability to view all three Tools, your computer is missing the advanced tool set. At this point you may be prompted to download the application because your computer will sense you're trying to access information you can't see. At this writing, Yahoo! doesn't allow you to manually change the settings on the MACD Tool like you can do on MSN. But it does allow you to view different moving averages, timelines, and other indicators.

Whether you've got a high-speed Internet connection or not, it won't take you long to get the program downloaded. At Yahoo!, you may need to create a user ID and password, which is also totally free, to view all of its financial research tools. All of Yahoo!'s tools are found under "Charts," and specifically under "Technical Analysis" on the left-hand menu bar on every stock page.

To ensure you can access all the available information on a site like MSN or Yahoo!, it also pays to keep your browser up to date by downloading its most recent version.

STOCHASTICS

The second Tool in our kit is the Stochastic, developed by Dr. George C. Lane. This is a momentum tool that tracks the overbuying and overselling of a stock. Overselling occurs when a big institutional guy starts selling and others join in. That creates a lot of downward price pressure, which can generate a lot of short-term institutional concern; translate that as fear. When that happens, other institutional guys wait until they think the stock is as low as it's going to go and then start buying. When they do, the Stochastic Tool sees that and tells us to buy. Here's a sample Stochastic chart:

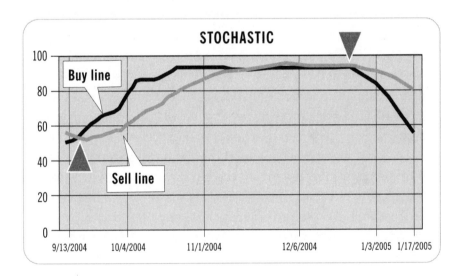

One of these lines is called the "buy line," and the other is called the "sell line." When the buy line crosses and gets on top of the sell line (I inserted an upright triangle), the Stochastic is signaling that the stock is going from oversold (too many sellers) to overbought. Time to buy. When the buy line crosses back (I inserted an upside-down triangle) it's the signal that it's now overbought (too many buyers) and heading for oversold. Time to sell. Nothing to it.

Buy line crosses up, buy. Buy line crosses down, sell.

The Stochastic looks at the high price and the low price of a stock over some period. Dr. Lane's research indicated that 14 trading days was best. The computer program he developed finds the high and the low price over 14 trading days and calculates how the current day's closing price sits in that range as a percentage. A score of 57 on the Stochastic means that in a range of zero being the lowest score over the last 14 trading days and 100 being the highest score over that time, today's price was in the 57th percentile, or about midway. All by itself that's not so wonderful except that Dr. Lane, and many researchers since, found that when the price went below the 20th percentile the stock was getting oversold—too many sellers and not enough buyers. Then when it moved up through the 20th percentile it often meant the big guys were starting to seriously buy and the price was likely to go up as it came out of an oversold condition and moved toward more normal trading. After the price moved well above the 80th percentile, the stock was going into an overbought condition—too many buyers and not enough sellers—and then as it dropped below the 80th percentile it often meant the big guys were seriously taking profits and the price was likely to drop. At MSN the Stochastic line is plotted against a five-day EMA that provides trigger points when they cross. This view of a Stochastic provides a warning of a trend change a bit earlier than the 20th to 80th percentiles.

As with the MACD, you can program how you prefer to view the Stochastic—how sensitively you want the signals to operate. Stochastics can be viewed in either a "fast" mode or a "slow" mode. I prefer to program the Stochastic for a moderate trading speed so I don't get whipsawed in and out all the time by the indicator (i.e., the slow Stochastic won't give off as many false signals as the fast one). The slow Stochastic that I like the best uses two numbers. The first number covers the number of periods, and I use 14 trading days. The second number creates a moving average to provide a trigger point. I like a five-day moving average. The default at MSN is 5-5, which I find makes way too many triggers. So the two numbers we'll use are 14-5. On the left of the chart are percentages. When the Stochastic line crosses up through the 20th percentile it's a positive signal, and when it crosses down through the 80th percentile it's a negative signal. That signal is usually preceded by a crossing of the 14- and 5-day lines as an early warning that change is in the wind. That's our buy sign. The 20th to 80th percentiles are just confirmations.

MOVING AVERAGE

The third Tool that I love to use is called a *moving average*. This Tool tracks an average of price during a specific time period. There are a lot of technical traders out there who trigger their buying and selling with a moving average. The moving average smooths out the peaks and valleys of daily price fluctuations and gives traders an easy view of the price trend. (Technical traders don't even think about what a business is worth. All they want to know is whether it's going to move up or down based on these or similar indicators. They're throwbacks to the EMT era, when investors were taught that all businesses were priced correctly all the time. That being the case, reason the technical guys, fundamentals are useless and all that matters is moving faster than anyone else.)

Moving averages are simply closing prices over a defined number of days divided by that number of days.

Specific moving averages are a kind of psychological barrier to the price of the stock moving up or moving down. You can think of them as a kind of floor or ceiling on the price. As the price goes above the moving average, it's breaking through the psychological ceiling by creating a new short-term high price, and that's a signal the attitude toward this stock has gotten positive. If it goes the other way, breaking through the floor, the attitude of the market has turned negative. And again, you have to control the settings on the website you're using for research by indicating at what speed to set the moving average.

At MSN you get two choices: 10-day and 50-day. I like to use a 10-day moving average because, unlike the MACD and Stochastic, I want this Tool to give me an early signal. The reason is that the moving average is usually the last signal to say "Buy" or "Sell," and by setting it to a fast speed, it syncs up better with the other two Tools.

The black line here represents the stock price, while the gray line represents the moving average. As the price line crosses the moving average line (I've inserted an upright triangle), that's the point when the stock price breaks through the ceiling and the psychology of the market turns positive. That's a buy signal for us. When it crosses the other way (I've inserted an upside-down triangle), that's the point where the price breaks through the floor and the psychology turns negative. Time to sell. Easy to follow.

When the price line crosses above the moving average line, buy. When the price line crosses below the moving average line, sell.

These three Tools cover the market trend, the market momentum, and the market psychology. They're all available on the Internet from lots of websites you can subscribe to, or you can get them free on virtually any online brokerage website, but they may be harder for you to read. Depending on where you get the Tools, it's going to take some time playing with them to get used to reading them all together. I suggest you do a lot of pretend trading, "paper trading" as it's called, which I'll explain shortly. Paper trading gives you an opportunity to use the Tools and become confident they're fantastic for doing one thing: keeping you from losing money.

Since you're new to using technical indicators (and if you aren't, lucky you; you already know how useful these Tools can be) we're going to keep it simple: When *all three* Tools are saying "buy," it's time to get in. When *all three* are saying "sell," it's time to get out. (Yes, wait for all three to give the signal.) The chart on page 210 shows Starbucks as an example of what can happen when you have a wonderful business selling at an attractive price with all three Tools saying "get in".

Notice that the first Tool to say "get in" was the Stochastic on September 20. The way we configure the Stochastic often makes it the early-warning signal. The next day, the moving average said "Get in" because the price made a new short-term high above the average — but we had to wait for the MACD. We just stay patient and check the chart sometime every day or night until we get all three signals saying "Get in." In this example it took two weeks for all three to say "Get in." At that point, by October 7, 2004, the MACD finally crossed the trigger line and all three Tools were telling us to get in. The price was $49.

Assuming we've done our Four M homework and we have a nice big MOS at $49, we buy it. No emotion, no guessing. We know our business, we know the big guys are getting in, and so we get in with them. From that point on, all we do is check this chart every day looking for

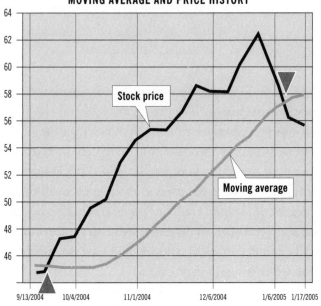

STARBUCKS CORP.
MOVING AVERAGE AND PRICE HISTORY

Stock price

Moving average

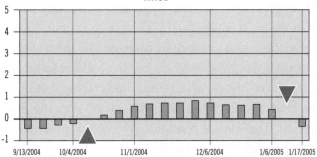

MACD

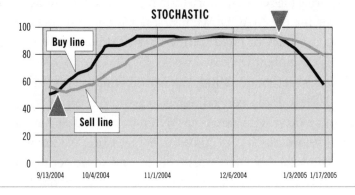

STOCHASTIC

Buy line

Sell line

the signals to get out. How long does checking it take? About 15 seconds — then it's time to go play. Nothing else to do. In this case, we check it every day through October, November, and December with no change. Then, at the end of December, we get our first signal to get out from the Stochastic.

Now we're really paying attention, since we don't want to give back any more than we have to (but at the same time, with only one negative signal, the stock could continue to run up, so we sit tight and watch to see what happens). The price is dropping, not a great sign, and then in January 2005, the other two Tools cry "Get out!" at about $57. And out we go. That single trade gives us a nice gain of 16 percent over a three-month period. And the best part is we did that without the risk of Starbucks' stock price dropping like a brick while we watched helplessly, guessing and wishing and hoping it would go back up. (After we got out, the price indeed dropped like a brick from $57, where we got out, to a low of $46 before it headed back up again.)

TOOLS ALONE WON'T MAKE YOU ANY MONEY

I get asked all the time, *If these Tools can tell us when to buy and sell, why do we need to do all this Four M stuff? Why not just buy and sell on the signals from the Tools?* Here's why: In the long run I feel confident you won't make money with Tools unless you know the value of the business you're buying. Remember that in the short run anything can happen to the price of a business, but Mr. Market has a set of scales and will properly weigh each and every company and give it its correct price at some point.

If you ignore the Four Ms and accidentally buy businesses that are priced above their value, the prices of those businesses will eventually correct themselves downward toward the Sticker Price. So, in spite of short-term trends, momentum, and psychology to the contrary, the longer-term trend, momentum, and psychology are going to be downward, as sure as there's gravity.

People who buy and sell based solely on these kinds of Tools find themselves losing a little here and a little there over and over as the price of the stock corrects downward toward its real value. Trying to use Tools to trade a stock that's headed down is like death by a thousand little cuts. You can lose half a percent or 1 percent or 2 percent only so many times before it starts to really add up to a shellacking. These Tools are fantastic at keeping you from losing money *if* you are buying businesses at prices below their value, the Sticker Price.

In my humble view (backed up by a few heavyweights like Mr. Buffett and Mr. Graham), the only way to make money with certainty in any kind of investment is to buy it well below its value. Doing that will make you very rich without taking the risk of being very poor. That's much more attractive to me than spinning a roulette wheel. I like certainty, and want to do everything I can to make sure I have it in my investments.

But what if you make a mistake and don't buy the business well below its value? What if you goofed on the EPS growth rate or the PE? What if you're actually (with 20-20 hindsight) buying at the top? Even then, the Tools will protect you far better than guessing and wishing and hoping.

In 2000, Apple was too difficult to understand and the Big Five were too inconsistent for me to figure out its Sticker Price, but it's a great case in point for how effective these indicators can be at getting you out of any stock. If you were winging it and buying Apple in September 2000, the business was priced at $30 (split adjusted) per share (reaching a high of $32 on September 8). During the last week of September, all three of the Tools said "Get out!" so what would you have done? You would've gotten out. The price continued to drift down, and two weeks later the business was selling for $28 per share.

Then Apple announced that it was going to miss all of its projections for the quarter and the year was going to be a lot worse than projected. It made this announcement after the close of trading, which is typical, so no one could buy or sell until trading opened the next trading day. When the market opened up the next morning, a lot of institutions wanted to sell Apple stock. But there were no buyers at $28. Zero. And there were no buyers at $27 or $26 or $20 or $18. There were no buyers at all until the stock got down to $13 a share. From there it continued to collapse on down to $7 by mid-December.

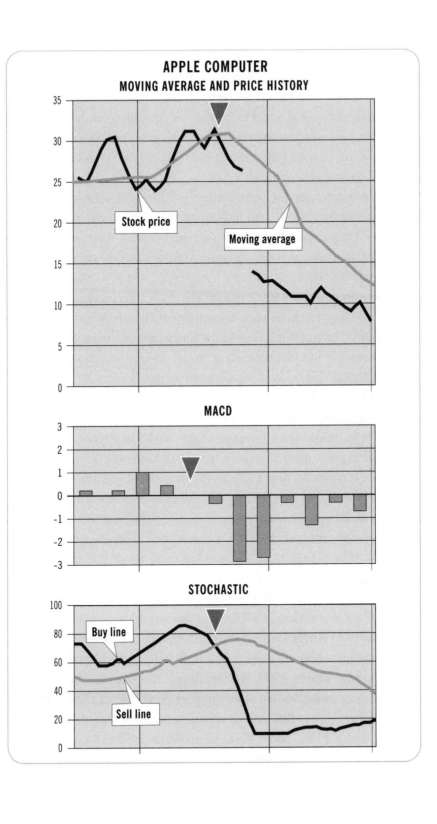

The lesson here is clear: If you'd had these Tools and used them, you would have gotten out at about $30. And if you still liked Apple as a Rule #1 stock—remembering that you have to understand the company before you buy it, and I'm not sure anyone understands Apple except Steve Jobs—but assuming you felt like you understood and could put a value on it, you could then buy it back for $8. That's how we use the Tools to protect ourselves.

As a side note, isn't it interesting that the Tools all said to get out two weeks before Steve Jobs announced the bad news? If you didn't know anything about these Tools, you might think they were psychic. But now you know who causes the signals to change: your fund manager and all the other institutional investors. These guys have billions in Apple, so do you think they talk to the guys who are high up in the company? Do you think they take them to baseball games and the Super Bowl? Do you think they know the names of the execs' kids?

I'm guessing the institutional guys call up the Apple execs and say, "How're things this quarter?" and the execs say, "Uhhhhh . . . well . . . I can't really talk about it. . . ." And the institutional guys hang up the phone and turn around to their computers and start the process of selling a whole truckload of Apple stock without anyone suspecting they're doing it. And that takes time. They know if the news is really bad they aren't going to get all the way out clean, but the earlier they start, the more of a jump they'll get on the guys down the street at that other fund. Of course, if they're asked on CNBC how they like Apple, they're going to tout what a great company it is. And when the reporter sticks the mike in their faces and asks the really tough question, "You're hyping Apple, do you own it?" the institutional guy will look sheepishly at the camera and say, "You got me. Yup, we own it." But what he's thinking is, *And I'm going to sell it to you, you moron.*

These Tools will get us out of a stock before it crashes, because the big guys almost always get an early hint that things aren't going to be so good, and start selling. Their selling triggers the Tools and we are outta there. Then, down the road after the dust clears, we can buy the stock back cheap. Those Rule #1 students who understood Apple well enough to buy it used these Tools to get out at $30 and back in at $8, and as a result they have seen their investment go to $40 from $8 in four years. That's a 500-percent return and a 50-percent compounded ROI. You can get rich doing that.

LITTLE REGRETS, BIG GAINS

If you decide to become a Rule #1 investor and learn to use these Tools, you might have a lot of little regrets about businesses you couldn't value, only to see them go through the roof. I have a friend who likes to point out the high fliers I miss because of my Rule #1 discipline. But I don't have any big regrets. Rule #1 and these Tools put me in cash well before the crash started in 2000. My friend doesn't invest in stocks anymore, and although I haven't asked why, I can guess he didn't know the difference between overpriced and underpriced businesses, and he didn't have any Tools telling him to get out.

The take-home point here is that the crash of 2000–2003 might be a mini-preview of what's coming. Again, who knows for sure what the market will do, but whatever it does, if you follow Rule #1 and use these Tools, you can grab Mr. Market's stick before he hits you with it. And then you'll have *all* of your money available to buy these great businesses back at fire-sale prices.

In the next chapter we're going to combine Rule #1 and the Tools and put it all together in one place.

Chapter 13

Take Baby Steps

Ideas are like rabbits. You get a couple and learn how to handle them, and pretty soon you have a dozen.

—JOHN STEINBECK (1902–1968)

YOU'VE LEARNED why you have to invest your own money: because the big guys can't. You've learned that the great secret of investing is simple: Buy a wonderful company at an attractive price. You've learned about the Four Ms, which help you identify and confirm a wonderful company at an attractive price.

You've learned there are two times to sell a wonderful company: when the Big Five show a breach in the Moat or when the price is above the Sticker. You've learned that the big guys control most of the money in the market and take weeks to move the money in and out of specific stocks. And you've learned about the three specific Tools (MACD, Stochastics, and Moving Averages) that can be utilized to know when to get in and when to get out. You've come a long way. Now the question is: Are you going to do it?

Here's the answer: Sure, if you go slowly, step by step. That's what I'm going to do in this chapter. We're going to take baby steps.

EXAMPLE FROM 2003, START TO FINISH

Remember Susan and Doug Connelly from Chapter 1? They were the couple who decided that if they really wanted to retire comfortably in 20 years, they'd have to do more with their money than just compound it in a treasury bond. Susan and Doug represent a lot of people who come to me in workshops trying to learn how to apply The Rule so they can begin reaping that golden 15-percent yearly return. They're middle-aged, with a combined income of about $60,000. They have kids still in school, a mortgage on a nice home, they like to travel, and eating out (a lot) is a form of entertainment. But one thing they don't have is a lot of extra money working for them—at least not so much that they can count on a comfortable retirement in 20 years. Susan and Doug have $20,000 in an IRA account, and they think they can contribute about $500 a month into that account. They believe they need about $4,000 a month in addition to Social Security to continue to live the way they are doing now.

Their big problem, what drove them to learn about Rule #1 investing, is that if they invest their nest egg with fund managers, they could easily see a zero rate of return in 20 years if the market doesn't go up. That means the Connellys would be trying to live on Social Security and a nest egg of about $150,000 (derived from their initial $20,000 grubstake and the $6,000 per year in savings accumulating over 20 years). The $150,000 invested in something safe like a T-bill once they retire will produce only $500 a month income without touching the nest egg. Not a pretty picture if they need $4,000. They'll be selling their home, leaving their friends in that neighborhood, and downsizing their lives in a huge way.

If, instead of investing with fund managers, they invest in a treasury bond for safety and a guaranteed return, they'll have about $235,000 to retire on, with an income of $800 a month. Still far from a good situation if they need $4,000.

The only other alternative (before they learned about Rule #1 investing) is to speculate on a piece of real estate or maybe in a commodity like gold. Speculation is paying the price Mr. Market is charging, without any idea of what the Sticker Price is, and then hoping someone will come along in the future and pay more than you did, also without regard to the real value. But the Connellys both know speculation is a gamble that could lose them everything, and neither of them is comfortable taking that kind of chance. Thus, Rule #1 investing seemed to offer a ray of hope in an otherwise bleak and scary financial picture.

Let's follow the Connellys through the steps of Rule #1 investing and see how they used Rule #1 in 2003 with that initial $20,000, and how they're doing by mid-2005.

Step One for a Rule #1 investor is always to decide what kind of business you'd be proud to own and that you understand. Remember the first M: *Meaning*. So Doug and Susan start by thinking about the Three Circles: Passion, Talent, and Money:

The websites I'll use to do the research for this example are Yahoo! Finance and MSN Money. Both are free.

They agree that the one thing that comes up for them on all three circles is restaurants. They love to go to restaurants of all kinds, they think they're really good at picking restaurants that will succeed, and they spend their money in restaurants as a form of recreation. Simple. True, they admit they've never owned a restaurant in the past and don't know the ins and outs of running a restaurant, but they also know they don't need to make this hard; they just need to stick to what has Meaning to them and what products or services they understand. The Connellys dine out so much, and approach the experience so much like a wine lover who discrimi-

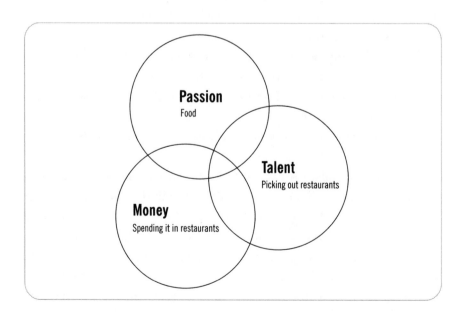

nates among fine wines, that they're confident they'd be able to make good decisions in the industry from a consumer standpoint.

The restaurant business is where they start diving into Rule #1. They go online to www.yahoo.com and on the top of the page they click the button for "Finance." There is a major heading called "Analyst Research" and below that is "Sector/Industry Analysis." This page comes up:

They click on the "Services" sector and get the list of industries shown on page 220. In the *R*s is "Restaurants." (If they weren't sure which sector includes restaurants, they could just click on any of the sector names and see if the industries that are listed are similar to restaurants. In a couple of minutes they'd find their way to the right place.)

Yahoo! My Yahoo! Mail

YAHOO! FINANCE **Sign In**
New User? Sign Up

Industry Center | Industry Index |

Industry Browser - Services Sector - Industry List

Enter symbol:
symbol lookup [_____] [View Industry]

Sectors > Services

Click on column heading to sort.

Description ▣

Sector: Services

Publishing - Periodicals
Railroads
Regional Airlines
Rental & Leasing Services
Research Services
Resorts & Casinos
Restaurants
Security & Protection Services
Shipping
Specialty Eateries
Specialty Retail, Other
Sporting Activities
Sporting Goods Stores
Staffing & Outsourcing Services
Technical Services
Toy & Hobby Stores
Trucking
Wholesale, Other

They click on "Restaurants" and get a list of businesses we all recognize. Here's a small piece of it:

Yahoo! My Yahoo! Mail

YAHOO! FINANCE **Sign In**
New User? Sign Up

Industry Center |

Industry Browser - Services - Restaurants

Enter symbol:　[　　　]　[View Industry]
symbol lookup

Sectors > Services > Restaurants (More Info)

Click on column heading to sort.

Description ▣

Sector: Services
Industry: Restaurants (More Info)

Boston Restaurant Associates I (BRAI.OB)
Boystoys.com Inc. (GRLZ.OB)
Brinker International Inc. (EAT)
BUCA Inc. (BUCAE)
Buffalo Wild Wings Inc. (BWLD)
California Pizza Kitchen Inc. (CPKI)
CBRL Group Inc. (CBRL)
CEC Entertainment Inc. (CEC)
Centerplate Inc. (CVP)
Champions Sports Inc. (CSBR.OB)
Champps Entertainment Inc. (CMPP)
Checkers Drive In Restaurants (CHKR)
Cheesecake Factory Inc. (CAKE)
CKE Restaurants Inc. (CKR)
Cosi Inc. (COSI)
Darden Restaurants Inc. (DRI)
Denny's Corp. (DENN)
Dreams Inc. (DRMS.OB)

They see lots and lots of restaurant-type businesses. They can click on any of these and get a lot of information about the company selected. They see the Cheesecake Factory, and since they like that restaurant, they click on it and get this page:

Cheesecake Factory Inc (CAKE)

MORE ON CAKE

Quotes
Summary
Real-Time ECN
Options
Historical Prices

Charts
Basic Chart
Technical Analysis

News & Info
Headlines
Company Events
Message Board

Company
▶ Profile
Key Statistics
SEC Filings
Competitors
Industry

Analyst Coverage
Analyst Opinion
Analyst Estimates
Research Reports
Star Analysts

Ownership
Major Holders

Profile

Cheesecake Factory Inc

DETAILS

Index Membership:	S&P 400 MidCap S&P 1500 Super Comp
Sector:	Services
Industry:	Restaurants

BUSINESS SUMMARY

The Cheesecake Factory Incorporated (TCFI) operates upscale, full-service, and casual dining restaurants in the United States. The company operates its restaurants under The Cheesecake Factory and Grand Lux Cafe trademarks. The Cheesecake Factory restaurants offer approximately 200 menu items, including appetizers, pizza, seafood, steaks, chicken, burgers, pasta, specialty items, salads, sandwiches, and omelets, as well as desserts, such as cheesecakes and other baked desserts. Grand Lux Cafe offers American and international

They can dig in on CAKE, but before they do, they note that Yahoo! gives them a lot more information about the restaurant industry. For example, one click tells them who the Cheesecake Factory's closest competitors are. Doug clicks on "Competitors." Here's what comes up:

Competitors   Get **Competitor**

DIRECT COMPETITOR COMPARISON

| CAKE | EAT | Pvt1 | DRI | Industry |

EAT = Brinker International Inc
Pvt1 = Carlson Restaurants Worldwide, Inc. (privately held)
DRI = Darden Restaurants Inc
Industry = Restaurants

RESTAURANT COMPANIES RANKED BY SALES

Company	Symbol
McDonald's Corp	MCD
Yum! Brands Inc	YUM
Darden Restaurants Inc	DRI
Starbucks Corp	SBUX
Autogrill S.p.A.	Private - \
Brinker International Inc	EAT
Wendy's International Inc	WEN
KFC Corporation	Private - \
Whitbread Group PLC	Private - \
Outback Steakhouse Inc	OSI

Just like that, they now have a whole bunch of similar companies to analyze to see if any of them meet the first M requirement. Just by clicking on restaurant symbols and then on their direct competitors, Doug and Susan can create a list of restaurants that have Meaning to them — that they like a lot and would be proud to own. They narrow the list down simply by thinking which restaurants they understand well enough to know why these particular businesses can continue to grow. Their list includes

1. CAKE: The Cheesecake Factory, Grand Lux Café
2. LNY: Landry's (Rainforest Cafe, Chart House, Joe's Crab Shack)

   3. DRI: Darden (Red Lobster, Olive Garden)

   4. EAT: Brinker International (Chili's, Macaroni Grill, Maggiano's)

(If you were doing this exercise, your list might include a different set of potential businesses. One key aspect of Rule #1 investing is that the first M means it's *personal*. It's up to you what you like and don't like. In other words, don't make the mistake of looking into buying businesses *other* people like.)

So far, these all look to Doug and Susan like wonderful companies that have Meaning to them. What to do next? They have to dive into the Moat.

As a Rule #1 investor, Susan knows that the Moat is critical to being able to predict the future. So the first question she and Doug discuss is what kind of a monopoly creates the Moat for these restaurant businesses. They refer to the Five Moats: *Brand, Secret, Toll, Switching,* and *Price.* The restaurant business is not based on secrets, you don't have to pay a toll to get a burger, and it's no big deal to switch restaurants. Some restaurants compete with a low price, but not these five. That leaves *Brand,* and sure enough, all of these restaurants are recognizable brands that deliver the expected product to the consumer over and over again. Clearly, these restaurant businesses are attempting to protect themselves with a Brand Moat.

Now Doug and Susan want to look at the Big Five numbers to confirm that the Moat is in good shape for each business. They can get some of the Big Five numbers on Yahoo! Finance, but MSN Money has ten years of numbers, so that's where they go (Susan clicks on www.msn.com/money). She wants to look at the most important Big Five number to confirm the Moat: ROIC. After getting into MSN Money, she plugs in the first symbol on the list: CAKE. And she gets this page:

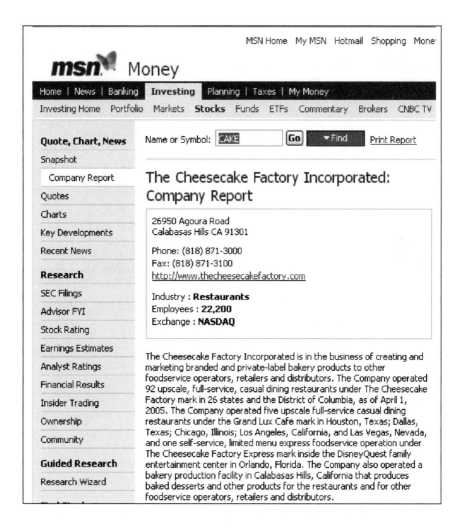

Now she clicks on "Financial Results," then "Key Ratios," and then finally she clicks on "Investment Returns":

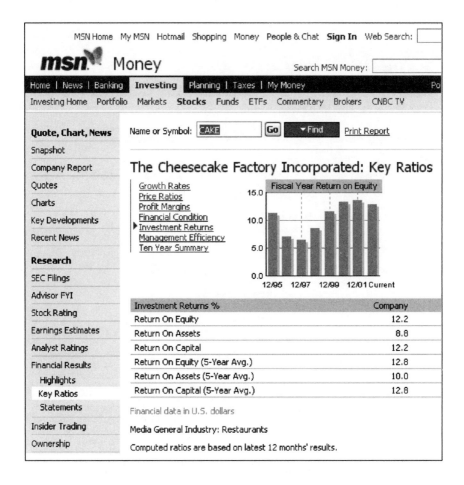

She sees "Return on Capital." That's our ROIC number. They have five-year and one-year ROIC: 12.8 percent and 12.2 percent. These are good (they are above our 10 percent minimum). ROIC is showing a big Brand Moat.

Now on to equity growth rate. Remember that according to Mr. Buffett, it's the single best substitute for the growth rate of the Sticker Price (which he calls "intrinsic value").

Reminder: Don't misunderstand the difference between what raw equity numbers mean and what equity growth *rates* mean. To determine Moat and MOS, we don't really care about how low or high the equity numbers are, but we care a lot about how low or high the equity *growth rates* are. Those are very different things.

For example, in mid-2005, McDonald's had a market cap of $42 billion with an equity value of $14 billion, while Google had a market cap of $86 billion with an equity value of $3 billion. ("Market cap" is defined as the price per share times all the shares—in other words, the actual "buy-the-whole-thing" price.) Google was priced twice as high as McDonald's, with less than one-quarter the equity. Obviously, market price isn't arrived at by looking at total equity. On the other hand, market price eventually seems to have a strong relationship to the equity growth rate. McDonald's equity growth rate for the last ten years has averaged about 7 percent a year while Google has been growing its equity at over 100 percent a year. That means McDonald's is increasing its surplus cash at a very slow rate while Google is increasing its surplus cash at a very high rate. The equity growth rate for any business is defined by growing surpluses, and surpluses are what a business makes that's valuable.

If I earn $20 per share in my lemonade stand, but I have to replace the tables, the juicers, and the warehouse space with that $20 per share, I, as owner, don't get to keep the $20. It isn't surplus. So what good is this business to me? It ain't worth nothing if it doesn't make anything I can keep. If I have to spend the profits just to stay in business, I'm not a happy owner. On the other hand, if I didn't have to buy that stuff with my $20 per share and the business could still produce a surplus next year, then I can let the business spend this year's surplus on advertising to grow the business so that next year I won't make $20, I'll make $30 per share. Surplus gives a business the cash to grow,

(continued)

> which is why businesses typically grow at about the rate that their surplus grows—i.e., the equity growth rate. If McDonald's is going to grow at only 7 percent a year and Google is going to grow at some insanely huge rate per year, Google could easily be worth double McDonald's today.

Even though Susan can click on "Growth Rates" to view the one-year and five-year average growth rates for sales and EPS, she really wants to see what the equity growth rates have been. This requires a little Rule of 72 work on her part (which she can then verify online with my calculators). So she clicks on "Ten Year Summary" and sees (among other columns) a column for book value per share and a column for PE:

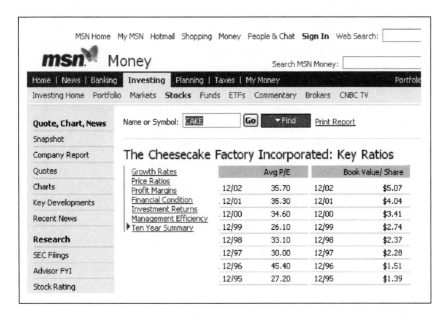

Book value per share is the same as equity. The numbers only go back to 1995, so we're going to see what the growth rate is for seven years. To get the growth rate, Susan rounds the oldest BVPS number, 1.39, to 1.40, then doubles it until it's close to the 2002 BVPS of $5.07:

- First double: 1.40 to 2.80
- Second double: 2.80 to 5.60.

Can't make sense of a company's free cash flow? Understand that when a company decides to put money toward capital projects, such as building more stores in new locations, its free cash flow can take a dive. That's not necessarily a bad thing. *Operating* cash flow is the leftover cash from a business's operations at the end of the period. It doesn't include cash from loans or selling stock, and it doesn't deduct cash spent to maintain the business. *Free* cash flow, on the other hand, is what's left over once the managers spend what's necessary to maintain the business. Since an ideal Rule #1 business doesn't spend a lot of cash to maintain its operations, free cash flow should be similar to operating cash flow in a potential Rule #1 company. But there are lots of exceptions and you shouldn't fuss over it.

So, when you're trying to decide whether a company's free cash flow struggles are serious or not, look into its "Operating Cash Flow" data and see if those numbers show consistency. You can calculate the growth rates of a company's operating cash flow as you do its free cash flow and compare. If operating cash flow is growing, you can just glance at the free cash flow and not worry so much about it.

Also keep in mind that the "priority" of the numbers—from most important to least—goes like this: (1) ROIC; (2) equity growth rate; (3) EPS growth rate; (4) sales growth rate; and (5) free cash growth rate. Always view the cash flow (whether it's "Free" or "Operating") within the context of the other Big Five numbers.

Doug and Susan decide that there's so much consistency, there must be a good brand Moat.

They also know they're going to use the Big Five to decide an appropriate EPS growth rate for the next ten years. Based on their understanding of the restaurant industry, Doug and Susan don't see any limit to CAKE's ability to continue growing as it's been doing for the last seven years, which, according to sales and EPS and book value, is to grow at over 20 percent a year. Deciding on a historical growth rate number from the Big Five is really just an educated guess. The key is that the guess shouldn't be a close call. Doug shouldn't guess that sales will grow at 28 percent or that equity will grow at 25 percent. They are ballparking this number, but need to keep it well within the ballpark.

Doug suggests they use the nine-year equity growth rate — 19 percent. Susan points out that 19 percent might be too conservative since equity has been growing at 24 percent or more lately, and EPS, sales, and cash are all growing at 20 percent or faster. They agree that the numbers — for the most part — hit at or above 20 percent, and that 20 percent is well within the historical range of the business's ability to grow. As such, they decide that's the historical growth rate they're happiest with.

At this point Susan suggests they look at Management, but Doug suggests that since they've found a good EPS growth rate number, to save time they should find out the Margin-of-Safety Price to see if CAKE is at an attractive price. (He's eager to buy it today if it all looks good.) If the price isn't right, Doug suggests putting off further research and focusing on finding something that's both wonderful and at an attractive price today. And if the MOS Price is available, then they can come back and finish the research on Management.

To do the Margin-of-Safety Price calculation, they need to know the Sticker Price. To figure out the Sticker Price, they need three things:

1. Current EPS — which they know from the company report is $0.64
2. Estimated EPS growth rate for the next ten years — which they are estimating at 20%
3. Estimated PE in ten years — which Susan found has been averaging 35

However, the estimated EPS growth rate is the lesser of the historical rate or the analysts' five-year estimate. To see what the pros are saying about it, Doug clicks on "Earnings Estimates" in the left menu and then clicks on the "Earnings Growth Rates" tab.

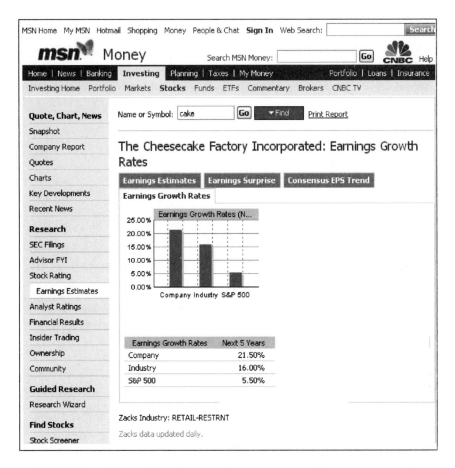

This chart shows him that, on the average, analysts are expecting a 21-percent growth rate, almost exactly what Doug and Susan thought. They congratulate each other on their accurate guess. It's always comforting to see your number match up well with the pros' number.

They also want to confirm that they have the right future PE number. The alternative method of finding the PE is to double the growth rate. Since the growth rate is 20 percent, doubling it gives CAKE a PE of 40. But because the historical PE is 35, they use 35 since it's more conservative. Now they have the three numbers they need for the Sticker Price:

1. Current EPS = $0.64
2. Estimated EPS growth rate for the next 10 years = 20%
3. Estimated PE in 10 years = 35

Susan asks herself how long to double once at 20-percent-a-year rate of growth (20 into 72, or 3.5 years to double once). Since she's doing a ten-year projection, 3.5 years per double means there are about three doubles in ten years. She rounds 0.64 to 0.60 and then does three doubles:

- First double: 60 to 120
- Second double: 120 to 240
- Third double: 240 to 480

She concludes the EPS in ten years will be about $4.80. Call it $5. Multiply $5 times the 35 PE, and she gets $175 per share in ten years. She knows her Rule #1 minimum acceptable rate of return is 15 percent—two doubles in ten years. Hence, to get the Sticker Price she simply divides the future stock price of $175 by four and—voilà—rounds off her Sticker Price to $44. Her MOS Price is half that, or $22 a share.

 Again, today Susan can go to www.ruleoneinvestor .com, click on the Sticker & MOS Calculator, input 10 years, 0.64, 20 percent, and 35 in the appropriate places, click "Calculate," and see the following:

1. Future Value: $150.70
2. Sticker Price: $37.25
3. MOS Price: $18.62

As you can tell, our Rule of 72 MOS is $22 and the accurate MOS is $19. It's better to be accurate, but the Rule of 72 gets you into the ballpark if you want to be self-reliant.

Doug checks the price that CAKE is selling for that day: $18.40. A few dollars below the MOS Price. Perfect. Now Doug and Susan are getting excited. They've found what appears to be a wonderful business, and it's available today at a very attractive price. They see a dollar of value available for 50 cents.

Time to dig in on Management.

Doug clicks on "SEC Filings" on the menu and quickly gets the latest company filings. He's looking for the annual report to the SEC, which is called a 10K Annual Filing.

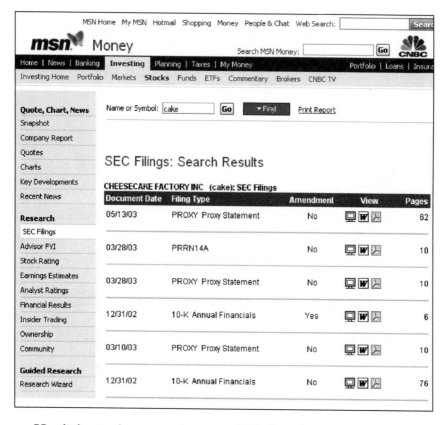

He clicks on the report (see page 238). In it he reads all about how the business got started, how they run the business, who their competitors are, all the risks of the business, management's discussion of operations — and, most important, who's running this enterprise.

Doug reads that the chairman and CEO is David Overton, who cofounded the business with his parents in 1972. Susan knows it's a good idea to invest with people who run the business as if it were the only thing that's going to feed their family for the next 100 years. So investing with the founders is a good start. Susan goes on the Internet and finds a lot of articles about Mr. Overton. She learns he went to law

employees worked in our corporate center and restaurant field supervision
organization. None of our employees are currently covered by collective
bargaining agreements, and we have never experienced an organized work
stoppage, strike or labor dispute. We believe our working conditions and
compensation packages are generally comparable with those offered by our
competitors and consider overall relations with our employees to be
favorable.

Trademarks

We have registered, among other marks, "The Cheesecake Factory",
"Grand Lux Cafe", "The Cheesecake Factory Bakery", "The Cheesecake Factory
Express", "The Dream Factory" and "The Cheesecake Factory Bakery Cafe" as
trademarks with the United States Patent and Trademark Office. Additional
trademark applications are pending. We have also registered our ownership
of the Internet domain name "www.thecheesecakefactory.com" and other names.
We regard our trademarks as having substantial value and as being important
factors in the marketing of our restaurants and bakery products. We have
registered, or have pending applications to register, one or more of our
trademarks in more than 70 foreign countries, although there can be no
assurance that our name and marks are registerable in every country for
which registration is being sought. The duration of trademark registrations
varies from country to country. However, trademarks are generally valid and
may be renewed indefinitely as long as they are in use and/or their
registrations are properly maintained, and they have not been found to
become generic.

Executive Officers

David Overton, age 56, serves as our Chairman of the Board and
Chief Executive Officer. Mr. Overton co-founded our predecessor company in
1972 with his parents.

Gerald W. Deitchle, age 51, serves as our President and Chief
Financial Officer. Mr. Deitchle has over 26 years of executive and
financial management experience with national restaurant and retail chain
operations. He joined our Company as Senior Vice President, Finance and
Administration and Chief Financial Officer in July 1995.

Michael P. Berry, age 54, joined our Company in July 2002 as
President and Chief Operating Officer of The Cheesecake Factory
Restaurants, Inc., our largest restaurant subsidiary. Prior to joining us,
Mr. Berry served as President of Barnes and Noble Booksellers. His prior
experience also includes service as a senior operations and foodservice
executive with The Walt Disney Company, Harvard University, the University
of California at Irvine and the University of California at Los Angeles.

CHEESECAKE FACTORY INC   Filing Date: 12/31/02

Peter J. D'Amelio, age 41, was appointed President and Chief
Operating Officer of our Grand Lux Cafe restaurant operations in October
2002. Mr. D'Amelio joined our Company in 1990 and steadily advanced through
our operations organization, with his most recent position as Senior Vice
President of Restaurant Operations.

Max S. Byfuglin, age 57, serves as Executive Vice President of The
Cheesecake Factory Bakery Incorporated, our bakery subsidiary. Mr. Byfuglin
joined our bakery operations in 1982 and worked closely with our founders,
serving in nearly every capacity in our bakery over the past 20 years.

---

school in California, became a successful rock-band drummer, and then
joined his folks in their small bakery business, designed a unique business model around his mom's cheesecake, and in 1972 they opened a
restaurant. The rest, as they say, is history.

Doug finds particularly interesting a quote he finds in an article about Overton: "But Overton says there's still much more work to do in safeguarding and promoting his business model. He remains unwavering in his determination that his concept's compelling mix of customer-pleasing qualities will not be diluted or impeded by corporate growth priorities."

In other words, the guy running CAKE isn't willing to screw up the Brand Moat just to meet the big guys' demands for growth for growth's sake. That's the view of a man with 100 years of success on his mind. Doug thinks that makes Mr. Overton a Rule #1 kind of manager— someone who's thinking long-term and for the good of the business and will not be driven by growth for growth's sake. That's music to a Rule #1 investor's ears, because we want to know this is still going to be a great business ten years from now; otherwise we can't predict earnings growth, and if we can't do that . . . we can't get Sticker or MOS Prices.

Susan and Doug read everything they can find on Mr. Overton and The Cheesecake Factory, looking for reasons *not* to buy this business, but they don't find any. Everything written about the Management and the business looks good. Time to see what Mr. Overton's been writing about his business.

They go to the CAKE website and read Mr. Overton's letters. He makes the point that "the only true limiter in accomplishing our annual growth goals is our ability to attract, train, and retain the quality people needed to manage our restaurants." He then goes on to explain how the company is dealing with that problem. Also, he explains how they're going to grow: Growth is going to come from expanding the number of Cheesecake Factory locations, and he believes the business can easily sustain 20-percent-plus growth for years. The fact they have a ten-year average investor return of more than 26 percent doesn't hurt Susan and Doug's confidence in the projection.

Susan and Doug decide CAKE passes the Four M test.

One down. Now they want to see if they can find an even better business to buy.

The next one on their list is Landry's. Susan types in its symbol, "LNY," and quickly goes to "Key Ratios" to evaluate ROIC.

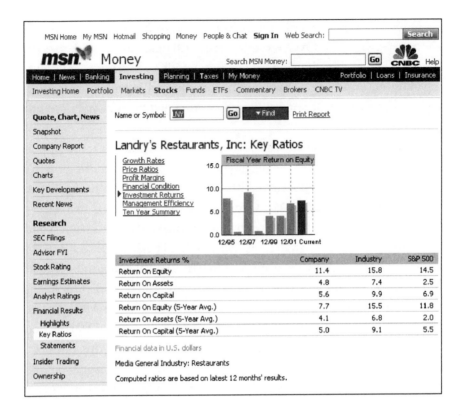

Landry's has a five-year ROIC of 5.0 percent and a one-year ROIC of 5.6 percent. These are low. Sadly. This ROIC isn't showing a big Brand Moat at all. This is a big red flag for Doug and Susan, and a deal killer. Too bad. It doesn't mean that Landry's won't be a great stock and make someone millions of dollars, or that it's a bad business for the long run. Maybe there are great reasons why the ROIC is too low, but Doug and Susan aren't MBA hotshots who love doing research. If it doesn't fit The Rule, that's the end of the story for Landry's. But there's a good lesson in doing this type of Rule #1 analysis: Remember to start with the most critical number — ROIC. If it isn't 10 percent or better, we're outta there without having to crunch a lot of numbers. Here's the order of analysis for the Big Five:

1. ROIC — if 10% or better, go on to . . .
2. Equity — if 10% or better, go on to . . .
3. EPS — if 10% or better, go on to . . .

4. Sales — if 10% or better, go on to . . .

5. Cash — if 10% or better, go on to . . . Management and MOS.

Next business.

Darden Restaurants (DRI). ROIC is good, but equity growth rate is 6 percent. Next business.

Brinker International (EAT). ROIC is good. Equity growth rate is 9 percent. Not good. And EPS in the last five years has slowed to an under-10-percent growth rate.

Doug and Susan have found one business that passes the Four M test: The Cheesecake Factory. They have $20,000 to invest right now. Now what?

Homework is done. It's almost time to buy, but first Doug wants to check what the insiders in CAKE are doing. Doug goes back to MSN Money, puts in CAKE, clicks on "Insider Trading," and sees that there's no significant insider trading. Nice.

MEASURING INSIDER TRADING

Use common sense when gauging whether some insider trading is a red flag or just a routine and harmless transaction. If many executives in a company are unloading 30 percent or more of their stock, I'd see that as a bad sign. Both MSN Money and Yahoo! Finance reveal how much each officer owns when it comes to company stock. While on the main stock page of any company, go to "Insider Trading" at MSN for this information, or refer to Yahoo! Finance's data under "Ownership," which contains links to "Insider Transactions" and the "Insider Roster."

Now Doug clicks on "Chart" to see if the institutional fund managers are buying or selling right now. He and Susan know that no matter how wonderful the business is, and no matter how great the Margin of Safety is, if the big guys are selling, it's going to go down even more.

The three charts (the MA, MACD, and Stochastics) for CAKE in

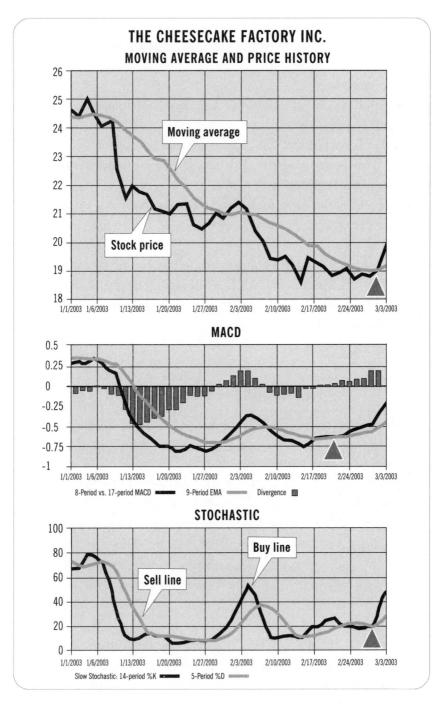

(Note: We can actually only see either the MACD or the Stochastic at any one time on MSN Money, but for clarity I put them together here.)

early 2003 show Doug and Susan that all three Tools are saying "Get in." That fact leaves Doug and Susan with no choice. CAKE is a Four M wonderful business at an attractive MOS Price, and the big guys are getting back in. The Connellys have already put their $20,000 into an online brokerage account. Now they put in a market order for 1,000 shares of CAKE, which will execute when the market opens the next day.

At 9:31 a.m., East Coast time, their online broker buys 1,000 shares of CAKE at $18.90. And here's what happens over the next two years:

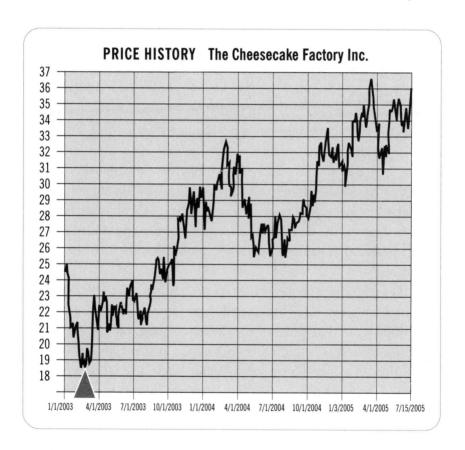

By getting in just below $19, and then moving in and out 11 times in two years with the big guys, and by adding in $500 a month they were saving, by July 2005, CAKE gives Doug and Susan a nice compounded rate of return of 56 percent per year, and their $20,000 is now worth

$78,000. Pretty good for two years. This is, of course, an incredibly high rate of return. Doug and Susan know that 50-percent-per-year rates of return are unlikely to continue for long periods of time. They also know they'd be criticized by almost all financial planners for not diversifying their portfolio. They have one stock, and everybody knows that's more dangerous than owning 50 stocks. Everybody except Rule #1 investors.

Granted, now that they have almost $80,000, they should be looking to spread that to a few other businesses, but only when they really do understand the industry, which entails learning about another industry. After two years, they feel comfortable they won't lose money in CAKE even if it starts to go down and they're now waiting for the other businesses they've found to be available at a great MOS Price. In that sense, as of the middle of 2005, they're in very good company. Mr. Buffett has about $40 billion in Berkshire Hathaway in cash and he's waiting for the same thing—an opportunity to buy another wonderful company at an attractive price.

The best part of what Rule #1 is doing for the Connellys is this: Now they know that 15 percent a year is well within their reach all through retirement. And that, my friends, changes everything for them because it means the size of the retirement nest egg they need to accumulate before they can quit working is much smaller than they originally thought.

If they continue making at least 15 percent with the $80,000 they now have, in just 10 years they'll have grown their nest egg to $323,000. From that time on they'll be receiving, on average, about $4,000 a month by continuing to bank 15 percent annual returns, which they can spend without touching their $323,000 nest egg. Instead of retiring badly in 20 years, they may be able to retire well in just 10. That's a huge motivation for them.

And there's one more bonus for the Connellys. Since they really don't expect to quit working for another 20 years, if they continue their savings and Rule #1 investing, by the time they retire, they'll have grown their nest egg to almost $1,500,000. From that point on they'll have to figure out how to spend an investment income of more than $220,000 a year. That's $18,000 a month, more than $500 a day they can spend instead of $500 a month. What a huge difference that'll make in their retirement. Instead of worrying about how to pay the electricity bill, they'll be discussing which Caribbean island to winter on and which country in Europe they want to take the kids and grandkids to next summer.

I hope you're anxious to get started yourself, even if you still feel a few steps behind the Connellys. That's okay. We have a few more lessons to help you find the baby steps you can take next. And in the next chapter we'll cover some of the natural barriers you must overcome before you can begin.

Chapter 14

Eliminate the Barriers

Money is better than poverty, if only for financial reasons.
—WOODY ALLEN (1935–)

BY NOW, if you've been following along, you may have found at least one business that has Meaning to you — that you would be proud to own and that you understand. In fact, let's assume you have. You've identified the Moat and confirmed it with the Big Five. You've researched the Management, Googled the company, and read the articles, and also gone to the company's website and read annual reports and the CEO's letters. You've calculated the Sticker Price and the MOS Price and checked that against the price being asked by Mr. Market. You've looked at the Tools to see if the institutional guys have been moving in or out of the stock. Some of you may even have found a business that meets every single Rule #1 criteria and has all three Tools saying "Buy." And now you're thinking about dropping money into a trading account today and buying that business.

Before you leap, though, you need to make sure you've eliminated the five most common barriers to successful Rule #1 investing:

1. Bad debt
2. Taxes on gains
3. Over-diversification
4. Your fund manager
5. Fear

GET RID OF BAD DEBT

The first barrier to success is bad debt. Yes, there's good debt and bad debt. Good debt is money you borrow at a low rate of interest, with which you make a high rate of return. This idea goes by the name of OPM (other people's money) or *leverage*. An obvious example is the money you borrow to buy an apartment complex. The debt is covered by the rental income — or it will be in a few years. Bad debt, by contrast, is consumer debt—money you borrow at a high interest rate to buy things that don't produce income or grow in value. Things like cars, refrigerators, clothing, and trips to Europe. All of us have done it, and all of us have paid the price. The price of bad debt is the impact of compounding rates of return working *against* you instead of *for* you. If you have credit cards or bank loans costing you 18 percent or more a year, that's 18 percent compounding against your retirement. Since Rule #1 is all about not losing money, the first thing most of us must do to become successful Rule #1 investors is to pay off bad debt.

Think about it: If our target rate of return for The Rule is 15 percent and we have credit card debt we're paying 18 percent on, essentially that means we're borrowing money at 18 percent and making only 15 percent on it. Even though we're doing well as a Rule #1 investor, we're going backwards at the rate of 3 percent compounded per year. That's a heck of a barrier to successful investing. The only way you'll get rich that way is to hit the lottery. Otherwise, you're going broke with great certainty. But notice that if we turn that around and take the money we were going to invest and instead pay off the 18-percent-interest-rate debt, then instead of losing 3 percent a year, now, even if we don't have any money left to invest, at least we're breaking even and we're not violating Rule #1. And as long as you don't violate Rule #1 and you keep on practicing, learning, and saving, you're going to be rich one day.

There's good debt as a Rule #1 investor, too. If you can borrow money at 4 percent and you're an experienced Rule #1 investor who can compound money at a consistently high rate of return, say 16 percent, it makes sense to borrow. If we can pay 4 percent and make 16 percent, we're using leverage to accelerate the overall rate of return on all of our money. So here are the three guidelines for taking on debt. Only consider taking on debt (or keeping it) if:

1. You're an experienced and successful Rule #1 investor.
2. The interest rate on the debt is less than 33 percent *of your expected rate of return*. For example, if you expect over 21 percent, you can borrow at 7 percent.
3. The total debt that you carry (not including your house and car) can be paid off in less than one year of savings from your income after you pay for all your monthly stuff.

That said, taking on debt to accelerate your overall rate of return is "advanced tactics," and I hate to even mention it here for fear of encouraging you to do it. Don't. Unless you *really know* what you're doing, just stay out of debt—or focus on getting rid of your debt first. While doing so, you'll still be able to practice and master the Rule #1 technique by paper trading, which I'll explain below. Simulating real trades using Rule #1 while not actually having real money in the market is extremely important for the beginner. It'll give you all the training you need so that once you have your debt cleared away, you'll be ready to jump in and get going. Soon enough, you'll be generating riches instead of debt. How cool is that?

TAXES

If we could just buy and hold, there wouldn't be a tax issue. Unfortunately, we're not geniuses enough to know the stock can't go lower, and Mr. Market is far too irrational to be trusted. So we use the Tools, get in and out with the big guys, and avoid the danger of holding in a market that can crash. Great. Except now the Feds can tax us. As much as possible, it's our duty as good citizens who intend to take care of ourselves in our wobbly old age to avoid paying taxes whenever it's possible to legally do so. In fact, our government has seen fit to provide us with a vast array of tax loopholes we can use to defer taxes. These loopholes are called SIMPLE IRAs, Roth IRAs, SEP IRAs, 401ks, and

DON'T EAT THE SEED CORN

A lot of people spend all their income on living expenses and, as a result, don't have enough to retire today and won't have enough to retire tomorrow, either. Back in the old days, farmers would say, "Don't eat your seed corn." Seed corn is what farmers save to plant next year to get a crop to live on in the future. If you eat the seed corn, you may live well this year, but then you could have huge problems next year. A lot of you need to take a lesson from the farmers, because you're eating your seed corn.

If you want to retire in 15 years but your lifestyle eats up all of your income, what do you do? You make some hard choices and take action:

Choice 1. Study and learn The Rule while you get another job and make $500 a month extra to put in an IRA, then start practicing The Rule and banking 15 percent.

Choice 2. Study and learn The Rule while you cut down on your expenses by $500 a month, put the savings in an IRA, and then start making 15 percent under The Rule.

Here's the good news: Once you learn Rule #1 and can make 15 percent a year, the total amount of money you'll need to retire is going to be a much smaller pile than you thought. A Rule #1 investor who is okay with a $50,000-a-year lifestyle needs only $300,000 to retire. Even with $0 saved today, a Rule #1 investor who can save $500 a month will have $300,000 in less than 15 years.

If you'll do that, you can retire in 15 years with $50,000 a year income for the rest of your life. And if you have $50,000 right now (the average for a baby-boomer family) you can retire in ten years or less.

You can do this.

Just don't eat the seed corn.

Defined Benefit Plans (among others). We can even set up a trust that'll defer taxes for us.

Since I'm a river guide and not a tax attorney or CPA, I'm not going to advise you about how to set up these plans. I will tell you I'm not a huge fan of the 401k programs because most of them force you to invest in mutual funds. The only time a 401k is better than an IRA is when the company you work for is matching at least 50 percent of the funds you put in there. In that case, take the free money, but put in only the amount they're going to match. Beyond that point, open up an IRA and max it out, because you can do Rule #1 investing in an IRA that's self-directed. Roth IRAs are tax-free forever! You put the money in after you pay tax on it, and it grows inside the Roth tax-free, and then when you retire and take it out, you never have to pay tax on the gains. I like that one. That's the one my kids have, because they're in a very low tax bracket and will be for some time, so it makes a lot of sense to jam as much into a Roth as they can after tax, and then never pay tax on the gains.

Any online brokerage can tell you over the phone how to set one of these up. It's easy and takes about five minutes. They can also show you how to roll over a 401k that's no longer being matched by your employer. Some of the plans have a very limited amount you can put in, and are of much more use to people in their twenties than to people in their fifties. (Your accountant can help you determine which one is best for you, as well as how much you can allocate to it on an annual basis.) But plans like a SIMPLE IRA are excellent — you can pack away a huge amount every year tax-free if you qualify. The key thing is to get the money into a tax-deferred or tax-free account.

Obviously, not all of the money all of us are able to invest is in a tax-free account. Some of us have more money to invest than Uncle Sam lets us put away in a retirement account. Some of the money you're investing might be in a taxable account. Let me summarize my feelings about taking your profit versus leaving it in the business for the long term to avoid short-term taxes. You can do the math and convince yourself that staying in for the long term is clearly the better choice, but I don't stay in.

The reason I don't is that a stock market that's been overpriced for as long as this one may be in for a serious crash sometime. It doesn't have to happen, because the past does not necessarily predict the future, but it certainly *can* happen, and if it does and you're in for the long haul, the long haul just got very long indeed. If you ride a stock down from $100 to $20 in a serious market meltdown, that stock has to go up 400 percent just to break even. Wouldn't it make more sense from a risk perspective to just pay the taxes and take your gains off the table every time the big guys start to get out? Up to you.

I think it's criminal that I can't roll my gains over into another business in some reasonable amount of time. Why doesn't Congress understand that every time it strips away 40 percent of my gains to pay for their little boondoggles, it removes from the investment pool capital that creates jobs? Congress seems to get it with commercial real estate. You can roll that over in a 1041 exchange. So, if you can do that in real estate, why not in businesses? I never saw a society get rich by building apartments and skyscrapers. Wealth is created by businesses that create products that make our labor more efficient. So how crazy is it to penalize investors in businesses and encourage investors in real estate? Real crazy.

DIVERSIFICATION

A word about diversifying yourself. The idea gets a lot of play on TV, but it's usually badly done and vastly overrated. You already know how I feel about diversifying in the market. It's for the ignorant, which you no longer are, so you're not going to diversify by buying 50 stocks. Dumb. And you're not going to diversify by buying one mutual fund made up of 100 stocks. Dumb. Dumb. You're going to focus your money on a few businesses that have Meaning to you. Do not buy some tech biz you don't understand so that you're "diversified" and if tech goes up you'll make money. We don't play that game even if as great an investor as Jim Cramer is urging us on.

I love Jim Cramer, and I love his show. If you really enjoy all this, I encourage you to watch him. You'll hear some great commentary about investing, and even though he doesn't call it Rule #1, he's a fundamentals guy and that puts him in the same ballpark with us. Cramer does it his way because he's Cramer. The guy is holding about 50 rules in his head that he learned as a hedge-fund manager, but if you didn't already know it, Jim Cramer is one very smart guy. Way smarter than I am. He's smart enough to know a lot about a lot of things. Me, I'm only smart enough to know one thing: Rule #1.

The other difference between us is that Jim can be in the market all the time. Me, I'm in the market only some of the time — and then only when the big guys are moving my way. And Jim is very up front about the time commitment to invest the way he does it. Ain't gonna be no 15 minutes a week, my friend. He tells you it's going to take about five hours a week to handle the minimum research load, Cramer-style. Now, you know Cramer loves what he's doing. Be hard to miss that! But, frankly, not all of us are all that excited about stock investing. Some of us just want to go fishing and still be able to make 15 percent a year. If that's you, you're Rule #1 all the way! Rule #1 investors put in the research to learn a few businesses very well.

It's okay to put all of your eggs in one basket. Just watch the basket.

There's another kind of diversification: diversification across asset groups. Cash is an asset group. Real estate is an asset group. Equities are an asset group. Bonds are an asset group. For me, I consider my investments in the public stock market to be both the cash and equities groups because I can get my money out of the market in seconds. Investments in real estate and private businesses are far less liquid, and much more difficult to turn into cash immediately. Bonds, to me, are a short-term place to store cash. I prefer U.S. government short-term T-bills. Anything longer than a year or two has a lot of market risk associated with it. Bonds are for when I can't find any businesses to buy and there's too much cash sitting in my trading account for comfort from an insurance point of view. You won't have that problem for a while.

But that's about it for my level of diversification: cash and businesses, short-term government bonds, and, of course, some real estate. Three groups.

I used to own a *lot* of real estate. A lot more than I own now. That was before I learned how safely I could invest in equities with The Rule and the Tools. Since then, I've cut back on real estate mostly because

I'm lazy and real estate can be like real work. I had to manage property managers, deal with mortgage bankers, keep track of income and expense reports, and in general I couldn't see the difference between owning a lot of real estate and running a real business. Both of them are *work.* As you know, I'd rather be riding my Harley. So today what real estate I do have I pretty much forget about. I'm going to give it to my kids.

And the rest of the money is working in Rule #1 investments, most of which are completely liquid.

Because most financial planners are not Rule #1 investors, they often recommend changing your asset mix as you get older to lower your risk. They have their special formulas for asset allocation, such as "When you're 30, you should have everything in equities, and when you're 60, you should have x percent in bonds, no matter what." But for a Rule #1 investor, age doesn't matter. As long as you're thinking clearly, you can invest in the stock market. And you've seen the difference in the way you live when you compound your retirement nest egg at 15 percent versus 4 percent—especially once you retire. As a Rule #1 investor, you can retire earlier and you can retire better, as long as you follow The Rule.

SAYING GOOD-BYE TO YOUR FUND MANAGER AND HELLO TO FINANCIAL LITERACY

Like the Simon and Garfunkel song says (sort of), there are 50 ways to leave your fund manager . . . and set yourself free. Remember, your fund manager wants to keep your money. (That's as important a part of his job as finding investments for the fund.) So does your broker and any other financial services professionals who happen to have their hands in your pockets. They're going to make an argument as follows:

1. You don't know what you're doing.
2. You don't have any experience.
3. Investing, like brain surgery, is best left to the professionals.
4. Nobody beats the market anyway.

5. For the amateur, 15 percent a year is very unlikely, so don't try.
6. If the pros can't do it, you certainly can't.
7. If you could do it, everybody would be doing it.
8. Who is this Rule #1 guy anyway?

Think about it like this: Centuries ago, little guys like us lived as peasants in villages in Europe. Each village had a guy who read our letters and wrote replies. He was literate. Certainly he was held in awe. He could read and write. If you asked him if *you* should learn to read and write, he might chuckle and pull a heavy bound book off the shelf and open it and show you the intricate Latin designs on the page that somehow made sense to him, but to you were no more enlightening than the patterns of stones on a beach. He might have said, "Certainly, you could learn if you had the *time*. But it does take teachers and tools like this book—both of which are very expensive. I doubt you could afford it, even with your fine job as associate smith in the stable. Also, the writing's in Latin. Do you understand Latin, *tu assimus dumbus*? Besides, you don't need to do it. That's what I do for you, and I'm happy to do it. If you need something read, just bring it and I'll see to it immediately. After all, I'm here for you."

And off you'd go, putting out of your head any thought of reading and writing, chalking up the idea as a silly fantasy and a waste of time. A few years later, though, Gutenberg would come along and invent a technology for getting books into the hands of many, many more people. And soon enough, the notion that the average citizen should be able to read and write would gain currency.

In much the same way, I think financial literacy is on the way, and just by reading this book, you're already a part of that revolution. It's easy, and soon everyone will be doing it. If you continue to practice and learn Rule #1 investing, you'll benefit by being among the first to go on your own (excluding, of course, the very small group of investors who've been practicing Rule #1 for decades). I get asked all the time what would happen if all of the world's investors took their money out of the hands of mutual fund managers and invested it on their own, as if something terrible might occur. Owning a business is not a zero-sum game. No one has to lose for you to win. Businesses create value out of thin air. Someone invents something, and suddenly an endeavor that used to take ten hours now takes ten seconds. The savings of ten hours of costly labor is wealth. No one had to lose for that wealth to benefit all of us, and if you own the company that figured that out, you win big-time because everyone is going to want that thing, whatever it is, and your business is going to become very large and profitable.

So if all of us investors take control of our own money, all that will happen, if we're Rule #1 investors anyway, is that businesses will stop being priced irrationally, which means it's going to be hard to get a great Margin of Safety when you buy in. But the trade-off will be that Management that's untruthful to owners will not have any investors, businesses that are unethical will not have any investors, Mr. Market may get out of the bipolar psych ward, and our country will benefit from a class of investors who act like owners. Our overall rate of return might drop because it'll become harder to find a huge MOS, but the risk of the market's crashing will likely go down as well. In the long run, it seems like a good trade-off. But that will be a long time coming, if it ever happens. In the meantime, those of us who are Rule #1 investors will enjoy the benefit of Mr. Market's irrational pricing.

Which brings us to fear.

OVERCOMING YOUR FEAR

Remember ERI? The Emotional Rule of Investing dictates that once you buy a business, its price will go down. And that's exactly what you fear. The only way to really overcome fear of loss is to know you won't lose.

I get asked all the time, "What's the minimum amount of money I can do this with?" Here's the answer: Zero. And that's the amount I want all of you to start with. Zero dollars invested.

Remember, Rule #1 is all about not putting hard-earned dollars at risk. If you start investing without knowing what you're doing, you could make mistakes and lose some of that hard-earned money, even as a Rule #1 investor. And you might be scared. I don't want you to be afraid of losing your money. That isn't fun, and this should be a blast. If you've never experienced it, believe me, making hundreds of thousands of dollars in a short time is really a lot of fun. So, no fear . . . because we're not going to take any risks.

Instead of starting with real money, you're going to use pretend money. It's called paper trading (or simulated trading). All you'll need to get started is a notebook to keep track of your decisions and the willingness to become a millionaire. (Alternatively, you can also find online programs that allow you to open an account and paper-trade for practice. These sites simulate the market and help you keep track of your profits and losses.)

To paper-trade, you start by searching for a business that's wonderful and available at an attractive price. Do the Four M analysis on businesses until you find one that works for you. In your notebook, write down the name of the business and the symbol, the Sticker Price, and the MOS Price. Also write in one column your total cash balance. You can make up a number like $100,000 to invest, or use the amount you think you'll be starting with. Your call. If you use more money, you're going to be able to invest in more businesses, which will speed up your learning process. So I'd use the $100,000.

Review the Tools for the businesses you want to buy, and when you have three Tools that say "Get in," buy the business on paper. You'll need to record the actual price you would've bought at were you using real money, so on whatever site you're using for research, say MSN Money, look at the price the stock is selling for right now. If it's after trading hours in New York (9:30 a.m. to 4:00 p.m.), wait and look at the price the next morning at 9:30 (EST) if you can. There's a 20-minute delay at most free sites like MSN Money, so the price you see is not exactly the price the stock is selling for right now. To be more accurate, if you can open a trading account (which I talk about in the next chapter; you may have to deposit money to open one), do so and get the up-to-the-second price from your online broker.

In your notebook you'll now write the date you bought the stock, the price you paid per share, the number of shares you bought, and the total cost of the transaction. Don't forget to include a commission of $10 per trade in your total. Subtract that amount from your cash balance.

I put an e-trading journal on www.ruleoneinvestor.com, which you can use as a template for a paper journal in Excel, as is. Just go download it and do something about making your future better, starting right now.

Now watch the Tools. Once you have your money in a stock, all you're doing from that point on is looking at the Tools to know when to get out. That takes seconds. After you do this a bit, you'll see why, once you've picked a few great businesses, your total time per week really is about 15 minutes.

When the Tools say to get out, look for the price and record it and charge yourself another $10 commission. Put that amount down as the total return on the transaction. The difference between the amount you put in and the amount you took out is your profit or loss on that trade. Put that amount down in the notebook, too. And now add the total remaining cash back into your cash balance.

Here's a trading journal that I created based on the Connellys' CAKE investments, which shows they started investing in February 2002 with $20,000, managed to add $5,500 from savings, and have $39,500 by the end of 2003. (If you use the journal on my website, the math is automatic.) Of course, once you start investing with real money, your brokerage will keep track of all of this for you automatically.

Buy Date	Stock symbol	Buy Price	# of Shares	$ Out	Broker Comm	Total $ Out	Sell Date	Stock symbol	Sell Price	# of Shares	$ In	Broker Comm	Total $ In	Banking Date	Deposits and Withdrawals	Cash Balance
														15-Jan-02	$ 20,000	$ 20,000
13-Feb-03	CAKE	$ 19	1000	$ 19,000	$ 10	$ 19,010										$ 990
														15-Feb-02	$ 500	$ 1,490
														15-Mar-02	$ 500	$ 24,000
							4-Apr-03	CAKE	$ 22	1000	$22,000	$ 10	$22,010			$ 24,000
														15-Apr-02	$ 500	$ 24,500
6-May-03	CAKE	$ 22	1100	$ 24,200	$ 10	$ 24,210										$ 290
														15-May-02	$ 500	$ 790
														15-Jun-02	$ 500	$ 1,290
														15-Jul-02	$ 500	$ 27,100
							7-Aug-03	CAKE	$ 23	1100	$25,300	$ 10	$25,310			$ 27,100
														15-Aug-02	$ 500	$ 27,600
28-Aug-03	CAKE	$ 21	1300	$ 27,300	$ 10	$ 27,310										$ 290
														15-Sep-02	$ 500	$ 790
														15-Oct-02	$ 500	$ 1,290
							18-Nov-03	CAKE	$ 25	1300	$32,500	$ 10	$32,510			$ 33,800
														15-Nov-02	$ 500	$ 1,290
2-Dec-02	CAKE	$ 25	1300	$ 32,500	$ 10	$ 32,510										$ 1,790
														15-Dec-02	$ 500	$ 1,790
							30-Dec-03	CAKE	$ 29	1300	$37,700	$ 10	$37,710			$ 39,500

The amount of time you should continue paper trading depends on your confidence level. The main idea at this point is for you to become comfortable that you can do this and not lose money. If you're losing little bits (1 to 2 percent), be patient. That can happen even in the best of businesses. But, over time, if you've done your Four Ms well (and if the whole market isn't in a free fall), you'll see your stock run up in price. A single run-up will usually offset several small losses. For some novice investors, paper trading can last six months or more. Don't be discouraged if you aren't ready to go in under a year. The market isn't going anywhere, and you're learning every time you do this. For others, the paper-trading process may take only two months. If you've done well, you'll experience a deep regret that you didn't use real money. Everybody feels that way. Start with paper trading anyway.

I got a letter from a guy whom I'll call Fred (to help preserve his marriage). Fred learned how to do this Rule #1 stuff and told his wife he was going to start investing their money himself. She said, "Over my dead body. I know you, and I know you don't have any idea what you're doing." He told her not to worry, that he was going to paper-trade. She watched him as he paper-traded for two months — making an average of 19 percent — and then said, "Fred, why in the world didn't you use real money?" The truth is, doing this on paper can be frustrating — especially if you're doing really well. You're seeing big gains and they aren't real. If you start feeling that way, it might be time to think about putting some real bucks into the market. The next chapter shows you in some detail how that works, especially if you're new to this.

Chapter 15

Prepare for Your First Rule #1 Purchase

Create a definite plan for carrying out your desire and begin at once, whether you're ready or not, to put this plan into action.

—NAPOLEON HILL (1883–1970)

WHEN I first started investing, the industry wasn't geared for a really small investor. Brokers didn't want to work with someone who had less than $100,000, much less someone with $1,000. It took me weeks to gather information. I'd call for an annual report and it would show up ten days later. I had to get information from the library, and it was always hard to find. I never heard the phone calls between the fund managers and the executives of the business where they'd talk about the future. I never got insider trading information soon enough. The insider trading was hardly reported, and if it was, it emerged too long after the deal to be useful.

And there were no technical Tools I'd ever heard of. If I didn't have somebody taking me by the hand and helping me each step of the way, there was no way a river guide like me was going to become an investor. For a hundred years in the financial services industry, that was just the way things had always been. It was always geared toward the big and the rich — those who could afford to pay for access to the information held so tightly by people in the industry. No wonder the financial services industry is *still* locked into thinking the small investor is better off letting a pro invest his or her money (financial managers and advisers still want to make a living off you). For one hundred years, they were probably right to say they were the only ones who could invest your money wisely. But not anymore.

You've already seen how much financial information is right there on your computer with the click of a mouse. In fact, today the problem has reversed itself. With the SEC enforcing rules that level the playing field and the Internet facilitating the transfer of critical information quickly, there's now so much information for the little guy to access in an instant that it's easy to get intimidated. Rule #1 solves that problem by focusing our precious time and resources on exactly what to look for and how to find it. It gives us the knowledge and the Tools to overcome ERI. But even so, we still have to overcome the intimidation factor of putting real money in the market if we've never done it before.

In this chapter I'm going to walk you through the process of taking money out of your checking account and getting it set up properly so you can put it into a business you think is wonderful and is available at an attractive price. And I'm going to congratulate you in advance for taking these important steps, because once you have, you can relax and enjoy the benefits of Rule #1 investing.

OPENING A BROKERAGE ACCOUNT

While you and I can buy a piece of a business from the business itself without a broker, just as we can buy a house directly from the owner, it's not as easy to sell it by yourself once you own it. Brokers, whether in real estate, oil and gas, business, or stocks, play a very important role in making it easy to buy and sell stuff. What they do is let you know what people are willing to pay for an item, and if you want to buy or sell an item, they make sure both sides do what they're supposed to do to complete the transaction. They then handle all the paperwork and make it easy to get the deal done.

Real estate transactions move so slowly that you can see the process as your broker presents the real estate listings for sale, shows you the properties, helps you decide on a price to pay for a certain property, does the paperwork, conveys the offer to the seller, does some more paperwork on the counteroffer, then gets everybody happy and puts the thing into escrow for some more paperwork. And finally gets the deal done. All of this happens, more or less, when you buy a piece of a business, too, but it happens quickly and you don't see any of it. Instead of taking 60 days for the process to be completed, it takes about six seconds. Compared to buying stock, a real estate broker moves at the speed of a glacier.

Stock brokers make transactions happen in seconds by having a lot of the same kind of product (identical shares of stock in a business), lots of buyers and sellers in the market, and sometimes by buying and selling stock themselves. And the speed of stock transactions isn't affected at all by the fact that the average number of shares bought or sold at any one time is 345, with a value of about $5,000. Small deals move a lot faster than big deals. (Remember how the big guys have to sneak in and out?) Over the years a process has evolved that makes it incredibly easy to buy and sell stock compared to anything else I know of, including going to the grocery store.

The first thing you have to do to be part of this process is to open an account with a broker. You have three choices: full-service brokers (e.g., Merrill Lynch), discount brokers (e.g., Scottrade, Schwab, TD Waterhouse), and online brokers (e.g., E-Trade). The spectrum of discount brokers is huge (believe it or not, some are called "premium" discount brokerages and other are called "basic" discount brokerages), so it's worth your while to find one that suits your needs. Trading commissions and fees can range enormously from one "discount" brokerage to another, but, luckily, fierce competition among brokerages in recent years has brought many fees down. When comparing one brokerage to another, think about the extent of the services offered, the costs and the ease of use.

Full-service brokers like Morgan Stanley, UBS, Smith Barney, and Merrill Lynch offer personal service to investors, but they generally cater to those with more than $250,000 (and often the floor is more like $500,000). But even if you have $500,000 with a full-service broker, usually what you're buying is a personal relationship, not great advice. Most brokers don't have the skills or the tools to show you how to make 15 percent a year. The few who do aren't going to work for you unless you have millions. Nonetheless, some people want handholding more than results, and don't mind paying the higher commission. With $500,000, the fees for a full-service account are around $10,000 a year compared to $500 for 50 trades with an online broker. That's a lot of extra to pay for someone to tell you everything's going to be okay. To paraphrase Mr. Buffett, "Wall Street is the only place in the world where the customer shows up in a Rolls-Royce to give his money to someone who comes to work on the subway."

Open an account with an online broker who answers phone calls, and you'll have the best of both worlds. To pick a good online broker, start by Googling "online broker ratings." (You know how to Google, right? Go to www.google.com and type in "online broker ratings" and hit "Google Search.") You'll get a list of broker rating services.

> Brokerages are among the many businesses that get ranked every year by various firms. Finding lists of the pros and cons on all the popular brokerage houses is quite easy—another task made simple by the Internet. The following are links to a few independent ratings and rankings of online brokerage firms. This can be a useful starting point.
>
> - **SmartMoney:**
>   www.smartmoney.com/brokers/index.cfm?story=intro
> - **Weiss Ratings, Inc.:**
>   www.weissratings.com/News/Broker/20020514broker.htm
> - **JD Power:**
>   www.jdpower.com/cc/finance/search.asp?CatID=5
> - **Keynote Systems:** www.keynote.com/measures/brokers/
>
> Don't make a big deal out of this. Pick one on the list and open an account.

To make a final decision on which online broker to use, decide if you want to pay bills online from your brokerage account, and make sure your broker will do an IRA for you and that you're not restricted to mutual funds. If you're going to open an account with less than $2,500, be sure your choice allows that.

> Basic questions to ask your potential brokerage house:
>
> - What are your trading and commission fees?
> - What types of accounts do you offer?
> - What minimums do you require in certain types of accounts?
> - What interest rates do you pay for cash accounts?
> - What kind of banking amenities do you offer?
> - Am I restricted in any way as to what I can buy?

Essentially, opening a trading account is much the same as opening a checking account at a bank. Pick one, download the forms (or have the brokerage house send you the forms in the mail), and send them a check for the minimum account balance, which is going to range from $1 to $2,500. Your account will be open in a few days with whatever dollars you've placed in it. You're now set to invest with that amount.

Note that there are lots of types of accounts you can open. I mentioned a few of them in the preceding chapter when I discussed taxes on gains. The two most common choices are Individual and IRA accounts. I strongly recommend that you open at least an IRA account so you can invest your retirement money without taxation. Every good online broker has someone on the phones who can tell you how to get your current retirement account rolled over without any tax penalty into an account you can invest. There's nothing to it, and they do it thousands of times a week, so there's no reason why you shouldn't be completely in charge of your retirement money.

I also noted previously that many retirement accounts have restrictions, such as how much money you can contribute on an annual basis. The kind of account you should open will depend on your income and how much you have to invest. The goal is to contribute the most you can to the most tax-protected account. Again, as I pointed out in the preceding chapter, discuss your particular situation with your accountant or tax adviser if you're confused. Your online broker may also be able to help you out.

PURCHASING SHARES OF STOCK

Once your account is open, when you buy a stock, the broker will take the money out of your account, buy the number of shares you specified, and hold the stock certificates until you sell those shares. When you sell the shares, the money from the sale is put back into your account. Your account balance will always show the current value of the shares you own and the cash you have left to invest.

All online brokers charge a commission every time you buy and sell shares. The commission for almost all of them is a set amount and, for our purposes, you can buy as much stock as you want and all you pay is that single commission for that transaction. For example, whether you buy 100 or 1,000 shares, the commission is still only $9.99 or whatever your broker is charging. Commissions range from $4 to $20, and you get what you pay for. For example, Sharebuilder charges $4, but only for "automatic" trades executed on Tuesdays. Pretty much for the buy, hold, and diversify crowd, and not informed Rule #1 investors. I'd recommend putting your money into a well-known brokerage with online sites — firms like Scottrade, Fidelity, E-Trade, Ameritrade, Options Express, or Schwab (there are others, so do your homework). You'll pay around $10 a trade; if you buy and sell ten times a year, your commission charges will be about $100 a year. They deduct the commission charges from your cash account each time you buy or sell.

The commission charges, as low as they are compared to the old days, still can add up if you don't have much money to invest. Consider that if you invest only $1,000, the commission of $10 is 1 percent when you buy. And when you sell, it's another $10, another 1 percent. That means the stock has to go up 2 percent for you to break even. I make a lot of money on 2-percent moves, and so should you. For this reason it's important to move up the amount you're investing as soon as you're comfortable (or as quickly as you can get it), to about $5,000. At

$5,000, the two $10 commissions aren't a very big chunk of your profit.

Once you have your account open, you've done your Rule #1 homework, and you're ready to invest, you'll have some choices to make.

When you open up your account and click on the "Trade" button, you'll see a place to input the symbol of the stock you want to buy. It might say something like "Get Quotes." When you click on that, the brokerage will find the up-to-the-second price that the buyers are offering. This is called the *Bid*. It'll also tell you the up-to-the-second price that the sellers are offering. This is called the *Ask*. And finally it'll tell you the *Last*, the last price at which the stock was actually bought and sold.

Whole Foods, WFMI, at this writing, has a Bid of $134.62, an Ask of $136.68, and a Last of $135.95. Notice that the Last is in between the Bid and the Ask. A good online broker will get that middle price for you whether you're buying or selling. A bad one will buy for you at the high price — the Ask — and sell for you at the low price — the Bid — and you get screwed out of a buck or two. The well-established brokers don't do that, which is why it's best to go with one of them. Sometimes there's a big difference between the Bid and the Ask, but on most businesses that will qualify as Rule #1 wonderful companies, the difference is going to be very small.

When you click the button that says "Buy," the website is going to ask you to input the number of shares and the symbol of the stock you're buying. I usually divide the Last price into the amount of money I'm going to invest in that business and then round the number of shares off. For example, if you want to buy $10,000 of Walgreens, which has a Last price of $34.51, you divide $34.51 into $10,000 and get 289.77 shares. It may be easiest to just round up to 290 shares, add the $10 commission, and make the total investment $10,017.90. Or, if the ten grand was all you had in the account, you could round down to 289 and make the investment $9,983.39 with commission, which would leave $16 cash in the account.

You enter the number of shares and the symbol, and then the website is going to ask you to choose between a Market-type order and a Limit-type order. If you click on Market order, you're telling the broker to buy the stock at the price it's selling for at that instant. In this case, something around $34.51 is probably where you'll get the order placed, since the Last price is the best indication of Mr. Market's price. You might pay a little more if the stock price is moving up, or a little less if it's moving down. Since you're buying only 290 shares, the order will likely be done in one trade because the average number of shares per trade is about 345. If, on the other hand, you're buying 1,000 shares, you'll probably see two or three trades executed of 300 to 500 shares in each trade, with similar prices but not necessarily exactly the same. You'll be charged for only one trade, though. (I like to use Market order trades because they execute in seconds while I'm watching, and then I can go snowboarding.) Market orders are fun because they happen very quickly, usually before you can click to see if the order was placed.

LIMIT, STOP, AND STOP-LOSS ORDERS

Sometimes, however, we're going to want to buy a business that's bouncing around in price so much that one trade might be a dollar difference in price from the last trade. Generally speaking, this isn't typical for a Rule #1 business because such big swings happen more often in new, small businesses that don't qualify as predictable. But if we want a stock where that's happening (possible especially if we're working within our Risky Biz portfolio, which I'll explain below), we need to protect ourselves from paying way more than we have to by putting in a so-called limit order.

When you click on "Limit Order," the website is going to ask you to spell out what price is the most you'll pay. Let's say the most I want to pay for Walgreens is $34.80. If I put in a limit order at that price, the broker will try to get me the best price below that, but will not execute the trade above $34.80. If no one will sell his stock at that price or below, my limit order will just sit with the broker unless the price comes down to $34.80. If it does, the broker will buy it, again at the best price available. Lots of savvy investors use only limit orders. You might also be able to limit the length of time your order exists before being canceled if the set price is never reached.

In reality, you're going to be tempted from time to time by small businesses and perhaps by IPOs. Try to restrain yourself for a couple of years until you know what you're doing. Stick to *predictable* businesses. Having said that, occasionally you're going to find a wonderful business at an incredibly attractive price that doesn't have much stock trading. A lack of active trading makes the stock "illiquid," which means you can't easily get out without dropping the price dramatically. I like to see at least 500,000 shares trading on average every day in a given stock. I know that sounds like a lot, but it really isn't. Microsoft trades about 50 *million* shares a day. If you're getting tempted by a business that trades only 50,000 shares a day, I promise you, if you buy it, you'll get to experience what it's like to be the big guy and not be able to get out without dropping the price.

I once bought into a small business that was trading about 20,000 shares a day, and I bought 30,000 shares. I got to watch the price go up as I bought, and a couple of weeks later, when I came to my senses, I got to watch the price drop like a brick when I sold. I unloaded and the price went from $1.20 to $0.80 before I got all the way out. That's what the institutional guys feel like every day, and I don't like that feeling at all and neither will you, so stay away from the thinly traded businesses until you're a lot more experienced.

A *trailing stop* is a great way to protect yourself from a drop in the price even when you aren't paying attention. This is a stop-loss order that's set at a percentage level below the current price. The actual price at which the stop-loss will execute automatically adjusts as the stock price moves up. This is a great tool for those of us who don't like to pay attention. It lets the profits run while cutting losses at the same time. It's especially important to use a stop or a trailing stop once the market price is within 20 percent of the Sticker Price. That's the range where the big guys start bailing out, so a lot of things can happen suddenly. A typical percentage to use for a trailing stop is 5 percent.

Check with your brokerage house to know how it allows you to use these tools. Stop orders typically don't entail an extra charge, so they're simply part of your regular trade. To execute a trailing stop, click on the "Sell" button on most websites and simply choose "Trailing Stop."

"Market capitalization" refers to the total dollar value of all out-standing (sold and held by investors) shares. A business's "market cap" is calculated by multiplying its number of out-standing shares times the current market price.

Here's a good rule of thumb for evaluating market caps and whether a business has enough market cap to consider it a sound investment at all. Generally, you want to find businesses that trade more than 500,000 shares a day. If each share is priced under $1, make the trading threshold over 1 million shares a day. The idea is to have enough trading going on so you can get out without affecting the price.

Another rule of thumb is to make sure the amount of stock you own is less than 1 percent of the average volume in trading dollars. For example, Whole Foods trades about 900,000 shares a day at $130 a share—that's about $120 million. I wouldn't want to have more than $1 million invested in Whole Foods at any one time. NowAuto, an auto dealership company, trades about 250,000 shares a day at $1—about $250,000. Applying my rule, I wouldn't want more than about $2,500 in that stock. If you in-vest more than that, you can trigger a big sell-off the moment you try to get out all at once.

Remember that before you can use real money, you have to have some. My recommendation is that you tighten up the belt from the day you start learning to be a Rule #1 investor, and stop spending money on things you're buying to impress people you don't know. One of my few great advantages as a new Rule #1 investor was that I was completely comfortable living out of a sleeping bag and a rucksack. Before I met the Wolf and started investing, I'd been living that way since I was 19, or for 13 years. It wasn't a problem to hang on to every dime I was mak-ing. I just kept trying to live the same way, more or less. Well, I confess to buying a house and a Jaguar pretty quickly once Rule #1 generated wealth for me, but other than that I kept plowing my money back into wonderful businesses. (The Wolf convinced me I needed to relax a little

How many businesses should you own? Mr. Buffett has about 30, but then he also has $60 billion he's investing. If you have up to $10,000, you should own one business. If you have up to $20,000, you can get two. Max it out at five or so. Granted, in time you'll be tracking 30 or 40 on your Watch List. These companies should be in different parts of the market and meet all Rule #1 criteria, but are either not available at an MOS Price or not getting Mr. Market interested enough to attract the institutional buyers, who would then push the price up and get the Tools to say "get in." You'll watch these potential buys, and as they come back into favor, you can consider purchasing them and dumping others that have ceased to be at attractive prices or have fallen out of institutional favor. At any one time you should keep your money focused on between one and five specific businesses that you understand well and are still priced at Sticker or below. Lou Simpson, Warren Buffett's choice to manage GEICO's funds, invests $2.5 billion in about eight businesses. (By the way, Mr. Simpson has compounded GEICO's money at over 20 percent per year for 24 years— beating the S&P 500 by 7 percent! What this really means: $10,000 in the S&P since 1980 is worth $240,000 today. That same $10,000 with Mr. Simpson is now worth $1 million.)

about money. So I got the Jag. I was embarrassed at first, then got used to it. When I started having problems with it—it was, after all, a *used* Jag—I was embarrassed all over again, so I sold it . . . for more than I'd paid for it the previous year! Went out and bought a Jeep. More my style. (Remember, Rule #1 works in lots of markets—real estate, cars, diamonds. All you have to do is buy $1 for 50 cents and you're going to come out okay.)

If it's okay to own a stock that's at Sticker Price, why not skip the whole MOS thing and just buy at Sticker? Because MOS means what it says: It's a Margin of Safety against having the wrong Sticker Price, among other wrong things that can happen. And if we have the right Sticker Price, we get to ride the big rise up from MOS to Sticker. On that ride we hope to see our returns go far above the 15-percent target. Once we catch that ride up, we can stay with a stock as long as it continues to accelerate up to and through the Sticker Price, but from that point on, (1) it's unlikely it will continue the same rate of return for us; and (2) there are bound to be other Rule #1 businesses available at MOS if we're willing to look. Why accept 15 percent if you can continually pick up 20 percent or more with a little extra homework?

YOUR FIRST $1,000

Now you're ready. So buy the business that meets all the Rule #1 criteria with the whole $1,000. Even if you have more to put toward investing, start with $1,000 only. You'll add more once you become confident in "real-world" investing. Buy one business. Use the Three Tools. And for the next days, weeks, or even months, you must check those Tools *every day at some point*. It isn't necessary to check the market as soon as it opens. Just commit to checking the Three Tools each day. A time will come when one of the three shows a negative signal — a sign to get out. Usually the price starts to go sideways, and then either the MACD or Stochastics gives a negative signal. You then carefully watch for the third Tool to go negative. When it does, you go back to your online brokerage account and sell all of your stock in that wonderful business. Then you wait for those three indicators to tell you the big guys are going back in.

Prepare yourself for this. What these Tools do is (1) protect you from a crash; and (2) get you in front of a big run-up. That's all you need.

A reminder: Don't ever forget that these Tools will probably not make you any money if you're trying to buy a business that's already priced far above the Sticker Price. If you make a significant mistake in determining the Sticker Price, you're probably going to have a lot of break-even trades with the Tools as Mr. Market keeps pushing the price down below what you think it's worth. Be sure you do the entire Rule #1 analysis (the Four M test) before you invest. If you have several trades in a row that break even, you might want to review the Four Ms on that business to confirm, in particular, that you understand the business.

The reason I want you to start with $1,000 no matter how much you have to invest is that I want you to see for yourself that you're investing with real money with the same success you had paper trading. Once you're truly confident you won't lose money doing Rule #1 investing even if you figure the Sticker Price wrong, you're ready to add more funds to your account. Bring your account to $3,000 and continue making sure you don't change the way you handle the emotional aspects of investing. When you know you have ERI under control, then, if you have it, bring your capital to $5,000.

Once you're at $5,000, the commissions you're getting charged to get in and get out are no longer significant. At Scottrade, for example, you can move in and out of one business five times in a year for $70. With $5,000 invested, the $70 is a 1.4 percent overhead for the year. Obviously, you do not want to be paying tax on your gains, so do as much investing through an IRA as you can where you don't get taxed. You get the idea: Pick a wonderful business at an attractive price (i.e., a big MOS), don't get taxed on your gains, and don't worry about $10 commissions. Just get in and out with the big guys.

RISKY BIZ

Once you become a whiz at Rule #1, and you've got a decent amount of money working for you in the market—say, $50,000—you're going to get curious. You're going to want to mix things up a bit and try to put to the Rule #1 test relatively new companies you have a really good feeling about. Are there any exceptions to The Rule?

Every once in a while I see a relatively new company or a technology business I think passes the majority of the Four M tests but that can't completely qualify as a Rule #1 business because it's either too new to have a ten-year track record or too high-tech to thoroughly understand if you're a river guide. Still, I think I understand it enough, and the Big Five, as far back as possible, are simply awesome and Management is world-class. Oh, and it's on sale by Mr. Market far below Sticker. Google springs to mind. *Sooooo* tempting. In fact, I gave in to temptation long ago. It simply is not in my makeup to play it safe all the time, and I really do love owning a business that can change the world. So I created the so-called Risky Biz portfolio. Here are the rules:

1. You have at least $50,000 in the stock market.
2. You'll invest only 10 percent of your total basket in the Risky Biz portfolio.
3. You actually believe you do understand the business, even if you probably don't.
4. You watch the Tools like a hawk.

Risky Biz is fun. And, even better, if you get good at it, your biggest gains can come from this portfolio. I've done it very successfully just a couple of times, which is why I call it my "Risky Biz" portfolio. The first investing coup was a small biotech company, and the second was a small software company. Neither got very big before they were acquired by bigger businesses, but the return on my investment was a monster! It's fun to watch $1,000 of risk capital become $1 million in four years. And with the Tools, the downside risk is a whole lot less than it would be otherwise. (By the way, the Risky Biz portfolio is where my friends do "call options," which is a trading technique that automatically makes it a Risky Biz, no matter how predictable the business is or how well you understand it. Once you leverage up with a call option, lots of bad things can happen too quickly to avoid breaking The Rule. I'm not going to get into options in this book except to say that you need to know the risks before you consider doing an option.)

Bottom line: Finding a hot business that explodes is great fun. You can take your portfolio to the next level by adding a Risky Biz to it, but only when you're getting bored with 15 to 20 percent a year, okay? (And don't assume it bears no risk!)

SO GO DO IT

I got to this point and my teacher said, "Okay, now go do it." Take it one baby step at a time. There's no rush. Because Mr. Market is a maniac, there'll always be wonderful companies available at attractive prices. Your job is to take your time and never violate Rule #1. At the beginning, I'd say don't spend more than 15 to 30 minutes a day. Later, when you have a list of wonderful businesses you want to buy, your time will drop to 15 minutes a week. So go shopping, find a bargain, and have fun getting rich with The Rule.

Chapter 16

Q&A

There is no reason for any individual to have a computer in his home.
—Ken Olsen (1926–), President, Digital Equipment, 1977

Q. —What if I'm a complete novice? I've never invested in the stock market. I don't understand it. Will I be able to do this?

A. —You're my favorite student. Of course you can learn to do this. You can learn correctly from the start. Just take it one step at a time, don't use real money, and remember Rule #1. Start going shopping for a business to buy today. The sooner you get your shopping list together, the sooner you can buy something and start letting those smart businesspeople make you rich. Do *not* allow yourself to be told you can't do it by someone who isn't doing it himself. Why should you allow him to decide how well you will live in 20 years?

Q. — How does investing money in the market actually work? Do I need a broker?

A. —You need a broker, but you don't need to pay a lot per trade. Somewhere between $5 and $14 is the most you should pay. Use any online search engine, such as Google, and look for "online brokerage." You'll get a list of websites for brokerages. Scottrade was the first on the list when I Googled "online brokerage" at this writing. Good company, $7 per trade. Ameritrade is good, too, at $11 a trade.

Pick one, call the toll-free number, and a nice person will guide you through opening an account. You may choose to pick a brokerage that has a brick-and-mortar office nearby, but that's not necessary. You can do most everything these days over the Internet or through the mail.

Opening a brokerage account is just like opening a checking account. You deposit some money, say $1,000, in an account and you're ready to go. It may take you some time and practice to get used to your particular brokerage's website functions, but most of them operate similarly. You click on the trading button, input the symbol of the company you want to own and the number of shares, click "market order," review your soon-to-be purchase, and then, if it looks right, click "buy." Simple as that. The broker will immediately buy the stock at the best price and take the money from your account. When you sell the stock, you repeat similar steps, and the broker will reverse your order and put the money back in your account. (Of course, if you don't sell your stock at the same price you bought it, the broker won't be putting the same amount of money back into your cash reserves. When you sell, your broker is buying back your stock at the price at which the market is asking for it — so you get more back, or less.) Simple.

Q. — How much time will it take me to get used to being a Rule #1 investor? And how much work and family time is going to be sacrificed?

A. — It takes me about 15 minutes a week or so to review my portfolio and run my numbers. Some weeks it's longer, and can be several hours if I'm playing around doing searches. Lots of weeks, I spend less than a minute a day. What makes it so quick is having a fairly short list of businesses that I am interested in owning, and having good tools that do most of the work. If one of the businesses on my list starts getting a lot of institutional money into it, it's time for me to take action. Otherwise there isn't anything to do. Some investing gurus differ with me on this. Some think it takes about an hour per company per week, and you need at least five companies. That's five hours a week. But then, those guys are in the market all the time and trying to make huge rates of return. I'm doing it so I don't lose any money, and I'm happy to be out of the market for months at a time.

Q. — How do I get started? Once I set out to invest, what are my first steps?

A. — Here are my ten steps to Rule #1:

1. Remember your goal: to buy $1 for 50 cents.
2. Do your homework until you find a few businesses that meet the first three of the Four Ms — *Meaning, Moat,* and *Management.* Remember, the only kind of business that has a predictable future is a "wonderful" company. You must understand it, want to own it, and be able to spot great leadership as well as a durable Moat.
3. To know that you've found $1 for 50 cents, you have to know the value of the business, which requires that you can predict its future to some degree. Do your calculations to come up with a conservative Sticker Price. And from that . . .
4. Set your Margin-of-Safety Price.
5. Make a Watch List of your companies.
6. Wait patiently.
7. When Mr. Market names your price, prepare to ACT!
8. Watch the Three Tools for when to get in, and buy when all three say "Go."
9. Follow the big guys in and out of the market with the Tools until Mr. Market's price on your wonderful company gets at or above your Sticker Price.
10. When Mr. Market's price is higher than the Sticker Price, put this one back on your Watch List and go find a new business to buy.

Q. — Is there a website where I can get help doing this Rule #1 stuff?

A. — Yeah. Mine: www.ruleoneinvestor.com

Q. — Do I need high-speed Internet access?

A. — No. You can do this easily with dial-up. And if you don't have any Internet access, visit your local library, Internet café, Kinko's, or wherever you can access the Internet cheaply and easily in your area. These days it's not difficult to find Internet access, and it's quite painless to learn how to navigate the Internet with a little practice. (Trust me, it's easier than your ABCs, even for computerphobes.)

Q. — Can you tell us what you — Phil Town — have bought or avoided in the past?

A. — If you're asking for stock tips, you've missed the point of this book. I want you to focus on learning how to become a Rule #1 investor by finding businesses that have Meaning to YOU — that YOU understand, and that YOU'D like to own, which is a very personal experience. My telling you what has made me win or lose in the past will do nothing to help you become the best Rule #1 investor you can be. Recommending stocks goes against my Rule #1 philosophy. Remember, Rule #1 is about owning a business, not investing in stocks. Owning a business is an intimate expression of individual values, knowledge, and understanding. It is a very personal reflection of who you are as a person. That said, I owned and avoided the stocks I talk about in the book.

Q. — Will I make mistakes along the way? Have you ever made huge mistakes?

A. — Sure, I've made big mistakes, but I haven't made big mistakes that cost me my money. I lost some of my gains because, like Mr. Buffett with Coke, I held on too long. Without naming names, I bought into a software business once that made me a million dollars on about $500,000 invested, but I thought it would go to $20 million. It did, but it was massively overvalued and then — surprise — it crashed back down. I got out with my million, but just barely. From this I learned to unload at or just above the Sticker. (This was in the days before Tools, too, so now it's less risky to ride the business well above the Sticker and then bail at the first sign of trouble.)

Q. — You talk so much about Buffett, I wonder: Should I invest
in his company? And should I invest in companies he's investing in?

A. — I love Mr. Buffett's principles of investing, and he's such an icon
that he's easy to lean on for credibility. If you've read this book, you
actually already know the answer to that question: You put
Berkshire Hathaway through the Four Ms and see if (1) you think
it's a wonderful business, and (2) it's available at an attractive price.
If it's wonderful to you and cheap, buy it.

　　As for the businesses that Mr. Buffett owns through Berkshire,
some are public like Coke and the *Washington Post.* Do the Four Ms
on them, and if they're wonderful to you and cheap, buy them.
What you might find is that they're wonderful and not so cheap.
Put them on a Watch List, update their Sticker Prices about four
times a year, and if they become cheap, buy them then. But NEVER
buy a business because someone else bought it. Mr. Buffett buys
businesses all the time for arbitrage or convertible bond plays. So if
a business doesn't meet Rule #1 standards, I don't care who owns it,
go shopping for something else.

Q. — If you were to do a Rule #1 analysis on Berkshire Hathaway,
what would it look like?

A. — Here you go:

A RULE #1 ANALYSIS OF BERKSHIRE HATHAWAY
(circa Sept 2005)

Current Price: $82,990
Current TTM EPS: $4,736

BIG FIVE	old	5	3	1
ROIC	11%			
Equity	21%	9%	15%	12%
EPS	24%	27%	144%	-10%
Sales	37%	25%	25%	16%
Cash	21%	23%	-2%	-16%

Big Five growth rate: 17%   (my estimate)
Analyst growth rate: 11%
Rule #1 growth rate: **11%**

Historical PE: 22
2 × Growth Rate PE: 34
Rule #1 PE: **22**

Future EPS: $13,447.50
Future Value: $295,845
Sticker: **$73,128**
MOS: **$36,564**

Remix with my guesses instead of those of the analysts:

Future EPS: $22,765.14
Future Value: $500,833
Sticker: **$123,798**
MOS: **$61,899**

If you give Buffett the benefit of the doubt and put the growth rate closer to the company's historical growth rate of 21 percent, the stock is buyable if you've been buying it, but just barely. So I still move in and out of it. However, if you think the analysts are right, it's overvalued at this writing. That makes this a more advanced decision than most Rule #1 investors should make. Find a business where you can agree with the analysts or where your projection is more conservative (lower than the analysts' projection).

Q. — **Let's say a smart person looks at a company, does all the math, and sees vast potential, but no fund managers agree and the stock price never goes up. So isn't the key to investing predicting what most people will do — in other words, step into the shoes of the majority and see the market as they see it?**

A. — The problem with this question is that it relates to speculating and stock investing. I cannot reiterate this enough: As Rule #1 investors, we have to act as business buyers buying businesses — not stocks. We don't care what others are doing. We don't care about the stock market. All we want is to buy a wonderful business at a great price. What others do or think is none of our concern, and the less attention we pay to the pundits on television and to the stock market's ups and downs, the better we will be.

If we get the right business at the right MOS Price, we know we are going to make money, we just don't know when. We know this because Mr. Market always prices things correctly — at some point. In other words, the fact that the "majority" don't agree with us is irrelevant to our decision because we know that at some point they will come to agree with us.

And you can take that to the bank.

Q. — **What if I can't watch the market for a period of time, say when I go on vacation, or know I won't have access to the Internet and trading for days on end? What about stop-loss or limit orders?**

A. — If you aren't going to be able to watch your investment, a stop-loss is a good idea. Stop-loss orders are a way to minimize losses; you place an order with your broker that instructs him to sell a certain stock when it reaches a certain price, such as 10 percent below what you paid for it. When I use such an order, I set it at 5 percent below the current price because I know that a 5-percent drop usually produces technical signals to get out. (All three Tools will say "Get out" once it drops 5 percent. So if I'm not around to access and see those signals, I know that my order will take care of the sell for me if and when those Tools tell me to sell.)

If you can put in a *moving* stop-loss that keeps moving up with the price, do that. On most brokerage sites, this is referred to as a *trailing stop*. Of course, you can always go to cash and just forget about it for a few weeks with no harm done. When I went to Rome with my kids last year, I did exactly that and forgot all about it for three weeks. This is when trading within a tax-protected account is particularly beneficial.

Q. — Where can I go to learn about options? What are they?

A. — Options give you a way to make a lot of money with a little money — with the risk of losing all of the money. That said, a lot of very smart investors use options to lower their risk. I think success in options comes first from being a solid Rule #1 investor, and takes training. See my website for links to the best options courses and products. (See the Glossary for a more technical definition, as options are beyond the scope of this book.)

Q. — What about cyclical stocks? Are any Rule #1 businesses cyclical? And if not, then can I still invest in them using the Tools when they are uptrending?

A. — First let's define what *cyclical* means. Cyclical stocks are stocks that rise and fall with the waves of economic growth, especially during their specific industry's own cycle; for example, automakers and aircraft manufacturers are affected by the economy (people don't buy cars when the economy is bad, and, likewise, the airlines buy new airplanes when the economy is strong), whereas health-care companies generally are not cyclical because people will buy drugs no matter what. Other examples of cyclical industries include steel, paper, heavy machinery, and furniture. Cyclical industries are sensitive to the business cycle and price changes. On the other hand, companies whose products or services are in demand regardless of how the economy is doing are referred to as "secular" businesses.

Rule #1 is about buying $1 of value for half price, period—no matter what kind of business it is. Truth is, that's very hard to do with cyclical businesses simply because, by definition, the business is going to slow down and there's no way to know for sure how long that slowdown is going to be. And if you don't know that, how do you know that it's worth a dollar? You don't. Nonetheless, with the Tools, you can buy into a cyclical business when it's off-cycle and, if you catch it right, do very well. Just use the Tools and don't hang around if nothing happens in a few months.

Q. — How long will it take me to create a good list of companies that I like?

A. — Figure about four to ten hours of research per company that ends up on your Watch List, depending on how much you already know. For most of us, we already have a pretty good idea of what we would like to own, because we shop all the time and have already decided, for example, that we might like Whole Foods Market better than Ralphs, or Wal-Mart better than Kmart (or vice versa on both). Obviously, you won't put four to ten hours into everything you look at, but when it gets narrowed down to a few candidates, that's when you put in more time on those choice few. The financial research is very quick with the best tools, and it's slower with the free stuff, but so what? There's no rush. The market isn't going anywhere, believe me! You're shopping for a bargain. It's fun to shop, so take your time and enjoy it.

Q. —Where do I go to get research if I can't afford professional tools?

A. — Before I even get into this, let me remind you of an analogy: farming is just digging a hole and putting in a seed. Some farmers still dig the hole with a stick. Some do it with a big tractor. The tractor is a lot faster, but — and here's the point — you don't *need* the tractor. Is it better? Yeah. Faster? Yeah. Does it do a better job? Yeah. But you can still farm if you can't afford a tractor. Investing is just like that. The "stick" way of investing (to beat this analogy to death) is to get the annual reports and dig through them. Slow, painfully slow, but doable. If you look around, you'll find some free Internet tools (MSN Money, Yahoo! Finance, CNN Money) that have data on thousands of stocks. Their search tools were mediocre at this writing, but once you know the company you want to research, the Internet's free information highway can give you about 70 percent of what you need if you don't mind digging around to get the data out. Don't let it intimidate you the first time around. Again, once you get used to using the Internet to access the information, extract what you need, and make sense of it, it'll be a piece of cake. Who knows, maybe by the time you read this book the free online search and function tools will be even better — easier to use and more comprehensive.

Beyond that, you'll need to use a powerful search engine, such as Google, for news and Management. Log on to my website and you can access my Rule #1 calculators. Then add a few key indicators: MACD, Stochastics, and Moving Averages from either a financial site or your brokerage site.

Q. — What is the best set of Tools?

A. — Deciding who has the best tool set is an ongoing hobby of mine because I get onstage and show people how to do this stuff the way I do it, so of course I show them the Tools I've been using. Since Tools change, instead of stating that some specific tool set is the best, I invite you to visit my website, where I keep updating the best-of-breed Tools. I'll link you to pro Tool sites and give you a rundown on which ones are best for which kinds of investing. A few examples I'll mention here: Investors Business Daily, Zacks, Morningstar, and Success.

Q. — The Tools are only as good as the data. Is every Nasdaq/NYSE company in the database?

A. — Depends on the database. The pro databases have them all in there along with Toronto, Montreal, and over-the-counter stocks.

But they charge you. The free databases at MSN and Yahoo! have about 60 percent of the businesses in their databases. But, hey, it's free, and it's a good place to start. Don't let that stop you.

Q. —What are the best online sites for *free* financial data?

A. —MSN Money and Yahoo! Finance. MSN is best for individual stock information while Yahoo! is better at industry information.

Q. —What if I have a lot of debt?

A. —One of the great advantages of being in Special Forces a long time ago is that I don't get too worked up about the little things that go wrong in my life now. Once you've been shot at, everything else seems relatively minor. So the first thing I can tell you about having too much debt is to keep it in perspective. Think about it the way Special Ops soldiers do after something bad happens: Nobody died, we're still healthy, we're still in the game.

BUT, let's be realistic here, it's still hard to shake the pressure that debt puts on you. It's like you're on a treadmill, and no matter how fast you run, you get nowhere. So to fix this we've got to get better training and we've got to do stuff differently.

First, the training: Read books by people like Suze Orman, William Danko, and David Bach. Their books will help you start finding money even while paying down the debt.

Based on what you learn, make a plan and stick to it. Keep the goal in mind, and in a couple of years (or maybe five or so, doesn't matter) you will be debt-free and you will have money to invest.

Meanwhile, while you are paying off the debt, you are going to be banking the most important thing you can bank: investing experience. I would recommend this whether you have debt or not: If you are just starting Rule #1 investing, then I want you to paper-trade $300,000 until you know you know what you are doing. (I discussed paper trading in Chapter 14; you basically keep track of your profits and losses in a notebook, as if you'd actually bought and sold in the real market. You can also find online market "simulators" that facilitate your fake paper trades and track your investing. I want you to use $300,000 because when you have that for real, you can retire if you are knocking out 15 percent a year. Start at my website, where

I give you some tools and information to get going.) It might take you two months; it might take you two years. But that's okay because you are banking experience. And, meanwhile, you are getting rid of the debt.

Q. — What are the tax consequences of buying and selling stocks regularly?

A. — If you are using one or more of the many IRA and other retirement plans, there are no tax consequences. Inside an IRA you can buy and sell as much as you want, and you don't pay tax on the gains. If you work for a small business or are self-employed, you can put thousands of dollars into an IRA every year. It is a huge advantage. If you have money to invest that you can't get into a tax-protected account, you still want to invest it without watching it go down 50 percent because you didn't want to sell for tax reasons. That's sort of dumb, huh? So, if you have to pay taxes, pay them. If you make 15 percent and end up with 10 percent per year, isn't that better than losing your money? (See Chapter 14 for more on this topic. I'll tell you why it's not a smart idea to buy and sell based on tax consequences.)

Q. — If you had to say which number is *the* most important number of the Big Five, which would it be? And why?

A. — The most important number is ROIC, because it tells us so much about how well the business is being run. Next most important to me is the equity growth number, because it's a proxy for the growth rate of Sticker Price (aka intrinsic value or retail price). If equity is going up at 24 percent a year, eventually the Sticker Price will reflect that growth. But all five numbers are important.

Q. — What are the fees/commissions paid to online accounts? Are there any benefits to going with a broker who has higher fees/commissions? Or are there downsides to using a cheap broker?

A. — Commissions range from $5 to $20 for unlimited trading. The higher-priced brokers like Schwab have checking accounts and online bill-paying, which may be worth it for you. If those banking services are not important, use a cheap big-time broker: Brown, Scottrade, Fidelity, E-Trade, and Ameritrade are all fine.

Q. — I know I have to keep up with the news and data on my businesses, but how much should I be keeping up with worldly events, and the news in general? And what about all those TV (and especially cable news) financial programs?

A. —You do have to keep up enough to understand what you own. Beyond that, personally, I'd rather be snowboarding or riding my horse in the mountains than watching a bunch of talking heads. I just take a quick look at the three Tools once a day to keep an eye on the institutional guys. Believe me, they are always going to know a lot more about what's going on and how that will impact your business than you or I ever will. So, once you've picked your biz, watch what the big guys do with buying and selling your stock. That will tell you a lot more than reading or watching the TV will. If they start dumping it like crazy, you might want to check the news!

And if you do watch the talking heads, please remember that you are watching a game. These guys have big money invested and they are going to do and say whatever they can to promote whatever they own, especially if they want to sell it. That said, I do like to watch Jim Cramer. He's a maniac, but a smart one. You can do worse than take a look at the businesses he likes on his program.

Q. — Is there any right time to buy into an index or sector fund?

A. —You can buy indexes just like stocks. They are called Exchange Traded Funds or ETFs. The advantage of buying indexes lies in not having to find a wonderful company that meets the requirements of all the Four Ms. Instead, you just own all of those stocks in that index or sector (read "good ones and bad ones"). The biggest disadvantage is that the index is going to go up at the average of the stocks in the index, whereas a wonderful company that passes the Four Ms test has no such limitation. Example: In the last five years the food retailers and wholesalers index went up 0 percent while Whole Foods went up 600 percent. That's significant. On the other hand, if you don't want to take the trouble to learn Rule #1 investing, your next best choice is long-term index investing.

Q. — My company offers a 401k, but does not match, and we can't choose individual stocks (we're stuck with mutual funds). Should I stop putting money toward my 401k and instead set up another kind of account? Which kind?

A. — I'm not a fan of 401k plans because they assume you are incapable of making your own investing decisions, so they force you to give your money to the mutual fund managers and then you could end up with a zero return for 20 years or so. Even so, if they are matching funds, it's a good deal, and if you can, get a SIMPLE IRA plan put together in your business. You can bank some serious money pre-tax. In your case they aren't matching, so forget it. Go get an IRA. (For more on this topic, see Chapter 14. Depending on your income level and access to certain types of retirement accounts, your situation may be different. There are many different kinds of IRAs, each with its own features and limitations. An accountant can also help you determine which one will be best for you. The key is to have the most tax-saving account possible and be able to freely buy whatever you want in the market, with no restrictions. You want the account to be "self-directed," meaning you control it.)

Q. — I have a lot of money tied up in a 401k, and I'd like to roll that money over into another type of account that I can self-direct and buy individual stocks (my 401k is very limited). But I'll get penalized if I cash out of the 401k. What should I do?

A. — Call any of the online brokers, and they will point out how to do a rollover without any penalty. They do it all the time. However, sometimes you can't because of company policy, so you are stuck with the 401k mutual funds. In that case, put each of the available funds on a Watch List, then use long-term Tools and pull out when they go red and go to the money market account. If you'd done that between 2000 to 2005, a fund like the Janus 20, which dropped 40 percent of its value, would have given you a 15-percent-per-year return.

Q. — If a company offers large dividends, is that a good thing or a
bad thing for the Rule #1 investor?

A. — Neither. It depends. We prefer a business that can use the excess
cash to build the business as long as the ROIC stays high. If it's
dropping, we prefer to get the dividends and reinvest them somewhere with a great MOS. (See Chapter 5 for more on dividends.)

Q. —When is the best time to check the market and trade?
Morning, midday, or after the market closes? And what about
the weekend? If I find a business to buy on Friday, do I wait
until after the market opens on Monday morning and "rings
up" the orders placed over the weekend?

A. — Check it when it's closed. Checking it during the day will just irri-
tate your ERI and make you nuts. Relax. Nighttime is good, but the
best time is whenever you'll take two minutes and do it consistently — even if that entails the weekend.

Q. — Is there anything to be gained by balancing a portfolio with
bonds, so that in years of flat equity returns, when bonds are
riding high, Rule #1 investors can participate somehow?

A. —Try to remember this: I don't care if you are buying real estate,
stocks, private businesses, gold coins, antique cars, or bonds, Rule
#1 investing isn't about "balanced portfolios," it's about buying $1
and only paying 50 cents for it. So, if you know that bonds are
cheap, buy 'em. And remember that there are wonderful businesses
available at attractive prices in almost any kind of stock market condition.

Q. —When Rule #1 investors are sitting in cash, awaiting Mr.
Market to name the right price on a wonderful company,
where's the best place to hold that cash? In a money market account? A few bonds? Savings?

A. — Most of you will eventually have enough money in your trading
account that your online broker will pay you short-term money market rates while your funds are in cash. Good enough.

Q. — Is it ever okay to buy a great business at or just below the Sticker Price? What if I find a wonderful business at a *semi-attractive* price?

A. — Charlie Munger, Warren Buffett's partner and a brilliant investor in his own right, has said that it's better to buy a wonderful business at a fair price than a fair business at a wonderful price. However, Charlie and Warren are really, really good at figuring out the value of a business. You and I . . . well, we're not Mr. Munger or Mr. Buffett. So we need to rely on a huge Margin of Safety to cover our rear ends in case we goofed on the Sticker Price. The closer you are to buying at the Sticker, the less margin you have for being dead wrong on the Sticker Price in the first place, and the less upside you can grab in a hurry. I suggest you wait to buy. If you can't help yourself and you just must have this particular business, be sure you have at least a 20-percent MOS Price off Sticker. Then watch very carefully what the big guys are doing. Always keep in mind that there are other wonderful and more attractively priced businesses out there if you just do more homework.

Q. — Some investing gurus say it's foolish not to consider interest rates when buying businesses. How much should I be aware of what the Fed is doing and what the current interest rates are?

A. — Not much, but not because we don't consider interest rates. We don't worry so much about it because we are demanding a 15-percent return in the first place and have a whopping 50-percent Margin of Safety in the second. Interest rates are factored into those two numbers.

Q. — Isn't it hard to make lots of money off huge, well-known companies? Don't the biggest rewards come from identifying *unknown* businesses at the beginning of their journey?

A. — Maybe the biggest psychic rewards come from finding the next Dell at the beginning, but the price you pay for buying unpredictable businesses far outweighs the gains most of the time. It is much safer and much more lucrative to buy a big, well-known business when it is massively underpriced because we can know it is massively underpriced. How are you going to know the value of a startup? Even the venture capital guys have no real idea. Stick with businesses that have already built big Moats. You might not have the thrill of a new venture blasting to the moon, but you will have the thrill of chillin' in your old age with no worries about money. And if, like me, you just can't stop yourself from investing in a few of these potential world-changers, do it in the Risky Biz portfolio with a small piece of your capital. (See Chapter 15 about Risky Biz rules.)

Q. — I usually do my taxes by myself with today's software that makes it easy. Once I start trading and setting up a Rule #1 account, however, will I have to find a good accountant and let him deal with the tax stuff?

A. —You probably aren't going to be doing all that much buying and selling. You can handle the accounting on your own — at least until the numbers are big enough where you're going to have an accountant anyway. Believe me, at that point, a good accountant will pay for himself or herself many times over.

Q. — My brother is a financial analyst and thinks I'm stupid for taking charge of my own money in the market. What do I tell him?

A. — Be gentle. He's like one of the guys who 500 years ago did the reading and writing for the village, and, as much as he loves you dearly, telling you to do this on your own goes against every paradigm he believes in. In addition, he really doesn't want you to become financially literate because then you won't need him. Tell him you know it's stupid to do this on your own, but you can't help it and you hope that he will be there for you down the road. Then go out and make 20 percent your first year while his recommended mutual funds did 0 percent. Show him what you did and then ask him if he thinks 20 percent is good. One of my students turned over his results to his very skeptical accountant at the end of his first year of doing Rule #1 investing and said, "How'd I do?" The accountant did the numbers and said, "You made 36 percent last year." My student said innocently, "Is that good?" and now his accountant is a Rule #1 investor.

Q. — I bought a wonderful company at an attractive price a few months ago, and it's done very well for me. But now it seems to have hit a wall, and while the indicators say I should sell, I *really* don't want to because I know the company will come back and continue to climb. Any advice you can give me?

A. —This is your call. You can definitely leave it in if it truly fit all the Rule #1 criteria when you bought it, but you take the chance of being wrong, or of being right but having to hold the stock through a very rough patch or a major market meltdown. Remember what I said about any stock in the market today: Even a wonderful company that met your Rule #1 criteria when you bought it can plummet for no reason at all due to a variety of market forces that only the fund managers can control. That's a lot of risk just to avoid being more active in your investments, or to avoid taxation. Bottom line: I say find a better, more currently wonderful company and keep the semi-wonderful one on your Watch List. You can always buy it back!

Q. —What is your take on commodity businesses? Don't some commodity businesses have better financials than a wide-Moat company simply because the former execute better? And if I'm going to buy commodities, say a metal, isn't it better to own the metal itself than a metal company?

A. —A commodity business, by definition, is a business without a Moat (i.e., it can't meet the full Rule #1 — the Four Ms — criteria). Regardless of the quality of its financials, a no-Moat business is not predictable in the long term because it has no ability to raise prices consistently. The price of corn last year was exactly what it was in 1948. Nobody knows what the price of corn will be in 2015, but I can bet you that Coke will be higher by at least the cost-of-living index. And if you're asking me about speculating in commodities, all I can tell you is that it is a game played by advanced investors like Warren Buffett. I've done a bit of it myself, but it is advanced investing. Stick with the basics for a while. A solid 15 percent or more returns a year will make you happy enough.

However (a *big* however), it's almost always a good thing to break

The Rule sometimes, right? So if you feel like breaking The Rule by buying a commodity, my recommendation is to buy a commodity ETF that mirrors the commodity prices. For example, you can own GLD (the ETF for gold) instead of gold stocks. Gold prices go up, GLD goes up. The Tools work well with ETFs.

Q. — What about REITs? What are they and are they for me?

A. — REITs, or Real Estate Investment Trusts, are a way of investing in real estate without actually buying a piece of property. Instead of buying real estate, you buy a company that buys real estate (either through properties or mortgages), and that company trades on an exchange like any other stock.

So, you can evaluate a REIT like you would any other company. Put any REIT to the Rule #1 test, and tell yourself that if you can buy $20 of real estate value for $10, that's a pretty good deal. Just be sure you know the Sticker Price, just as with any other business. Does it meet all of the Four Ms? Here's one big advantage to buying a REIT over owning real estate outright: If real estate flattens out or drops, it's easy to get out of a REIT. It takes eight seconds. It takes considerably longer than that to sell your Florida condo if nobody's buying. And think about all the fees and extra costs you had to bear just to buy that condo in the first place.

Q. — What about Dollar Cost Averaging? Doesn't Dollar Cost Averaging result in a long-term gain regardless of how the market does?

A. — Dollar Cost Averaging (DCA, which refers to investing regularly — e.g., the same dollar amount every month — so you are guaranteed to buy fewer shares when the price is high and more shares when the price is low) in either mutual funds or a stock does not guarantee a profit, much less a nice retirement, if the market or stock drifts for 20 years. Because of the price we insist upon as Rule #1 investors, and given the applications of Tools to ensure our safety, DCA is irrelevant.

Have more questions? E-mail me from my website and I'll keep a posting of the top questions asked!

Note to the Reader: The following terms represent a small fraction of investment and financial terms you'll likely encounter as you practice Rule #1 and begin to take charge of your own money in the market. This is not a comprehensive list, and is meant mostly to help you better understand key points made in this book.

For more definitions, refer to a financial dictionary, which you can find in a library or bookstore, or on the Internet.

American Stock Exchange (AMEX). The third-largest stock exchange by trading volume — after the NYSE and Nasdaq — in the United States. Located in New York City, it handles about 10 percent of all securities traded in the United States.

annual report. Found on most businesses' websites, it's the annual report to shareholders about what the business does and how well they did it. This report has in it the all-important CEO's letter to the shareholders. Another type of report done annually is called a 10K; it's the required report for public businesses that gives the public their financials for the last 12 months.

arbitrage. Simultaneously buying and selling stocks in order to profit from a differential in the price — usually as a result of the stock trading on different exchanges. For example, you buy a U.S. stock in the United States, and turn around and sell that stock on a foreign exchange where it's also selling, but for a different price owing to the lapse in the exchange rate's adjustment. Mr. Buffett sometimes does arbitrage on a takeover candidate. He exploits the difference between the market price and the takeover price.

Ask. The price asked by a seller.

asset. In a business, an asset is something the business owns that has a dollar value. (An asset in general is anything of value that can be traded.) An *intangible* asset is an asset that has a dollar value but may not be worth anything unless the business is successful. Typically this is an asset that was acquired through buying another business. The price paid in excess of that business's net worth is often called "goodwill" and is treated as an asset for GAAP purposes.

bear market. A market that's going down.

Bid. The price offered by a buyer.

bond. A debt investment, as in your loaning money to the U.S. government, which borrows from you for a defined period of time at a specified interest rate. The government issues you a certificate, or bond, that states the interest rate (coupon rate) that will be paid and when the loaned funds are to be returned (maturity date). These are often called T-bonds or T-bills, short for treasury bonds or bills.

book value. The net asset value of a company, calculated by total assets minus intangible assets (patents, goodwill) and liabilities. It's what the business is worth if you shut it down.

broker. An organization that's licensed to trade stocks for clients.

bull market. A market that's going up.

capital. Dollars. Money.

capital gains tax. A tax on the increase in the value of an asset; the difference in what you paid to purchase that asset and what you sell it for. (The gain is not realized until the asset is sold.) A capital gain may be short-term (one year or less) or long-term (more than one year). Long-term capital gains are usually taxed at a lower rate than regular income. So, if you sell stocks six months after you purchased them and take profits, you'll be taxed at a higher rate than if you sell them one year and one day after you originally bought them (assuming you can still take profits).

commodity. A bulk good that's traded on an exchange or in the cash market. Examples include grain, oats, coffee, fruit, gold, oil, beef, silver, and natural gas. A "commodity business," on the other hand, is what I call any company that produces a product that anyone else can similarly produce, thus eliminating a Moat. If you own a strawberry patch, for example, chances are a neighboring strawberry patch can easily compete with you. A strawberry from your patch is not going to be all that different from a strawberry from your neighbor. It's very difficult and expensive to create a Moat and protect it with a commodity business.

dividend. A distribution of cash, stock, or property by a company, based on its earnings, to its shareholders. Dividends are usually quoted per share. They are typically the "thank-you" notes for owning stocks in a stable company (which usually doesn't have stock prices that move rapidly).

dollar cost averaging (DCA). The practice of buying a certain number of shares in a given stock periodically, so you buy a certain dollar amount of shares regardless of the price per share. This allegedly helps reduce their risk of investing a large amount in a single stock at the wrong time. You buy more shares when the prices are low, and fewer shares when the prices are high. In long sideways markets, DCA will not reduce the risk of a zero rate of return. For Rule #1 investors, however, we already know what price we are willing to pay, so DCA isn't necessary.

Dow Jones Industrial Average. A price-weighted average of 30 significant stocks traded on the NYSE and the Nasdaq. Examples of DJIA companies include General Electric, Disney, McDonald's, and Coca-Cola. Invented by Charles Dow in 1896.

earnings. The net income or profit (usually after-tax) of a company during a given period. Earnings per share (EPS) is the profit from a company allocated to each share of stock held by shareholders. EPS shows the profitability of a company. "Diluted EPS" just means that all potential outstanding shares are included, such as stock options. Diluted EPS is a much more accurate reflection of a company's earnings. EPS is calculated by dividing the earnings by the number of shares that have been bought by shareholders. Diluted EPS is calculated by dividing the earnings by the number of shares that have been bought by shareholders plus the number of shares that are held by potential shareholders as options.

equity. (1) Stock or any other security representing ownership ("equities" are stocks). (2) On the balance sheet, equity refers to the amount of the funds contributed by the owners (the stockholders) plus the retained earnings (or losses). Thus, equity is essentially ownership in an asset after all debts associated with that asset are paid off. The importance of equity to a Rule #1 investor is in its growth rate. The growth rate of equity represents the growing surpluses, which in turn increase the value of the business.

ETF. Exchange-trade fund. A security that tracks an index and represents a basket of stocks like an index fund, but trades like a stock on an exchange, thus experiencing price changes throughout the day as it is bought and sold.

exchange. A market where securities, commodities, options, or futures are traded. Examples of exchanges include the NYSE, Nasdaq, and AMEX.

Four Ms. Meaning, Moat, Management, and MOS.

fund manager. The person responsible for investing a fund's money.

fundamental analysis. Evaluating a business by looking at its financial information.

GAAP. Generally Accepted Accounting Principles. The system of rules for certified accountants to create financial statements for a business.

hedge fund. A special type of fund that's usually limited by how many can invest in it, and is usually not regulated. Hedge funds are meant to get investors a maximum rate of return, and as such, these portfolios comprise both "safe" and risky stocks. Managers of hedge funds generally use sophisticated strategies involving options, short selling, and leverage.

index. An imaginary portfolio of securities (stocks and bonds) representing a particular market or a portion of it. The S&P 500 is one of the world's best-known indexes, and is the most commonly used benchmark for the stock market. Technically, you can't actually invest in an index. Rather, you invest in a security such as an index fund or ETF that attempts to track an index as closely as possible.

index fund. A portfolio of investments that are weighted the same as a stock-exchange index, such as the S&P 500, in order to mirror its performance.

insider trading. The buying or selling of stock by people who have access to private, i.e., nonpublic, information (*insider* knowledge) about a certain business. Insider trading typically involves executives, officers, directors, and managers within the business. The SEC requires all insiders to report all their transactions.

intrinsic value. The current value of a business based on its future surplus cash flow. I call it the Sticker Price.

IRA. Individual Retirement Account. Comes in lots of flavors, including SEP, SIMPLE, and ROTH. See your online broker for detailed explanation.

large-cap. Stocks with large market capitalization, between $10 billion and $200 billion.

Last. The last actual price at which a stock was sold.

limit order. An order to a brokerage to buy a stock at a price not to exceed a certain amount. If the sellers all want more than that amount, the order is not executed.

Management. The people who run the business. In the Rule #1 sense, the CEO.

margin. A loan by a brokerage of 50 percent of the purchase price of a stock (hence, "buying on the margin").

market capitalization. The total dollar value of all outstanding (sold and held by investors) shares. A business's "market cap" is calculated by multiplying its number of outstanding shares times the current market price.

market order. An order to a brokerage to buy or sell a stock for whatever the market price is either at that moment or, if the market is closed, the next day when it opens. I use market orders all the time. I put in a sell or buy market order at night when the market is closed, and when it opens my order is executed. I can do the same thing with a limit order.

Meaning. The concept of understanding a business well enough to own it. Includes the idea of pride of ownership.

mid-cap. Stocks with middle-range market capitalization, between $2 billion and $10 billion.

Moat. First coined by Warren Buffett, *Moat* refers to the competitive advantage a company has over other companies in the same industry.

money market account. A type of savings account that has the competitive rate of interest (real rate), and usually you have to meet minimum balance requirements to get the highest rate—or keep the funds in the account for a certain period of time. While you're waiting for Mr. Market to offer you a wonderful company at an attractive price, you may be keeping some of your cash reserves in a type of money market account. Sometimes these accounts are referred to as "MMDAs," which stands for "money market demand account" or "money market deposit account."

monopoly. A situation in which one company reigns as king over its industry and is said to control more than half the market for a given type of product or service. Examples are Microsoft and PG&E.

(MOS) Margin of Safety. A big discount to the Sticker or intrinsic value. Typically 50 percent off the Sticker Price.

mutual fund. A financial entity that allows a group of investors to pool their money for investing in the market, usually with a predetermined investment objective. A fund manager is responsible for taking that pooled money — usually billions — and buying securities (usually stocks or bonds). When you invest in a mutual fund, you are buying shares (or portions) of the mutual fund and become a shareholder of the fund. The vast majority of mutual funds fail to beat the market, as well as broad indexes like the S&P 500.

Nasdaq. An electronically traded exchange, created in 1971, and traditionally home to many high-tech stocks. Examples include Microsoft (MSFT), Intel (INTC), Dell (DELL), and Cisco (CSCO). Stocks traded on the Nasdaq typically have ticker symbols with four letters (as opposed to three letters on the NYSE).

NYSE. The New York Stock Exchange. The NYSE, located physically on Wall Street in New York City, is actually a corporation, operated by a board of directors, and is responsible for listing securities, setting policies, and supervising the stock exchange and its member activities. The NYSE uses floor traders (people) to make trades, whereas the Nasdaq and many other exchanges are computer driven.

options. The privilege to buy or sell an asset, such as a stock, at a specified price within a specified time. Options are typically for the advanced investor.

order. A contract between you and your brokerage that specifies what you want to buy or sell.

PE (P/E). A ratio of price to earnings (market value per share, divided by earnings per share). Sometimes the PE is referred to as the "multiple" because it shows how much investors are willing to pay per dollar of earnings. If Company X has a PE of 10, that means an investor is willing to pay $10 for every $1 of earnings. In general, a high PE means the analysts are projecting higher earnings in the future. When comparing PEs, it's best to compare PEs within the same industry, or against a company's own historical PE. The PE of the entire stock market—"market PE"—has historically been about 16.

portfolio list. A list of businesses that you have bought and may wish to sell. Rule #1 investors use a portfolio list to track the MOS and the Tools.

quarterly report. Often called a 10Q, it's the required report for public businesses that gives the public their financials for the last three months.

real time. Information that's up to the moment.

REITs (Real Estate Investment Trust). A security that sells like a stock on the major exchanges and invests in real estate directly, either through properties or mortgages. This is how you can invest in real estate, without actually buying a piece of property.

ROI (Return on Investment). The percentage return you've made on your investment. The ROI for a savings account is 2 percent a year. It's the total you got back from your investment, less the investment itself, divided by the investment. If I got back $120 from selling lemonade and my investment was $100, to find my ROI, I subtract $100 from $120 to get $20. And $20 ÷ $100 = 20%.

Rule #1. Don't lose money. Attributed by Warren Buffett to his teacher, Benjamin Graham. The essence of Rule #1 is the idea of certainty and low risk from buying businesses, not stocks, that are wonderful and only at an attractive price—in other words, buy a dollar of value for fifty cents.

Rule #2. See Rule #1.

Russell 2000. An index measuring the performance of the 2,000 smallest companies in the Russell 3000 Index, which is made up of 3,000 of the biggest U.S. stocks. The Russell 2000 serves as a benchmark for small-cap stocks in the United States.

S&P 500. An index of 500 stocks chosen for certain factors, such as market size, liquidity, and industry group representation. The S&P 500 is designed to be a leading indicator of U.S. equities, and is meant to reflect the risk/return characteristics of the large-cap universe. The S&P is one of the most commonly used benchmarks for the overall U.S. stock market.

Because the Dow Jones Industrial Average consists of only 30 companies, many say that the S&P 500 is a better representation of the U.S. market. For most, the S&P 500 is the definition of the market. S&P is Standard and Poor's, a financial services company that rates stocks and municipal bonds according to risk profiles. The company also produces and tracks its own indexes, such as the S&P 500, and publishes a variety of financial and investment reports.

sector fund. A type of mutual fund that invests in a particular industry or sector of the economy.

ticker tape. The scrolling stock symbols and prices you see crawling along the bottom of the CNBC screen during market hours.

T-note. A type of bond (debt investment) issued by the U.S. government debt security that has a fixed interest rate and a maturity between one and ten years. T-notes can be bought either directly from the U.S. government or through a bank.

trend. A direction that's discerned by trading data.

Watch List. A list of businesses that you don't own but may wish to buy. Rule #1 investors use a Watch List to track the MOS and the Tools.

Zacks. A Chicago-based firm that provides institutional and individual investors with analytical tools and financial information. You're likely to find financial data through outlets such as Microsoft Money, Reuters, Quicken, and Bank of America, which originated from Zacks.

Acknowledgments

This book begins with Ben Graham, Warren Buffett, and the Wolf, who, at his request, shall remain nameless. Graham did the exploring and Buffett created a well-beaten and simple path to follow: *Find a wonderful business and buy it at an attractive price.* But without the Wolf, I might never have been willing to walk the path. You can't go from 13 years living out of a sleeping bag to living rich without changing your thinking about some things. I might still think rich = bad. The Wolf had to teach me that a Rolls-Royce is just a car, not some symbol of decadence, before he could teach me that you don't have to be smart to make money — you just have to do what the best investors have always done.

The Wolf showed me the way, but what really got me moving was the birth of my first daughter, Danielle. And what kept me going for more was the birth of my second daughter, Alaina. Amazing how the arrival of these two souls made me stop thinking about the past and start thinking about the future — their future. They continue to give me the greatest joy of my life, and now that they know how to make money, I don't care what kind of bozos they marry.

And then along came Peter and Tamara Lowe and Brian Forte, who put me on the big stage in front of millions of people to tell my story and, in the process, have shown me more about how to live a successful life than anyone I've ever met. You would not be reading this without their support and encouragement.

A special thank-you to *Chicken Soup* author Marci Shimoff, for her friendship over the last 20 years, for encouraging me to write, and for introducing me to the best literary agent in the world, Bonnie Solow.

Bonnie and I met in her beautiful garden, and Lulu, her dog, liked me, so I got to hang out awhile. Bonnie was on her way to Alaska to explore some river with a bunch of guides, so right away I knew I was home and I was right. Since that day she put heart and soul into making this book happen and I can't thank her enough. She has become the quarterback of the whole Rule #1 enterprise and she has given me an experience that few first-time authors will ever know.

A critical part of this experience was finding the right publishing house. She dragged me to New York City and introduced me to amazing people in the industry and found the right home for this book: Crown Publishers/Random House. It was pretty much love at first sight when I met Jenny Frost and her wonderful team: Rick Horgan, Julian Pavia, Philip Patrick, Steve Ross, Tina Constable, Tara Gilbride, Jill Flaxman, and Brian Belfiglio. They immediately understood what this book could be. You are reading this because they are a fearless bunch of change agents who are willing to take on a first-time author who wants to shift the paradigm of investing.

A huge thank-you also to Sandi Mendelson and her fantastic PR team for their special efforts on my behalf.

The two people who made this book into something that you can read are Rick Horgan and Kristin Loberg. Rick believed in this book first of anyone in New York, championed it at Crown, and then edited and edited and suggested and edited some more until it was shaped into something that really does the job of teaching you how to do this investing stuff step by step by step. And the bearer of the brunt of my bludgeoning of the English language was Kristin Loberg, my collaborator, editor, and friend, who traded draft after draft after draft with infinite patience. She is an amazing person.

And since I'm on amazing persons, let me thank my old partners Dave Craig, Bob Kittell, Mitch Huhem, and Bill Witherspoon for teaching me so much over the years and Isabella DenHartigh and Mary Town for their support and encouragement.

Finally, I want to thank my mom for teaching me to be the best I can be, my dad for teaching me to do it with honor, and my God for making it all happen in just this way.

Index